Looking for Love in the Legal Discourse of Marriage

Looking for Love in the
Legal Discourse of Marriage

Renata Grossi

Australian
National
University

PRESS

ANU PRESS

Published by ANU Press
The Australian National University
Canberra ACT 0200, Australia
Email: anupress@anu.edu.au
This title is also available online at http://press.anu.edu.au

National Library of Australia Cataloguing-in-Publication entry

Author:	Grossi, Renata, author.
Title:	Looking for love in the legal discourse of marriage / Renata Grossi.
ISBN:	9781925021790 (paperback) 9781925021820 (ebook)
Subjects:	Marriage.
	Love.
	Marriage law.
	Husband and wife.
	Same-sex marriage.
Dewey Number:	306.872

Cover design by Nic Welbourn and layout by ANU Press

Cover image: *Ali and David asleep 12.01am-12.31* from the *Journey to Morning* Series by Blaide Lallemand and Hilary Cuerden-Clifford.

Contents

Acknowledgements

I owe gratitude to all the people who provided academic advice, guidance and enthusiasm, both formally and informally, throughout my doctoral thesis which forms the basis of this book. I would like to especially acknowledge my examiners, Kathryn Abrams and Hanne Peterson whose perceptive comments helped me to shape the thesis into the book. Equally as important were the comments of the anonymous referees who reviewed the final manuscript and provided useful advice as well as confidence in the project.

I would like to thank ANU Press, especially Don Anton for believing in me and Lorena Kanellopoulous for her efficient driving of the process. Thanks also to the editors Duncan Beard and Dave Gardiner who have much improved this manuscript. Inevitably, the manuscript retains some shortcomings and the responsibility for these is, of course, my own.

I would also like to acknowledge and thank The Australian National University for awarding me a publication subsidy.

A big thank you goes to all of my colleagues at the Herbert & Valmae Freilich Foundation, Penelope Mathew and Tristan Harley who have provided much-needed support and enthusiasm for the project all along. Similarly much thanks to Debjani Ganguly and Thomas Ford from the Humanities Research Centre at The Australian National University. A special thanks to Tom for helping me with the title.

Most importantly, my gratitude and my love go to all my friends (you know who you are) and to my family: my sisters Maria and Vittoria, my brother Luzio, my nephews Hugo, Francesco and Giosué, ma sopratutto un grande abraccio e bacio di gratitudine e amore per la mia cara mamma – Chiara!

Finally my deepest love to my partner David and to our daughters Harriet and Liliana. It is to the three of you that I dedicate this book.

Introduction

Law takes a very dim view of love.[1]
They say that the world was built for two
Only worth living if somebody is loving you[2]

The aim of this book is to test the (in)visibility of romantic love in the legal discourse of modern Australian marriage. Romantic love has become a core part of modernity and, unsurprisingly, a dominant part of the western marriage discourse,[3] but to what extent is this view replicated in the legal meaning of marriage? This question is important for two reasons. If love has become the reason people marry, then it is important that this is reflected in the law's content and application. This is self-evidently important for the legitimacy of law. Just as important is the question of how we understand law. Is law engaged with emotions, or separate from them? This forms part of a long-standing theoretical debate in the history of ideas.

To understand law's relationship with love is no easy task. While law names emotions, it deals with them only obliquely.[4] Emotions are not considered 'fit' for the study of law, and love even less so, with its 'stigma of association with women's magazines or frivolous trivia'.[5] Law is not alone in its scorn of emotions. The history of ideas has been dominated by a seemingly impenetrable distinction between reason and emotion, which not only distinguishes between the two, but values the former over the latter.[6] In this discourse, emotion is

---

1   ABC Television 'R v Dana' episode three *Rake* 18/11/2010.
2   Lana del Rey, *Video Games*, Polydor 2012.
3   Increasingly this is true also in non-western cultures. See, for example, the portrayal of 'love marriages' in Indian Bollywood films.
4   R F Moran, 'Law and Emotion, Love and Hate' (2000–2001) 11 *Journal of Contemporary Legal Issues* 783.
5   C Smart, *Personal Life* (Polity Press, Cambridge 2007) 58.
6   The opposition of reason and emotion has a long tradition dating back to the ancient Greek philosophers. Plato saw emotions as obstructions to the attainment of our true rational selves while Aristotle believed that a true understanding of the world around us could not be achieved without reference to our emotions. This debate has remained prominent in the history of ideas ever since. Underlying Aristotle's and Plato's difference is the view that they have of emotions themselves. A diverse number of conclusions have been reached about emotions. Emotions have been seen as bodily physical sensations, but also as expressions of our knowledge, ethics and value systems. Darwin saw them as vestiges of our evolutionary past, while others have argued that they are learned cultural phenomena. Anthropologists have reached different conclusions as to whether they are culturally specific or universal to all humans. Emotions are seen as phenomena that distract our purposes and lead us astray, but also as instruments that fine tune our thinking and help us to make 'rational' choices. If we see our emotions as devoid of meaning, as physical urges that can lead us into over-reactions, as blind passions, then one is more readily attracted to a view that emotions should be exorcised from any role in public life. On the other hand, if we accept a more 'cognitive' view of emotions, as purposeful aids to making ethical and rational choices, then we are not threatened by an idea that emotions are, and should be an integral part of public decision making. The important and positive role that emotions can play in public

relegated away from the important sphere of public discourse on the grounds that it is chaotic, unpredictable and therefore can too easily lead us into error.[7] A discourse of law that is inclusive of emotions in general, and love in particular, needs to overcome this hurdle.

This book will show that a careful study of love is neither frivolous nor trivial. In societies such as Australia, love is exalted, and is often presented as one of humanity's most powerful emotions. It is hailed as radical, liberating and equalising; as a progressive force capable of breaking down entrenched social barriers, delivering happiness and satisfaction; and of being at the forefront of a new humanism. The message that love is the most important thing in life is found all around us. It is not surprising, therefore, that love has permeated the institution of marriage.

The social discourse of marriage has changed radically during the last century or so, and yet it is still steeped in many traditional ideas. When considering the laws of marriage, the institution embodies a number of tensions. These tensions can be expressed as a variety of contests: Christianity versus secularism; patriarchal versus feminist; hierarchy versus equality; heterosexual versus queer; procreation versus love; traditional versus liberal; church versus state; status versus contract; duty versus agency. The tensions will be evident in the discussion and analysis of the book.

The substantive discussion of the law in this book is clustered around three main legal events that have explicitly challenged traditional legal understandings of marriage. The case of *Re Kevin (Validity of Marriage of Transsexual)*,[8] the case of *Garcia v National Australia Bank*[9], and the passing and subsequent overriding of the Australian Capital Territory's Civil Union Act (2006) by the

---

life has to some extent been accepted in some of the disciplines, however it remains persistent in law. For some studies in thinking about emotions see the following: J M Barbalet, *Emotion, Social Theory, and Social Structure: A Macrosociological Approach* (Cambridge University Press, UK 1998); C Calhoun and R Solomon, *What is an Emotion?: Classical Readings in Philosophical Psychology* (Oxford University Press, New York 1984); K Oatley and J M Jenkins, *Understanding Emotions* (Blackwell Publishers, Oxford 1996); K Oatley, *Best Laid Schemes: The Psychology of Emotions* (Cambridge University Press, Cambridge 1992); R Solomon (ed), *Thinking About Emotions: Contemporary Philosophers on Emotions* (Oxford University Press, Oxford 2004); P A French & H K Wettstein, *The Philosophy of Emotion*, Midwest Studies in Philosophy XXII (University of Notre Dame, Indiana 1998).

7   See D Evans, *Emotions: The Science of Sentiment* (Oxford University Press, Oxford 2001); Oatley & Jenkins, *Understanding Emotions*; Calhoun & Solomon, *What is an Emotion?*

8   There are two cases here: *Re Kevin (Validity of Marriage of Transsexual)* (2001) 28 Fam LR 158 (*Re Kevin* No1) and *Attorney-General for the Commonwealth v Kevin and Others* (2003) 30 Fam LR 1 (*Re Kevin* No2).

9   There are three *Garcia* cases in total: *Garcia v National Australia Bank Ltd* BC 9301944 Supreme Court of NSW Equity Division 1993; *National Australia Bank v Garcia* [1996] NSWSC 253; *Garcia v National Australia Bank Ltd* [1998] CLR 395.

federal government on the ground that the civil unions it legislated into being too closely resembled marriage.[10] Each of these episodes will be analysed with a view to answering these questions:

What meaning of marriage emerges from these episodes?

Do these episodes displace traditional meanings of marriage?

Is romantic love a part of the discourse and, if so, what is the meaning of the love that emerges from them?

Before turning to that substantive analysis, there are two important background discussions which frame the central questions of the book. The first is how this book is informed by the development of the law and emotion scholarship, and the second is how the discussion is informed by the understanding of romantic love that dominates contemporary society.

Framing the Questions of the Book

The Importance of Law and Emotion Scholarship

This book constitutes an example of how an emotional discourse (love) of a legal institution (marriage) enriches our understanding of that institution, helps us to understand how legal disputes are influenced by that understanding, and helps us to frame its regulation and reform (law). The importance of the question, however, goes beyond these important practical questions. At its heart, its aim is to challenge the exclusion of emotion from law and to challenge the dominant rhetoric of law that emerges from positivism.

Early positivists, such as Jeremy Bentham and John Austin, aimed to develop an intellectual framework in which law could be seen as rational, modern, and scientific. To achieve this, they disputed that law should be linked to morality and rights (natural law), and challenged the claim that law could consist in

---

10   These cases are not in family law. It could be argued that a book that examines the meaning of modern marriage should begin with an analysis of the Family Law Act (FLA). However, the legal episodes that this book relies upon exist for the most part outside of this revolutionary piece of legislation. This needs some explanation. My brief analysis of family law cases around those issues shows an unwillingness on the part of the newly established Family Law Court to engage in discussion, either explicit or implicit, about the question of marriage and its meaning since the repeal of the Matrimonial Causes Act. Presumably a return to such questions raised the spectre of the old law, which was to be avoided at all costs. To engage with Family Law Cases on the meaning of marriage, let alone its relationship to love, is therefore a difficult exercise. Courts circumscribe their reasoning to narrow points of law and go to great lengths to avoid any statements that can be read as being in any way normative. Because of this, despite the FLA appearing as a logical place to begin and end a discussion on marriage and love, the FLA is part of the back-story rather than the central story in this book. For more information on the impact of the FLA on marriage see chapter one.

unwritten and immemorial custom found in communities by the judge (common law theory). Instead, they wanted law to be associated with objectivity, certainty and neutrality.[11] Modern positivism continues to operate inside this paradigm, unified under two central assertions: that law is law as long as it is created in the approved political way, and that law and morality are and ought to be separate from one another. One of the many consequences of this framework is the exclusion of emotion from law.

Critical jurisprudence[12] has challenged this view of law and has contributed to an emotional discourse both generally and specifically. To begin with the general, critical jurisprudence, as part of the post-modern tradition, challenges meta-narratives. In so doing, it aims to liberate 'suppressed narratives' and 'subvert dominant paradigm[s]',[13] and in the process make room for alternative ways to understand law. Such an approach necessarily includes emotion. Furthermore, a central argument common to all strands of critical jurisprudence is its challenge to the idea of objectivity. For positivists, the claim that law can be objective (no matter how that is understood)[14] is central to the legitimacy of law. Critical jurisprudence challenges this claim from four distinct perspectives: critical legal studies (CLS) asserts that law is political, feminism that it is gendered, critical race theory (CRT) that it is racial, and queer theory that it is heteronormative.[15] In mounting these challenges, critical jurisprudence also undermines positivist claims that the law is value-neutral and rational.

As well as these general arguments, critical jurisprudence has developed a body of scholarship that has explicitly demanded an emotional engagement. This scholarship centralises the subject of law and the importance of identity based on sex, gender, race and sexuality.[16] Related to this, is the use of the methodology of storytelling,[17] a method that demands that law engages with

---

11   See K Lee, *The Positivist Science of Law* (Avebury, Aldershot 1989) and M Davis, *Asking the Law Question: The Dissolution of Legal Theory,* second edition (LawBook Co, NSW 2002).

12   Critical jurisprudence refers primarily to the schools of critical legal studies (CLS), feminisms, critical race theory (CRT) and queer theory, all of which can to some extent be characterised as post-modern. Critical jurisprudence can also include more general approaches to the study of law, such as law and society, law and literature and, of course, law and emotion.

13   A E Cook, 'Reflections on Post-Modernism' (1991–92) 26 *New England University Law Review* 751, 754.

14   J L Coleman, 'Truth and Objectivity in Law' (1995) 1 *Legal Theory* 33–68.

15   I feature queer theory in this book in order to show how it has advanced critical scholarship, challenged the objectivity of law, and exposed and critiqued the heteronormativity of marriage and of romantic love.

16   J M Balkin, 'Understanding Legal Understanding: The Legal Subject and the Problem of Legal Coherence' (1993) 103 *Yale Law Journal* 105–176. See also discussion of identity and emotion in Barbalet, *Emotion Social Theory and Social Structure* 11–12.

17   Storytelling is a method adopted in order to 'make arguments vivid' and 'to bring the raw experience of life as forcefully as possible into conceptual debates around law', Cotterrell, R *Politics of Jurisprudence: A Critical Introduction to Legal Philosophy,* second edition (Lexis Nexis, UK 2003). Tony Massaro describes storytelling in law as both a 'call to context' and a demand for more individualised justice, a method that implies that all voices are equal, and that diversity of voices is of 'paramount' political importance. The method, he says, embodies a number of demands that resonate throughout the legal system. He argues that this is evident in the lawyer-client relationship, where lawyers are now encouraged to let their clients tell

the way its processes impact upon real individuals rather than abstract entities or categories. It demands that law take into account 'existing social and legal arrangements and actual human behaviour'.[18] Furthermore, feminism's general project of making women's experiences central, rather than marginal to the way law thinks and acts has been central to the development of an emotional point of view in law, if nothing else by the long association of women with emotion.[19] This has been further assisted by the feminist project of exposing the private sphere, laden with emotional content, into public focus.[20]

According to Terry Moroney, the legitimation of emotion also owes something to the American Legal Realists of the 1920s and 1930s, who focussed the meaning of law on the practice of law and in particular on the role of the judge.[21] Maroney argues that the Realists should be understood as being among the first to argue that emotion is and ought to be understood as a part of the legal process. Accepting and demanding a judge's use of discretion entails an understanding of who the judge is that includes her sociological, political ideological and psychological aspects, none of which, Maroney claims, can be thought of independently of emotion.[22]

But the legitimacy of emotion in law has received its greatest boost from the recent development of a specific law and emotion scholarship. During the last few decades, a small group of legal scholars have begun to probe the scope of emotions in law. This scholarship has made substantial contributions to the way we think about the law. First and foremost, the scholarship has challenged the exclusion of emotions from law, arguing that law must recognise and include the rich normative depth of emotions.[23] The scholarship has developed to include

---

their story; in law teaching, where stories are being used to illustrate legal arguments, and in the work of judges and courts, where decision-makers are being asked to consider the uniqueness of the life experiences that litigants represent. All this promotes a variety of ends. Stories provide connections between people and experiences, they explore ways of thinking, and they heal and destroy experiences. For Massaro, storytelling is inextricably entwined with empathy, however it is difficult to extricate storytelling from emotion generally. T M Massaro, 'Empathy, Legal Storytelling, and the Rule of Law: New Words, Old Wounds' (1988–89) 87 *Michigan Law Review* 2106.

18 T M Massaro, 'Empathy, Legal Storytelling, and the Rule of Law: New Words, Old Wounds' (1988–89) 87 *Michigan Law Review* 2125.

19 S Mendus, *Feminism and Emotion: Readings in Moral and Political Philosophy* (Macmillan Press, GB 2000).

20 I have drawn upon feminist literatures to show the ways in which feminist legal theories have challenged the objectivity of law by arguing that law is gendered; the association between the feminine and emotion; the arguments that feminists have made against marriage, against love and against sex; and the impact that feminist ideas have had upon the same-sex marriage debate. Throughout the book I repeatedly use the term feminisms in order to indicate the broad movement and philosophy generally associated with the term. This is not to downplay the rich diversity of the views that the term embodies.

21 In particular, see Oliver Wendell Homes Jr, John Chipman Gray, Karl Llewellyn and Jerome Frank.

22 T Maroney, 'The Persistent Cultural Script of Judicial Dispassion' (2011) *California Law Review* 629–294.

23 H Peterson, 'Informal Law and/of Love in the European Community' in H Peterson (ed), *Home Knitted Law Norms and Values in Gendered Rule Making* (Ashgate, Dartmouth 1996) 114–155 and H Peterson (ed), *Love and Law in Europe: Complex Interrelations* (Ashgate, Dartmouth 1998) and P Goodrich, 'Law in the Courts of Love: Andreas Capellanus and the Judgements of Love' (1996) 48 *Stanford Law Review* 633–675.

more detailed work which has illuminated the role of emotions on different legal actors — judges,[24] juries,[25] lawyers,[26] witnesses and victims[27] — and in different legal contexts — criminal law,[28] family law,[29] domestic violence,[30] sexual harassment law,[31] and contract law.[32] The scholarship has also isolated the existence of specific emotions in law, for example, fear,[33] disgust,[34] shaming,[35] empathy,[36] mercy,[37] love,[38] and hope.[39]

Alongside and in partnership with this scholarship, practical approaches have developed in different jurisdictions which have accepted the important role that emotions play in the thinking and practices of law (comprehensive law movement). Practices such as problem solving courts and circle sentencing

---

24   N R Feigenson, 'Sympathy and Legal Judgement: A Psychological Analysis' (1997) 65 *Tennessee Law Review* 1–78; L Little, 2002 'Adjudication and Emotion' (2002) 3 *Florida Coastal Law Journal* 205–218; M C Nussbaum, 'Emotion in the Language of Judging' (1996) 70 *St John's Law Review* 23–30.

25   K S Douglas, D R Lyon & J R Ogloff, 'The Impact of Graphic Photographic Evidence on Mock Jurors' Decisions in a Murder Trial: Probative or Prejudicial?'(1997) 21 *Law and Human Behaviour* 489–509; B Myers, S Jay Lynn & J Arbuthnot, 'Victim Impact Testimony and Juror Judgements: The Effects of Harm Information and Witness Demeanour' (2002) 32 *Journal of Applied Social Psychology* 2393–2412.

26   S Bandes, 'Repression and Denial in Criminal Lawyering' (2006) 9 *Buffalo Criminal Law Review* 339–390.

27   S Bandes, 'Empathy, Narrative and Victim Impact Statements' (1996) 63 *University of Chicago Law Review* 361–412.

28   M C Nussbaum and D Kahan, 'Two Conceptions of Emotion in Criminal Law' (1996) 96 *Columbia Law Review* 269–374.

29   C Huntington, 'Repairing Family Law' (2008) 57 *Duke Law Journal* 1244–131.

30   N Seuffert, 'Domestic Violence, Discourses of Romantic Love, and Complex Personhood in the Law' (1999) 23 *Melbourne University Law Review* 211–240.

31   P Goodrich, 'The Laws of Love: Literature, History and the Governance of Kissing' (1998) 24 *New York University Review of Law & Social Change* 183–234.

32   H Keren, 'Considering Affective Consideration'(2009–10) 40 *Golden Gate University Law Review* 165–234; M A Eisenberg, 'The World of Contract and the World of Gift' (1997) 85 *California Law Review* 821– 866.

33   S Bandes, 'Fear Factor: The Role of Media in Covering and Shaping the Death Penalty' (2003–04) 1 *Ohio State Journal of Criminal Law* 585–598.

34   D M Kahan, (1999) 'The Progressive Appropriation of Disgust' in S Bandes (ed), *The Passions of Law* (New York University Press, New York 1999). M Nussbaum, '"Secret Sewers of Vice": Disgust, Bodies and the Law' in S Bandes (ed), *The Passions of Law* (New York University Press, New York 1999).

35   T M Massaro, 'Shame Culture and American Criminal Law' (1991) 89 *Michigan Law Review* 1880–1944.

36   L Henderson, 'Legality and Empathy' (1986–87) 85 *Michigan Law Review* 1574–1654.

37   J G Murphy & J Hampton, *Forgiveness and Mercy* (Cambridge University Press, Cambridge 1998); M C Nussbaum, 'Equity and Mercy' (1993) 22 *Philosophy and Public Affairs* 83–125.

38   P Goodrich, 'Law in the Courts of Love: Andreas Capellanus and the Judgements of Love' (1996) 48 *Stanford Law Review* 633–675; 'The Laws of Love: Literature, History and the Governance of Kissing' (1998) 24 *New York University Review of Law & Social Change* 183–234; 'Erotic Melancholia: Law Literature, and Love' (2002) 14 *Law & Literature* 103–129; *The Laws of Love: A Brief Historical and Practical Manual* (Palgrave Macmillan, London, 2006); Seuffert, 'Domestic Violence, Discourses of Romantic Love, and Complex Personhood in the Law; H Peterson, 'Informal Law and/of Love in the European Community' in Peterson (ed), *Home Knitted Law Norms and Values in Gendered Rule Making* (Ashgate, Dartmouth 1996) 114–155, and *Love and Law in Europe* (Ashgate, Dartmouth 1998).

39   K Abrams and H Keren, (2007) 'Law in the Cultivation of Hope' 95 *California Law Review* 319–382.

encompass therapeutic and restorative justice theories and practices,[40] and these consider 'extra-legal' factors such as emotions as essential to their operation and effectiveness.[41]

Law and emotion scholarship has developed to an extent where we can discern a variety of approaches within it. Maroney[42] identifies six commonly combined approaches: the emotion-centred approach (how an emotion is and should be reflected in law); the emotional phenomenon approach (how an emotion has been and should be experienced in law); the emotion theory approach (how emotion and theories of emotion are reflected in law); the legal doctrine approach (how emotions are reflected or should be reflected in legal doctrines); the theory of law approach (how emotions and their theories are reflected in theories of law); and the legal actor approach (how legal actors are influenced by emotions).

Kathryn Abrams has characterised the scholarship as embodying three different but not necessarily exclusive phases which she has labelled recognition, reconnaissance and regulation.[43] The recognition work is the general critical scholarship's challenge to the objectivity of law as discussed above, but also includes the scholarship which acknowledges the role that emotions have on the work of legal actors. Reconnaissance scholarship involved the importation of emotion scholarship from other disciplines into legal processes in an attempt to illuminate aspects of law which were not previously visible. The third phase, regulation, involves using the 'emotional' intelligence gained in law and emotion scholarship to influence the direction of law. As Abrams puts it, law and emotion scholarship has developed so that the question is not so much 'should or shouldn't a particular emotion be recognized through law but how, when, and — perhaps, most importantly — through what kinds of legal interventions', can the law affect emotions (express, reflect, channel, script, cultivate or destroy them).[44]

Above I have surveyed the discourse that has occurred between law and emotions in general. Much of this scholarship has involved the study of negative emotions and much of it has occurred in the field of criminal law. This book, however, is concerned with the emotion of love, and with laws outside of the criminal law

---

40   H Strang & J Braithwaite (eds), *Restorative Justice and Civil Society* (Cambridge University Press, New York 2001).

41   S Daicoff, *Law as Healing Profession: The 'Comprehensive Law Movement'* (New York Law School Clinical Research Institute Research paper series 05/06#12 http://cdn.law.ucla.edu/SiteCollectionDocuments/workshops%20and%20colloquia/clinical%20programs/susan%20daicoff.pdf accessed 17/07/10).

42   T Maroney, 'Law and Human Emotion: A Proposed Taxonomy of an Emerging Field'(2006) 30 *Law and Human Behaviour,* special issue on 'Emotion in Legal Judgement' 119–142.

43   K Abrams, 'Barriers and Boundaries: Exploring Emotion in the Law of the Family' *Virginia Journal of Social Policy and the Law* (2009) 16, 301–321.

44   Abrams, 'Barriers and Boundaries' 304.

context. The pioneer of the field of law and love is Peter Goodrich.[45] Goodrich's work crosses over a number of legal approaches. It can be classified as falling within the Critical Legal Studies school, the Post-modern school and the Law and Literature school. However we conceptualise his work, it contributes to the meaning of law and the meaning of love, and provides an example of a methodology that can be used in law and love scholarship.

In keeping with early law and emotion scholarship, a key element of Goodrich's work is a call to reject the exclusion of emotion in legal thought. The exclusion of emotion from law, he argues, reinforces the private and public distinction, and the male foundations of the legal system.[46] Moreover, the prohibition of *eros* from law leads to either a repressed or a deviant sexuality.[47] Goodrich's work goes one step further: he attempts to extract from predominately literary sources, the actual rules that govern, or should govern, love.[48]

My approach is different to Goodrich's in that I am engaged with an analysis of traditional legal sources, however, the importance of his work for this book lies in his pioneering and legitimation of the study of the relationship between love and law, and in his pioneering and legitimation of a critical approach to the study of law.

Returning to the broader law and emotion scholarship, in general we can say that it is seen as either marginal and irrelevant to the 'real' task of law or, alternatively, that it is received with suspicion and caution. For example, in relation to storytelling, both Paul Gewitz[49] and Tony Massaro[50] have warned against 'excessive emotion' and 'unguided emotion'. In relation to judging, Martha Nussbaum has stated that, to be useful, emotion must be tethered to evidence.[51] Restorative justice has been criticised for demanding 'compulsory compassion' in cases where it is not only inappropriate, but downright harmful.[52] In relation to the scholarship as a whole, Carol Sanger has described 'legislating

---

45 N Seuffert and H Peterson have explicitly named Goodrich as sparking their interest in the area of law and love. P Goodrich, 'Law in the Courts of Love: Andreas Capellanus and the Judgements of Love' (1996) 48 *Stanford Law Review* 633–675; *Law in the Courts of Love: Literature and Other Minor Jurisprudences* (Routledge, London 1996); 'Epistolary Justice: The Love Letter as Law' (1997) 9 *Yale Journal of Law & Humanities* 245–295; 'The Laws of Love: Literature, History and the Governance of Kissing' (1998) 24 *New York University Review of Law & Social Change* 183–234; 'Erotic Melancholia: Law Literature, and Love' (2002) 14 *Law & Literature* 103–129; 'Amatory Jurisprudence and the Querelles des Lois' (2000) 76 *Chicago-Kent Law Review* 751–778; *The Laws of Love: A Brief Historical and Practical Manual* (Palgrave Macmillan, London 2006).
46 Goodrich, 'The Laws of Love' 201.
47 Goodrich, 'The Laws of Love' 199.
48 See Goodrich, *Law in the Courts of Love;* 'Erotic Melancholia' 114.
49 P Gerwitz, 'On "I Know it When I See it"' (1996) 105 *Yale Law Journal* 1023–104.
50 T M Massaro, 'Empathy, Legal Storytelling, and the Rule of Law: New Words, Old Wounds' (1988–89) 87 *Michigan Law Review* 2099–2127.
51 M C Nussbaum, 'Emotion in the Language of Judging' (1996) 70 *St John's Law Review* 30.
52 A Acorn, *Compulsory Compassion: A Critique of Restorative Justice* (University of British Columbia Press, Vancouver 2004).

with affect' as a cheap crowd pleaser with the potential to be misused. She has warned that it constitutes a general tendency in society of an 'increasing socialization into having or at least displaying appropriate emotional responses in situations once unconnected to emotional involvement'.[53] Sanger has called for more caution and deliberation when we consider the legitimacy of law's role as a means of 'cultivating specific emotions'.[54]

These comments are to be considered carefully when evaluating the substantive issues that law and emotion scholarship gives rise to, however, we must be careful that they don't stifle the importance the scholarship has in legitimating emotion (and with it women and the private sphere), and the challenge it makes to positivism (and the view of law that is rooted in objectivity and a rational and scientific point of view).

The Meaning of Love

A book that asks whether law reflects love must engage with how we understand the concept of love itself, how it has developed and what it means in contemporary society.

The earliest discussion of love in western culture can be found in Plato's *Symposium*.[55] Here Simon May claims we find two lasting ideas of love.[56] In the speech of Aristophanes, we hear that love is a longing to find a part of ourselves and that, when we find it, it constitutes a unification, a merging of both our bodies and our souls which 'heal the human sore'.[57] From the speech of Socrates delivered as the ideas of Diotima (priestess and expert on love), we learn that love is the quest for the attainment of beauty, wisdom and the good. Love is represented as a ladder with the erotic at the lowest rung and ending with an abstract love at the highest. Love is aroused by beauty of a person's looks as well as their soul, character and deeds; it begins with sexual attraction but it is more than that; it raises us to higher things. Love has stages. In the first stage, a young lover will apply himself to the contemplation of physical beauty. A young lover will move from one lover to another, realising that beauty is not limited to one type. In the second stage, a lover will become a lover of beauty in a more general sense and will relax his passion for one person, as this will be considered beneath him. In the third stage, a lover will come to realise that the soul is more valuable than the body, and he will therefore come to appreciate

---

53   C Sanger, 'The Role and Reality of Emotions in Law' (2001–2002) 8 *William & Mary Journal Women & Law* 109.

54   C Sanger, 'Legislating with Affect: Emotion and Legislative Law Making', in J M Fleming (ed), *Passions and Emotions* (New York University Press, New York 2013) 63–64.

55   Plato, *Symposium* trans W R M Lamb, Loeb Classical Library (Harvard University Press, Cambridge 1975).

56   S May, *Love: A History* (Yale University Press, New Haven 2011) 40.

57   The Speech of Aristophanes in Plato, *Symposium* 141.

that beauty on the inside is more valuable than outward signs of beauty. The fourth stage consists of the realisation that the concept of beauty can encompass social and moral beauty. This will lead to a desire to acquire knowledge. The fifth stage is the realisation of absolute and pure beauty.[58]

Aristotle's *Philia* adds another, more ethical dimension to love. For Aristotle, friendship, love and justice are all linked. Friendship is the model for love, and justice is the model for friendship. A moral community needs both justice and friendship. The type of friendship that provides this model for love and justice is that which is based upon a sense of being good and doing good.

Christianity began the exaltation of love to the ultimate ideal it has become by asserting that there is nothing better than to love and be loved.[59] This message is found most strongly in the works of St Paul and St John the Evangelist. In the book of the Corinthians, St Paul says that love is greater than all knowledge, wealth, power and even faith:

> Love is patient; love is kind; love is not envious or boastful or arrogant or rude ... It bears all things, believes all things, hopes all things, endures all things ... And now faith, hope, and love abide, these three; and the greatest of these is love.[60]

St John the Evangelist preached that love brings us as close as possible to God: 'God is love, and those who abide in love abide in God, and God abides in them.'[61] This idealisation of love enabled the progression of western thinking about love to the courtly and romantic tradition. However, these largely positive developments came at a great cost. As will be attested to later, Christianity was brutal to sexual love.

The term courtly love was not used till the nineteenth century, but it refers to the idea of love that emerged in the twelfth century among a small section of the aristocracy, predominantly French. Its ideas were proselytised by troubadours who performed highly stylised poems whose themes were commonly embedded in a story of a poet or knight's love for an inaccessible aristocratic lady. The stories often depicted a struggle between love, desire and duty.[62]

---

58 Socrates' speech in Plato, *Symposium* 173–211.

59 For more discussion on love and Christianity see D'Arcy, *The Mind and Heart of Love: Lion and Unicorn a Study in Eros and Agape*; E Leites, 'The Duty to Desire: Love, Friendship, and Sexuality in Some Puritan Theories of Marriage' (1982) 15 *Journal of Social History* 383–408. See also A Nygren, *Agape and Eros: A Study of the Christian Idea of Love* trans A G Hebert (SPCK, London 1932–1939) and May, *Love: A History*.

60 1 Corinthians 13:1,2,4,7,13.

61 1 John 4:7–11 and 16.

62 See F R P Akehurst and J M Davis (eds), *A Handbook of the Troubadours* (University of California Press, Berkeley 1995). Tristan and Iseult tells a typical story of courtly love. Sir Tristan is a knight who is sent by his King to negotiate for the hand of a neighbouring princess and bring her home to him to be his queen. On the return journey they fall in love. The rest of the story is about their affair and how they try to keep their love and fulfil their respective duties to the King. *Tristan & Iseult a Twelfth Century Poem* trans J H Caulkins

Irving Singer characterises courtly love around five central features: that love between men and women is something splendid and is an ideal worth striving for; that it is ennobling for both the lover and the beloved; that sexual love is more than libido or a physical impulse but is something ethical and aesthetic; that love has rituals within it but it is not necessarily related to marriage; and that love is an intense and passionate relationship that establishes a oneness between the lovers. These developments paved the way for romantic love.[63]

Like courtly love, romantic love cherishes and idealises the love between men and women. It too ennobles lovers and sees love as ritualistic and spiritual, and as a means by which a oneness between lovers is created. It also sees sex as both pleasurable and good. It would be a mistake, however, to see romantic love purely as a restatement of the courtly tradition. Romantic love expresses many changes that occurred following the middle ages, and can be seen as reflecting a new kind of humanism which embodies ideas of liberty and equality, and, importantly, extends those ideas to the whole of society:

> By the nineteenth century every scullery maid could dream of dancing her way into some Prince Charming's heart, and every young aristocrat could yearn for the vampish woman of the streets who would elicit his true virility.[64]

Solomon echoes this, arguing that one of the features of romantic love is that it is appropriate only between equals. Like Singer, he relies upon the Cinderella story to argue that romantic love is a 'great levelling device' in society, a force that not only requires equals but is capable of creating them. It is for this reason that he claims that romantic love 'now finds its greatest popularity in self-consciously egalitarian societies'.[65] Hendrick and Hendrick claim that love must primarily accord individuals a certain freedom and autonomy, and love must itself be liberated from considerations of economy and politics.[66] These presuppositions

---

& G R Mermier (H Champion, Paris 1967). (For a quirky modern version of this story see the movie *Shrek* by Dreamworks 2001.) Another is the story of Lancelot and Guinevere, E Vinaver, *Lancelot and Guinevere: New Edition of the Romance of Lancelot and Guinevere* (The Folio Society, London 1953). Andreas Capellanus is often described as the prince of courtly love. See A Capellanus, *The Art of Courtly Love* trans J J Parry (Frederick Ungar Publishing, New York 1941). Capellanus states that everyone of sound mind can fall in love, but there is an age barrier. Men cannot be in love under the age of 14 (although true love for men really needs to wait till 18 as, before that, boys are too easily embarrassed) and over the age of 60. Women can only fall in love between the ages of 12 and 50. There are three avenues to true love: beauty, wit and excellent character. Great wealth and generosity of wealth can lead to love, but Capellanus is scathing of such love and says it should not be acknowledged by the courts of love. While beauty is important, men and women who adorn themselves excessively are not worthy subjects of love. To retain love, Capellanus advises secrecy, generosity and keeping good company. To increase love, he advises lovers to see each other rarely, to dream of one's lover and to feel jealousy. A Capellanus, *The Art of Courtly Love* book one 32–36 and book two 151–153.

63   I Singer, *The Nature of Love* vol 2: Courtly and Romantic (Chicago University Press, Chicago 1984) chapter one.

64   I Singer, *The Nature of Love* vol 3: The Modern World (Chicago University Press, Chicago 1987) 18.

65   R C Solomon, *About Love: Reinventing Romance for Our Times* (Little Field Quality Paperbacks, Lanham MD 1994) 45.

66   S Hendrick & C Hendrick, *Romantic Love* (Sage Publications, Newbury Park 1992) 39.

depend upon a modern western industrial society. In this way, romantic love becomes connected not only with individual freedom, but also modernity and progress. As Solomon argues:

> In essence, romantic love came of age only when newly industrialized and increasingly anonymous societies fostered the economically independent and socially shrunken ('nuclear') family, when women as well as men were permitted considerable personal choice in their marriage partners, when romantic love novels spread the gospel to the multitude of women in the middle class (whereas courtly love had been the privilege of a few aristocratic heroines) and, philosophically most important, when centuries-old contrast between sacred and profane love had broken down and been synthesized in a secular mode (like so many ideas of the Enlightenment).[67]

The idea that romantic love is radical, liberating and modern has spread beyond western societies. It finds expression for example in challenges to common (mis)perceptions of arranged marriages in India.[68] In the 'Red Love' context, it is equated with the shattering of capitalism.[69]

Contemporary love has developed many of the features of love that were begun during the romantic period. If love was extended to the masses during that time, the message has now reached saturation point in our culture. Beck and Beck-Gernsheim claim that love is now considered the major existential goal of our times, capable of providing all of us with a sense of worth and a way of being in the world.[70] Illouz claims that love has become the 'cultural core of modernity',[71] a supreme value capable of delivering happiness — a 'collective utopia'.[72] Bruckner has described it as the general ideology of the West,[73] and May, as the 'undeclared religion of the west', 'the ultimate source of meaning

---

67 Solomon, *About Love* 60.

68 Reuters, *Just Woman@asiaOne* 21/12/2007. http://www.asiaone.com/Just%2BWoman/News/ Women%2BIn%2BThe%2BNews/Story/A1Story20071221-42037.html accessed 19/05/10. It is a common theme in Bollywood films to show the tussle between a couple's romantic love and the interests of their joint families. See R Majumbar, *Marriage and Modernity: Family Values in Colonial Bengal* (Duke University Press, Durham London 2009).

69 The concept of 'Red Love' originated from the novel of the same name by Alexandra Kollontai. Red love appears to be used to signify the coincidence of romantic love with Marxism and, at least for some, implies free love. See http://www.solidarity-us.org/node/1724 accessed18/05/10. For another look at the revolutionary nature of romantic love, especially its connection with free love outside of the 'western context', see E Tipton, 'Sex in the City: Chastity vs Free Love in Interwar Japan' (2005) 11 *Intersections: Gender and Sexuality in Asia and the Pacific*intersections.anu.edu.au/issue11_contents.html accessed 11/05/2010.

70 Beck & Beck-Gernsheim, *The Normal Chaos of Love* trans M Ritter and J Wiebel (Polity Press, Cambridge 1995) 193–194.

71 E Illouz, *Why Love Hurts: A Sociological Explanation* (Polity, Cambridge 2012) 120.

72 Illouz, *Consuming the Romantic Utopia: Love and the Cultural Contradictions of Capitalism* (University of California Press, Berkeley 1997) 2.

73 P Bruckner, *The Paradox of Love*trans S Randall (Princeton University Press, Princeton NJ 2012).

and happiness'.[74] According to these writers, the key messages in contemporary society are that love is a selfless, unconditional 'gift', that affirms the loved one, that transforms us to a higher state of being, is eternal, benevolent, harmonious and redeems us from our suffering.[75] Love gives us a feeling of 'living in high altitude',[76] and represents a 'Dionysian affirmation of life'.[77] We seek love because it makes us feel at home, it roots our life, it validates and solidifies our existence, it 'deepens our sense of being', it enables us to 'experience the reality of our life as indestructible', it offers us a promise of 'ontological rootedness'.[78] We crave this because we are born with an 'intense feeling of vulnerability'.[79] It achieves this because it is the 'central link – in the long chain of interaction rituals'.[80] Its prominence is assisted by the fact that it is a common theme in mass culture, especially film and advertising, and has become associated with mass consumption and the ethics of consumerism.[81]

Contemporary love also continues the themes of liberty and freedom. Beck and Beck-Gernsheim assert that love requires individuals who are free, active and accountable agents,[82] and a context free of any external rules and pressures: love is a blank form whose actual content is a 'subjective and mutual invention'.[83] It is these features of contemporary love that, for Anthony Giddens, make it a potential for significant social transformation. Giddens claims that the rise of romantic love today has led to the democratisation of the private sphere. It has given rise to the 'pure relationship' which is a durable emotional tie that can be established according to another person on the basis of the tie itself rather than to anything extrinsic to it.[84] He says that the pure relationship is 'part of a generic restructuring of intimacy' which can emerge in contexts other than heterosexual marriage.[85] Essential to the emergence of the 'pure relationship' is the emergence of 'plastic sexuality', a sexuality which 'functions as a malleable feature of self, a prime connecting point between body, self-identity and social norms'.[86] Romantic love has given way to 'confluent love', an ideal of love that gives everyone a chance to become sexually accomplished that is not necessarily

---

74   May, *Love: A History* 1.
75   May, *Love: A History* 2.
76   Bruckner, *The Paradox of Love* 75.
77   Bruckner, *The Paradox of Love* 128.
78   May, *Love: A History* 6.
79   May, *Love: A History* 10.
80   Illouz, *Why Love Hurts* 120.
81   Illouz, *Consuming the Romantic Utopia* 28. Hsu-Ming Teo has argued that love in twentieth century Australia has undergone a change that brings it closer to an American, white, middle-class, consumerist model. Hsu-Ming Teo 'The Americanisation of Romantic Love in Australia' in A Curthoys and M Lake (eds), *Connected Worlds: History in Transnational Perspective* (ANU E Press, Canberra 2005).
82   Beck & Beck-Gernsheim, *The Normal Chaos of Love* 193–94.
83   Beck & Beck-Gernsheim, *The Normal Chaos of Love* 193.
84   A Giddens, *The Transformation of Intimacy: Sexuality Love and Eroticism in Modern Societies* (Polity Press, Cambridge 1992) 2.
85   Giddens, *The Transformation of Intimacy* 58.
86   Giddens, *The Transformation of Intimacy* 15.

heterosexual or monogamous. In the model of the pure relationship and confluent love, the relationship holds only while each partner is gaining sufficient benefit from it. Importantly for same-sex love, confluent love differs from romantic love because 'while not necessarily androgynous, and still perhaps structured around difference, [it] presumes a model of the pure relationship in which knowing the traits of the other is central'.[87] As such, sexuality is only one of the factors to be negotiated as part of the relationship. While Giddens' formulation of love in modern society has been criticised for not reflecting reality,[88] its importance is in its formulation of a democratic way of understanding love. For Giddens, 'pure relationship', 'plastic sexuality' and 'confluent love' are all 'part of a generic restructuring of intimacy'[89] representing a formulation of love that is more democratic and inclusive than any in the past.

To round off this discussion on love, something must also be said about sex. Indeed, it is often the case that the two are discussed as if they were the same thing. This slippage is understandable. The relationship between sex and love throughout the ages cannot be easily separated. As Zygmunt Bauman claims, 'sex eroticism and love are linked yet separate. They can hardly exist without each other, and yet their existence is pent in the ongoing war of independence, the boundaries between them are hotly contested — alternatively, but often simultaneously, the sites of defensive battles and of invasions.'[90]

In the classical Greek tradition, sexual intercourse was not necessarily a part of love. Sex could be an expression of love but, as we saw above, love itself was primarily seen as an ideal for the attainment of something else.[91] Christianity's view of sex was largely negative. Christian love was chaste, pious, dutiful and stable, tied to 'an eternal being, a pure love',[92] barely tolerated even within marriage.[93] St Augustine describes sexual impulse and orgasm as 'an almost

---

87 Giddens, *The Transformation of Intimacy* 63.

88 L Jamieson, 'Intimacy Transformed? A Critical Look at the Pure Relationship' (1993) 33 *Sociology* 477–494.

89 Giddens, *The Transformation of Intimacy* 58.

90 Z Bauman, 'On Post Modern Uses of Sex' (1995) 15 *Theory Culture and Society* 19.

91 Sexual intercourse was also disconnected from heterosexuality. Stephen Garton says that sex in classical times was understood as an act between an active and a passive partner. He argues that the 'central trope of Greco-Roman sexual culture was activity/passivity not homosexuality/heterosexuality. S Garton, *Histories of Sexualities* (Equinox Publishing, London 2004) 32.

92 Goodrich, *Law in the Courts of Love* 31. In a discussion on the view of sex in western civilisation mention needs to be made of the Victorian period. One reading of Victorianism is that it represented sexual repression and prudery of all kinds. Foucault, however, has argued that the opposite was actually true, that it produced the discourse of sex because it spoke about it relentlessly in a variety of contexts. M Foucault *The History of Sexuality* trans R Hurley (Pantheon Books, New York 1987).

93 Solomon, *About Love* 57–58. Christianity still has a strict view on what constitutes legitimate sexual acts even within marriage. See G Grisez, *The Way of the Lord Jesus* vol 2: Living a Christian Life (Franciscan Press, Quincy University 1993) 639. However it is important not to overstate this, David West says that over two millennia of Christianity a wide variety of views about sexuality have been accommodated. D West, *Reason and Sexuality in Western Thought* (Polity Press, Cambridge 2005) 26.

total eclipse of acumen and, as it were, sentinel alertness'.[94] Christianity turns sex and sexuality into something more important than personal desire or even personal moral choices. They become important issues that determine a person's relationship with God and consequently influence their afterlife.

A more positive view of sex emerged with courtly love and was continued by romantic love. Romantic love centralises sex, and is often wrongly equated with free love,[95] but in fact it does not equate love with sex. While sex can represent the intensity associated with love, it is not the same as love. They are different pursuits.[96] Zygmunt Bauman claims that to seek sexual delights for their own sake has now become a cultural norm of modernity. Illouz agrees, claiming that in modern western society sex and love form separate and parallel life narratives.[97] And yet it is still the case that love and sex are difficult to separate. Neil Delaney says that any plausible understanding of contemporary love needs to acknowledge its sexual nature. Love necessarily includes 'mutual longings for sexual intimacy together with a more sweeping delight in each other's physicality'.[98] Paul Johnson argues that sex is still always in the service of love. Ultimately, he claims, 'love exerts a normative force over sex that cannot be easily escaped.'[99]

Outline of the Book

Chapter one documents the changing legal discourse of marriage by outlining major reforms during the nineteenth and twentieth centuries. This history shows the ways in which marriage has become disconnected from traditional

---

94   St Augustine, 'The City of God extract' in Solomon & Higgins (eds), *The Philosophy of (Erotic) Love* 45. From this emerges a general view, prominent in Christianity, that to have a body is a trial to be borne. According to D P Verene, personal morality is therefore 'largely body-denying morality based upon a set of restrictions on bodily activities. Classical Christian morality directs me to relate to activities that heavily involve the passions of my body only in certain ways (only through marriage, etc.) and not in others. This is done in order that I can relate properly to my soul and relate my soul properly to God.' D P Verene (ed), *Sexual Love and Western Morality: A Philosophical Anthology* (Jones & Bartlett, Boston c1995) 45.

95   This is especially so in the 'red love' context. Tipton, 'Sex in the City'.

96   Singer, *The Nature of Love* vol 3 10.

97   Illouz argues that this is both a good thing and a bad thing: on the one hand, it can be seen as bringing about equality between the sexes, but, on the other, it has also led to a loss. She says '[b]ecause sexuality need not be sublimated in a spiritual ideal of love, and because "self realization" is perceived to depend on experimentation with a variety of partners, the absoluteness conveyed by the experience of love at first sight has faded away into the cool hedonism of leisure consumption and the rationalized search for the most suitable partner.' Illouz, *Consuming the Romantic Utopia* 289.

98   N Delaney, 'Love and Loving Commitment: Articulating a Modern Ideal' (1996) 33 *American Philosophical Quarterly* 339–347.

99   P Johnson, *Love, Heterosexuality and Society* (Routledge, London 2005) 223. See also Wouters, who argues that sex in contemporary society is being seen once again as an element of an intimate relationship, rather than a goal in its own right. Wouters C, 'Balancing Sex and Love Since the 1960s Sexual Revolution' (1998) 15 *Theory Culture and Society* 201.

meanings and more closely connected to ideas of romantic love. Having established this connection, the book considers the extent to which romantic love forms part of the legal discourse of marriage via an examination of a number of established meanings of marriage derived from its traditional connections with sex (embracing both sexual intercourse and sexual identity), economic considerations and sexuality.

Chapter two analyses the connection between sex (sexual intercourse) and marriage and evaluate its importance. The analysis shows a shifting narrative where sex moves from being inseparable from marriage, and a 'right' for the husband, to being the subject of negotiation between equal partners in the pursuit of mutual pleasure. This shifting narrative makes room for the insinuation of love into the relationship.

Chapter three documents and analyses another shifting narrative - the one between marriage and economic considerations.

Chapter four turns to the connection in marriage between sexual intercourse, sexual identity, and sexuality, and considers the same-sex marriage debate in Australia. In this context, I document how love has come to be considered the most important defining characteristic of the marriage relationship and demonstrate how it has thereby been able to disrupt the traditional requirements of heterosexuality.

This analysis undermines the positivist hold on the understanding of law, as well as the meanings traditionally associated with marriage. In doing so, it opens the discussion on what romantic love means in contemporary society.

1. Love and Marriage

Cuz if you liked it then you should have put a ring on it
If you liked it then you shoulda put a ring on it.[1]

Introduction

William Eskridge argues that 'marriage is an institution that is constructed, not discovered by societies'.[2] The history of marriage seen through its laws certainly bears this out. Marriage has meant different things at different times. It has transmogrified from being a religious sacred institution to a contractual legal one, from a patriarchal institution to a more equal partnership based on freedom and equality. Over time, marriage has been understood in many different ways. It has been considered central to sexual expression and the procreation of children, the formation of community and of social and political alliances. It has been considered as an important way to regulate property, citizenship and the giving and receiving of care. While many of these functions are not denied by a contemporary understanding of the institution, a significant argument now exists that marriage in contemporary society is, and should be understood primarily as an institution that gives expression to love. It is the aim of this book to test the visibility of this view in the legal discourse and to assess the consequence of this for the meaning of both marriage and love.

This chapter will briefly outline the development of the law of marriage in England and Australia, from old common law principles, to reforms in the nineteenth and twentieth centuries, before turning to a discussion on how we can best now understand the institution and the extent to which we can consider it a love institution. Finally, the chapter will turn to consider the consequences of connecting marriage with love, particularly in the light of feminist critiques of both marriage and love.

The Common Law of Marriage

A good place to begin a discussion on the common law of marriage is with Sir William Blackstone's *Commentaries on the Laws of England*, first published in

---

1   Beyonce Knowles, 'Single Ladies' (written by T L Harrell, B Knowles, T Nash & C Stewart) c2009. http://www.metrolyrics.com/single-ladies-lyrics-beyonce-knowles.html#ixzz0s85Xep6J accessed 28/06/10.
2   W N Eskridge jnr, 'A History of Same-Sex Marriage' (1993) 79(9) *Virginia Law Review* 1485.

1765–1769. The influence of this work and its author cannot be underestimated; it has been described by some as being the second most important text after the Bible.[3]

Blackstone makes the distinction between marriage as a civil contract and marriage as a spiritual union. As a civil contract, marriage must satisfy certain preconditions: the parties must be free and willing to enter into the contract, as well as meeting the conditions for being capable of entering into the contract (age or parental consent, mental competency, consanguinity and affinity). Apart from death, the only other way to end a marriage was to get a divorce. A divorce (*vincula matrimonii*) could be granted if the marriage was prohibited under canonical laws (consanguinity of the parties, consummation) or because the marriage had become 'improper or impossible' due to one of the parties having an ill temper or committing adultery (divorce a *mensa toro*).

The consequences of marriage were significant, especially for women. Blackstone sets out in the following paragraphs a regime of marriage which dogged married women for centuries:

> [B]y marriage, the husband and wife are one person in law: that is, the very being or legal existence of the woman is suspended during the marriage, or at least is incorporated and consolidated into that of the husband: under whose wing, protection, and cover, she performs every thing: and is therefore called in our law-french a *feme covert* … her condition during marriage is called her *coverture*.[4]

> But, though our law in general considers man and wife as one person, yet there are some instances in which she is separately considered; as inferior to him, and as acting by his compulsion. And therefore all deeds executed, and acts done, by her, during her *coverture*, are void; except it be a fine, or the like matter of record, in which case she must be solely and secretly examined, to learn if her act be voluntary.

> [T]he husband also (by the old law) might give his wife moderate correction. For, as he is to answer for misbehaviour, the law thought it reasonable to intrust him with this power of refraining her, by domestic chastisement, in the same moderation that a man is allowed to correct his apprentices or children; for whom the master or parent is also liable in some cases to answer.[5]

---

3 S B Presser, 'Marriage and the Law: Time for a Divorce?' in J A Nichols (ed), *Marriage and Divorce in a Multicultural Context: Multi-Tiered Marriage and the Boundaries of Civil Law and Religion* (Cambridge University Press, Cambridge 2012) 81.

4 Sir William Blackstone, *Commentaries on the Laws of England in Four Volumes*, vol 1 (Garland Publishing Inc, New York 1978) 442.

5 Blackstone, *Commentaries on the Laws of England* 444.

From this beginning, Susan Blake argues that marriage in the common law tradition can be understood via an analysis of the three inter-related concepts of unity, consortium and support.[6] The concept of unity is traced to the Bible and the creation of Eve from Adam's rib. She claims that it is this concept of unity that justifies the idea that upon marriage the couple became one person, and that person is the husband. This justifies the appropriation of the wife's property by the husband, and the almost total prohibition that the law placed upon a married woman's right to participate separately in any economic activity.

Consortium[7] is a very broad concept that can be understood around the idea of 'a sharing of two lives' and 'implies a companionship between each of them, entertainment of mutual friends, [and] sexual intercourse'.[8] The concept has in the past been used to justify legal principles such as: that a husband and wife should live together;[9] that each spouse has a duty to provide reasonable services to the other; and that a married couple has a right to privacy.[10] Finally, Blake claims financial support as another of marriage's central ideas. At common law a husband had an obligation to support his wife. So much so that the wife could evoke the common law agency of necessity and pledge her husband's credit if he was not providing essentials for her and her children. This would include the provision of food, clothing and housing. But the payback for this support was great.

Alongside these ideas of marriage, arguably the most decisive of the institution's meanings comes from the fact that it entrenched the dominance of the male/husband, and the complete subordination of the female/wife. This was so complete in the legal definition of marriage that it led many to have argued that historically, marriage was in fact a 'civil death' for women, who were treated like children, idiots, criminals and even slaves.[11] Lawrence Stone claims that the only thing that saved women from the hell that marriage could legally be was the 'skilful resistance of many wives and the compassion and goodwill of many

---

6   S H Blake, *Law of Marriage* (Barry Rose Publishers Ltd, Chichester 1982) 7–12.

7   For an argument as to the injustices that this concept had in Australia, see M Thornton, 'Loss of Consortium: Inequality Before the Law' (1984) 10 *The Sydney Law Review* 259–276.

8   *Crabtree v Crabtree (No 2)* [1964] ALR 820 quoted in Thornton 'Loss of Consortium' 265.

9   See *Dunn v Dunn* [1948] 2 All ER 822 and *Munro v Munro* [1950] 1 All ER 832.

10   Blake, *Law of Marriage* 8–11.

11   M Lindon Shanley, *Feminism, Marriage and the Law in England, 1850–1895* (Princeton University Press, Princeton New Jersey 1989) 10–11. The fact that children had more legal capacity is a point well recognised in an eighteenth century book on the laws of marriage. J Walthoe, *Baron and Feme or, the Law of Husbands and Wives* reprint of the 1700 edition, (Garland Publishing Inc, New York 1978). See this argument in D Post, 'Why Marriage Should Be Abolished' (1996–97) 18 *Women's Rts L Rep* 283–313. See also J S Mill & H Taylor (1869) 'The Subjection of Women' http://archive.org/details/subjectionofwome00millrich accessed 21/06/13.

husbands'.[12] It is worth noting here that feminists have been instrumental in the reforms that have taken place to marriage and continue to be careful and watchful over the institution.[13]

The common law tradition teaches us that a marriage is a unity between two people, but the relationship between them is not equal. The man is the superior of the two. In fact, the woman is not only inferior, but her existence is legally 'suspended' during marriage. This translates into a husband being entitled to act for her and any children of the marriage. Therefore, married women could not sue, could not be sued, could not sign a contract and could not make a valid will. Upon marriage her personal property became her husband's.[14] A husband had authority over domicile decisions and all matters relating to the upbringing and education of their children. The rights of the husband extended to his right to 'moderately correct' her if she misbehaved. This was emphasised by Lord Hale's much repeated maxim that a husband could beat his wife 'although not in a violent or cruel manner – not with a stick thicker than his thumb'.[15] Ultimately (as will be discussed in more detail in chapter two) the husband also had unlimited sexual access to his wife. Sir Matthew Hale in *History of the Pleas of the Crown* (1736) stated that a husband cannot be guilty of 'a rape committed by himself upon his lawful wife, for by their mutual matrimonial consent and contract the wife hath given herself in this kind unto her husband which she cannot retract'.[16]

To complete the picture, something must be said of the role of equity. At least in relation to the ownership and control of property, some married women could find some protection from some of these harsh laws from the courts of equity.[17]

---

12   L Stone, *Broken Lives* (Oxford University Press, Oxford 1993) 26.

13   See, for example, M A Fineman, 'The Meaning of Marriage' in A Bernstein (ed), *Marriage Proposals: Questioning Legal Status* (New York University Press, New York 2006); C Smart, *The Ties that Bind: Law, Marriage and the Reproduction of Patriarchal Relations* (Routledge & Kegan Paul, London 1984).

14   A husband could not alienate this property but he could dispose of any income that came from it as he pleased.

15   Lord Hale quoted in Lee Holcombe, *Wives and Property: Reform of the Married Women's Property Law in Nineteenth Century England* (Martin Robertson, Oxford 1983) 30. The impact that these laws had on married women was clearly harsh. Many accounts of horror stories can be found. For example, see Francis Cobbe's essay 'Wife Torture in England' in *The Contemporary Review* April 1878 http://www.keele.ac.uk/history/currentundergraduates/tltp/WOMEN/HANNAM/TEXT/HAN19IIA.HTM accessed 17/01/2013, and W Moore, *Wedlock* (Weidenfeld, London 2009).

16   Sir Matthew Hale, *History of the Pleas of the Crown 1736* vol 1 P R Glazebrook (ed), (Professional Books Ltd, London 1971) 629. This will be discussed further in chapter two.

17   This protection from Equity was realistically only available to the wealthy and therefore of limited protection for women in general. Leaving aside the expense of the courts themselves, the whole concept of the trust was really only workable in very wealthy families where it was possible to tie up property and capital. Furthermore, it was arguable as to whether the protection was for the benefit of the married woman, or rather for the protection of the assets of the family of origin against an interloping husband. A trust could, in fact, place a married woman in the power of multiple men, as she was then controlled not only by her husband, but also male trustees and solicitors. R Auchmuty, 'The Fiction of Equity' in Susan Scott-Hunt and Hilary Lim (eds), *Feminist Perspectives on Equity and Trusts* (Cavendish, London 2001). See also M Conway, 'Equity's Darling?' in S Scott-Hunt & H Lim (eds), *Feminist Perspectives on Equity and Trusts* 43.

Along with infants and lunatics, wives were considered a special group requiring protection from the equity courts. On some level this protection was given for all of the above injustices. In the case of ownership and control of property, women could have control over property by the use of trusts. Once a trust was created for her, this property was regarded as separate property over which she and her trustee had control. This trust would also enable her to have contractual capacity in relation to that separate property. Equity also recognised as her property, rather than her husband's, gifts given from friends and lovers and, on the question of custody of children, equity courts were willing to deny a father custody of his children if the welfare of the children justified it. Equity did nothing, however, to protect married women from physical and sexual abuse.

Nineteenth-Century Reform

The nineteenth century saw a number of significant reforms that began the erosion of some of the worst aspects of marriage. The Married Women's Property Act of 1870, despite being described as a legislative abortion,[18] was the beginning of some recognition that married women had some rights over property. In very simple terms, the Act gave women the right to own and control property acquired through inheritance, and retain as their own property money earned through employment and investments. The Married Women's Property Act of 1882 carried through the legislative aims of the 1870 Act and passed into law the principle that married women had the same rights in respect to property as unmarried ones. It established that women could acquire, hold and dispose of all property, could enter contracts, sue and be sued (civil and criminal actions) and could carry out any business separate to their husbands. Subsequent Acts were passed to fill gaps in the equality principle as they arose. The Married Women's Property Act of 1893, for example, bound women's separate property to any contract regardless of when it was acquired, and the Law Reform (Married Women and Tortfeasors) Act removed the idea of separate property and replaced it with the idea of married woman's property. This change removed the idea from equity that married women only had the right to own property as a special and separate right. Lee Holcombe argues that this reform constituted the abolishment of the wife as a *'feme covert'*.[19]

At the same time as reforms to women's right to own property were taking place, further change was coming to marriage with the erosion of the idea that marriage was an institution entered into for life. Notwithstanding the significance of the Reformation, divorce was difficult to obtain during the

---

18   Arthur Arnold quoted in Holcombe, *Wives and Property* 179. These outcomes were far short of what the original framers of the Act had sought.

19   Holcombe, *Wives and Property* 224.

eighteenth and nineteenth centuries. England's traditional divorce laws largely rested with the ecclesiastical courts and were thus rarely granted. Parliament could grant a divorce via a private act, but this was complex and expensive. Between 1670 and 1857, only 325 people obtained a divorce, and only four in total were obtained by female petitioners.[20] So difficult was the process of obtaining a divorce, Leonie Star asserts that for many, bigamy, murder and for a short time, wife sale, were the only alternatives.[21]

In 1857, the parliament of the UK passed the Matrimonial Causes Act. This Act created a civil court that was empowered to grant divorces without any reference to ecclesiastical courts. It created a new Court for Divorce and Matrimonial Causes. The grounds upon which divorce could be granted were different for men and women (the infamous divorce double standard). A husband only needed proof of his wife's adultery, whereas for a wife, a divorce could only be granted if her husband's adultery was accompanied by other offences such as incest, bigamy, sodomy, bestiality, cruelty or desertion. This view was in keeping with the general double standard that existed in society that tolerated male infidelity while simultaneously punishing women severely for it.

Early colonial Australia provided an interesting context for these laws. The States were encouraged to pass their own version of the 1857 Act, and did so. South Australia was the first in 1857 and New South Wales the last in 1873. Conditions in early Australia were not ideal for permanent and monogamous relationships. Many convicts had left families behind with little hope of ever seeing them again, there was a high mobility rate ,with many moving frequently in search of 'better conditions and greater wealth', and there was a general shortage of women. These conditions made for a greater need for a clear-cut divorce law. As Henry Finlay argues:

> There was a major need for the availability of a law of divorce that would allow a deserted wife an independent existence without a husband, where the latter absconded. In a colony where there was a scarcity of women, it also made her free to contract another marriage with a provider for her children, in preference to the greater uncertainty of de facto habitation.[22]

---

20   L Star, *Counsel of Perfection: The Family Court of Australia* (Oxford University Press, Australia 1996) 25.

21   Star, *Counsel of Perfection* 26–27. See also L Stone, *Road to Divorce: England 1530–1987* (Oxford University Press, Oxford 1990).

22   H Finlay, 'Divorce and the Status of Women: Beginnings in Nineteenth Century Australia' Australian Institute of Family Studies seminar paper http://www.aifs.gov.au/institute/seminars/finlay.html accessed 21/03/2013.

As a result, bigamy based on the presumption of death was much more widespread in Australia than in England. Despite the different conditions and attempts to pass laws that were more in keeping with the social conditions in Australia, the laws followed more or less the same pattern as they did in England.

By the end of the nineteenth century, married women had won a number of important rights in relation to the ownership of property and the right to leave a marriage. There were other significant reforms in relation to the custody of children. The Infant Custody Act 1839 allowed the Court of Chancery to award mothers custody of their children under the age of 16. Some protection was also won in relation to domestic violence. The Matrimonial Causes Act of 1878 allowed women who had been beaten by their husbands to get a separation order from a local magistrate, putting an end to the idea that he could chastise her physically. Such an order would thereafter prevent her husband from seeking a restitution of conjugal rights, an action that was otherwise not abolished till the late twentieth century.[23] Another victory came in 1891 in the case of *Regina v Jackson* when the Court held that a husband does not have the right to make a prisoner of his wife in the home.[24] These changes in the law did not change the fact that women had the right only to apply to a court to be able to leave an abusive and brutal husband, they did not have the right to leave per se. As Shanley points out, to do so would leave a wife open to being guilty of desertion, receiving an order for restitution of conjugal rights, lose her right to claim maintenance, and affect her claim to her property (before 1882).[25] Furthermore, as it is still the case, there is a significant gap between the law as written and the law as practiced. Francis Cobbe's essay 'Wife-torture in England' documents a shocking tolerance by the courts towards domestic violence during this period.[26] The economic realities also meant that it was difficult for women to leave an unhappy marriage and support themselves and their children. Nevertheless, significant reform did take place in the nineteenth century and continued into the twentieth century.

Twentieth-Century Reform

Reform to marriage during the twentieth century was substantial. The introduction of no fault divorce, the removal of some old common law vestiges of patriarchy and the general development of a rights and equality based discourse had significant impact.

---

23 Matrimonial Proceedings and Property Act 1970 UK; Family Law Act 1974 AUS.

24 *R v Jackson* [1891] 1 QB 671.

25 Shanley, *Feminism, Marriage, and the Law in England, 1850–1895* 174.

26 Cobbe, 'Wife Torture in England'.

The federal jurisdiction for marriage was exercised for the first time in Australia by the passing of the Matrimonial Causes Act of 1959. This Act legislated 14 grounds for divorce. The grounds mirrored some already existing state legislation. Some of these grounds were adultery, desertion, wilfull refusal to consummate the marriage, cruelty, rape, sodomy, bestiality and habitual drunkenness and habitual intoxication as a result of drug use. These causes were applied equally to men and women thus removing the infamous divorce double standard.[27] This Act also removed the inability to consummate a marriage as a ground for the making of a declaration of nullity, another significant departure from the religious meaning of marriage. The importance of consummation, however, remained ambiguous given that a possible ground for divorce was to wilfully refuse to consummate a marriage. The Act was predicated on the idea that divorce would be granted if one of the parties was at fault, the only provision which would allow parties to divorce without this requirement was if the parties had been separated for five years. Out of 24,500 divorces granted under this Act, the most popular of the grounds were desertion (9,000), adultery (8,000), separation and cruelty.[28]

No-fault divorce was introduced with the passing of the Family Law Act (FLA) in 1975 (Matrimonial Causes Act 1973 in the UK). This Act can be seen as both a reaction to, and a scaffolding of the many social changes that had occurred in the previous decades. Nonetheless it remains one of the most contentious pieces of legislation ever passed in Australia.[29] The FLA removed from the process the attribution of blame and the need to provide clear and graphic evidence of that blame, and instead replaced all 14 grounds with a single one, 'irretrievable breakdown',[30] evidenced simply by a 12-month separation.[31] The granting of a divorce thus became an administrative rather than an adversarial process, it provided a marriage that was no longer working with 'a decent burial with the minimum of embarrassment, humiliation and bitterness'.[32]

---

27 For a discussion of the divorce double standard see A S Holmes, 'The Double Standard in the English Divorce Laws, 1857–1923' (1995) 20(2) *Law and Social Inquiry* 601–620.

28 Starr, *Counsel of Perfection* 57. The 'fault' scheme under the Matrimonial Causes Act has been described as creating incentives to commit abuses, encouraging collusion and perjury, and blackmail. L Young & G Monahan, *Family Law in Australia* seventh edition (Lexis Nexis Butterworths Australia 2009) 189. The process required for divorce under this legislation has been described as sordid and highly adversarial. See E Cox in ABC Radio National 'Finding Fault' *Hindsight* 15/08/10 http://www.abc.net.au/rn/hindsight/stories/2010/2977277.htm accessed 02/09/2010. See also S Swain, *Born in Hope: The Early Years of the Family Court of Australia* (UNSW Press, NSW 2012) 51.

29 Star *Counsel of Perfection* 51.

30 The FLA however also empowered the newly established Family Law Court to make determinations on spousal maintenance; child maintenance; child custody and contact, and property distributions. All of these are ancillary to the granting of a divorce. The Act also abolished the right for damages for adultery, enticement and criminal conversation.

31 FLA s 48(2).

32 Great Britain Law Commission, 'Reform of the Grounds of Divorce: The Field of Choice' report no 6 in Star, *Counsel of Perfection* 55.

The FLA makes a number of other important provisions. In regard to the custody of children, it legislated the principle that custody decisions must be made according to the principle of what is 'in the best interest of the child', and a rebuttable presumption exists that parental responsibility be equally shared between fathers and mothers.[33] In regard to property distribution, the court has wide discretion to make orders according to the parties' contribution (financial and non-financial) and their future needs. There no longer exists any assumption that property obtained during a marriage belongs to the husband alone. In regards to financial support, both parents are now considered responsible for the maintenance of the children of a marriage and spousal maintenance is regarded in gender neutral terms, it is no longer automatically assumed, and it is usually granted for only limited and short term circumstances.[34]

Furthermore, in keeping with a more individualistic view of marriage, the FLA encourages parties to come to their own agreements in relation to their financial settlement, maintenance payments and custody arrangements, giving courts power in these areas only when the parties themselves cannot reach agreement or when the agreements reached are considered unjust or inequitable.[35]

There were other legal changes that had significant impact upon the institution of marriage. In 1991, (much later than one would have believed) the common law finally removed the marital immunity against rape. In *R v L* the High Court of Australia said that the notion 'was out of keeping with the view society now takes of the relationship between the parties to a marriage'.[36] Justice Brennan went so far as to question the validity of the common law principle itself arguing that sex in marriage, according to ecclesiastical law, was always subject to consent.[37] Other legal reforms such as the recognition of de-facto relationships[38] and civil unions,[39] as well as reforms that removed the distinction between children born in wedlock and outside of it,[40] further challenged the centrality of marriage in organising intimacy, family and procreation.

---

33   See sections 60CA, 60CC, 61C, 61DA.

34   See Part VII.

35   See sections 63AA, 63B and 85–89.

36   *R v L* (1991) 174 CLR 390 (Mason CJ, Deane & Toohey JJ). In England the immunity was also removed in the same year in the case of *R v R* [1991] 2 WLR 1065.

37   *R v L* (1991) 174 CLR 396 (Brennan J). This case will be discussed further in chapter two.

38   State legislation recognising de-facto relationships began to be passed in the 1980s. See M Harrison, 'The Legal System and De Facto Relationships' (1991) 30 *Family Matters* 30–33. See R Probert, *The Changing Legal Regulation of Cohabitation: From Fornicators to Family 1600–2010* (Cambridge University Press, Cambridge 2012).

39   Civil Union legislation currently exists in Victoria the ACT and Tasmania. Tasmania was the first state to pass legislation in 2004.

40   In the mid-nineteen seventies most states passed legislation to remove disadvantages for ex-nuptial children. See Law Reform commission of NSW Issues Paper 1 (1981) — De Facto Relationships http://www.lawlink.nsw.gov.au/lrc.nsf/pages/ip1chp3 accessed 16/01/2013.

Finally, mention must be made of international and national human rights discourse. The signing of international treaties against the discrimination of women (Convention for the Elimination of Discrimination against Women 1979), and the subsequent passing of anti-discrimination laws such as The Sex Discrimination Act (1984), outlawed both explicit and implicit discrimination based on sex and gender. These international and domestic laws catapulted society into a discourse of rights which has led to a general rethinking of how men and women were and are treated in the workplace and in the home, and has further added to the erosion of marriage as a patriarchal institution.

The Meanings of Marriage: Holy Estate, Oppressive Patriarchy, Equal Love

This brief legislative history shows considerable changes to the meaning of marriage in the past 300 or so years. There are now a plurality of meanings to marriage.[41] Some have described marriage as an institution at a crossroad.[42] In the introduction I expressed this as marriage embodying a number of contests. Returning to Blake's three concepts of unity, consortium and support, we can say that in many ways the institution still reflects these principles, but the way that we understand the principles themselves has now changed.

Marriage is no longer overwhelmingly seen as a religious, life-long or patriarchal institution. Despite the fact that churches continue to take a very active interest in marriage, as evidenced by the public discourse around same-sex marriage, statistics show that, for many, marriage is more secular and contractual than religious. In 2007, 63 per cent of marriages were conducted in a civil ceremony alone;[43] this reflects a radical departure from the idea of marriage as 'a state of existence ordained by the Creator', 'a holy estate' and a 'sacred obligation'.[44] Similarly, marriage is no longer a life-long institution. In Australia, a third of all marriages end in divorce.[45] The other significant change that has occurred to marriage is the slow removal of men's total power and control over their wives. Reforms during the nineteenth and twentieth centuries slowly eroded the idea that husbands own their wives and can use, and abuse, them as they see fit.

---

41   As Martha Fineman says, the reasons for marrying are as 'diverse as the inhabitants of our contemporary, secular state'. 'The Meaning of Marriage' 33.

42   See M Garrison and E S Scott (eds), *Marriage at the Crossroads: Law, Policy and the Brave New World of Twenty-First-Century Families* (Cambridge University Press, Cambridge 2012). See also Martha Fineman, *The Autonomy Myth: Theory of Dependency* (New York Press, New York 2004) and 'The Meaning of Marriage'.

43   C Frew, 'The Social Construction of Marriage in Australia' (2011) 28 *Law in Context* 81.

44   J Witte jnr, *From Sacrament to Contract: Marriage, Religion and Law in the Western Tradition* (Westminster John Knox Press, Louisville Kentucky 1997) 194.

45   http://www.mydivorce.com.au/divorceadvice/divorce-statistics-australia.htm accessed 10/01/2013.

Even though much has changed, marriage still remains a problematic institution for feminists. Dianne Post,[46] for example, has described marriage as an enterprise that has a 50 per cent failure rate, which results in domestic violence in 63 per cent of cases, and which results in child abuse in up to 80 per cent of cases. She says that if this was any other enterprise it would be abolished, instead, 'politicians extol it, courts ruminate over its value to society, and business, religious and cultural leaders pander to its mystique'.[47] This view leads many to question the worthiness of the existence of the institution *in toto*.

Martha Fineman, for example, has consistently argued that the state should not support and privilege the family unit as defined via marriage. Marriage, Fineman argues, has become a largely irrelevant institution, whose primary and important functions and goals can and are being met elsewhere.[48] She argues that the state should, in fact, abandon civil marriage as an institution and instead support relationships which ensure that human needs are met humanely and justly.[49] Abolishing marriage would take gender equality seriously by letting individuals themselves bargain for the content of their agreements.[50] Disputes arising from such agreements would be dealt with according to general principles of equity and common law rather than specialised principles of family law. This would ensure 'that a lot more regulation (protection) would occur once interactions between individuals within families were removed from behind the veil of privacy that now shields them'.[51] By abolishing marriage, the state would be removing protection for such behaviour and exposing women and children to the same protections that the law offers all citizens. In fact, Fineman says, 'we would even begin to develop theories of tort to compensate sexual affiliates for conduct endemic to family interactions but considered unacceptable among strangers'.[52]

---

46   D Post, 'Why Marriage Should be Abolished' (1996–97) 18 *Women's Rights Law Reporter* 283–313.

47   Post, 'Why Marriage Should be Abolished' 283. How Post arrives at these figures is not clear, but her point is valid, there are many unhappy and failed marriages and much domestic violence and child abuse by any measure of the statistics.

48   Fineman argues that the functions that are currently fulfilled by marriage can be and are being fulfilled by other relationships. She claims that marriage is expected to do a lot of essential work in our society, 'children must be cared for and nurtured, dependency must be addressed, and individual happiness is of general concern', but all of these tasks can be met by transferring the legal status and the social and economic subsidies to the relationship of caretaker and dependent. This change would not only be fair but it would also be more reflective of current realities. Fineman quotes US data which shows that less than a quarter of households are made up of married couples and their children. Fineman, 'The Meaning of Marriage' 30, 39, 42.

49   M Fineman, *The Autonomy Myth*. See also N D Polikoff, 'Why Lesbians and Gay Men Should Read Martha Fineman' (2000) 8 *American University Journal of Gender Social Policy and Law* 167–176. However this is not to say that marriage is universally condemned by feminists. See, for example, Pat Maniardi who said, 'I believe women — and men — would like love, security, companionship, respect and long term commitment to each other. Women rarely get much of this, in marriage or out, but we want it.' P Maniardi, 'The Marriage Question in the Feminist Revolution' cited in C A Douglas, *Love and Politics: Radical Feminist and Lesbian Theories* (Ism Press, San Francisco 1990) 169.

50   Fineman, 'Meaning of Marriage' 58.

51   Fineman, 'Meaning of Marriage' 58.

52   Fineman, 'Meaning of Marriage' 59. Furthermore, abolishing marriage would be of benefit to same-sex couples whose relationships currently do not enjoy the same status of marriage. If the state does not prefer

While many are calling for the abolition of the institution altogether, it is important to acknowledge that, for many, marriage still retains importance through its traditional meanings. Churches still see the institution primarily in religious terms. Empirical studies also show that religious believers are more likely to marry than non-religious believers,[53] and that, at least at the time of entering into marriage, people intend it to be a life-long relationship.[54] And many still argue that the institution is largely constructed around patriarchy.[55] Every now and then we are reminded of some of these meanings of marriage. For example, take the case in 2008 of Italian bishop Lorenzo Chiarinelli, who refused to allow a young paraplegic man to marry in the Catholic Church on the grounds that he would be unable to consummate the marriage.[56] Consider also the fact that, in 2012, the Anglican Sydney diocese approved a new form of words for marriage vows that includes a promise by the wife to submit to her husband.[57]

For those who reject traditional meanings, a number of different theories to understand modern marriage have been postulated. Witte claims that by the turn of the twenty-first century marriage is viewed as 'a private bilateral contract to be formed, maintained, and dissolved as the couple sees fit'.[58] This would imply that marriage is now to be understood by the same forces that underlie all contracts, freedom, equality and intention. This is undeniably so, but it ignores other important aspects of the relationship associated with for example happiness, satisfaction, care and altruism. In other words, a contractual understanding of marriage does not make room for an understanding of its emotional underpinnings.

Wilcox and Dew argue that marriage today has become an expressive 'super relationship' for soulmates, whose primary focus is the emotional fulfillment of

---

a form of sexual affiliation then 'none would be prohibited', and if 'substantial economic and other societal benefits currently afforded to certain heterosexual units would no longer be justified', then 'punishments of "deviant" sexual connections would no longer be permitted'. Fineman, 'Meaning of Marriage' 59.

53   See B Hewitt and J Baxter, 'Who Gets Married in Australia?: The Characteristics Associated with a Transition Into First Marriage 2001–6' (2012) 48 *Journal of Sociology* 43–61.

54   Empirical studies show that a major reason given for getting married is the desire to make a life-long commitment to another person. See Relationships Australia, 'Relationships Indicator Survey' http://www.relationships.org.au/what-we-do/research/australian-relationships-indicators accessed 16/02/2013.

55   See also Martha Fineman, *The Autonomy Myth* and 'The Meaning of Marriage'. See also Post, 'Why Marriage Should Be Abolished'.

56   Discussion of this case on a blog featuring the story brought this telling comment from a reader, again reminding us of the importance that is attached to marriage as procreation. The blogger said, 'apparently the secular media decided to present this unremarkable and perennial fact as "news", as part of the evil campaign to convince people that "marriage" can be redefined to mean simply a public declaration that two people love each other'. 'No Church Wedding for Impotent Man' *Cath News* 12/06/2008 http://www.cathnews.com/article.aspx?aeid+7581 accessed 07/13/2009.

57   This new form of words requires the minister to ask the bride: 'Will you honour and submit to him, as the church submits to Christ?' and the bride is required to pledge 'to love and to submit'. K Burke 'To Love and to Submit: A Marriage Made in 2012' *Sydney Morning Herald*, 25/09/2012 http://www.smh.com.au/action/printArticle?id=3581935 accessed 1/06/2013.

58   Witte, *From Sacrament to Contract* 195.

each of the spouses in the marriage. This is in contrast to the traditional model of marriage that has focussed on the norms of permanency, fidelity, mutual aid, parenthood and gender complimentarity.[59] It is the emotional content of the relationship, therefore, that one must look to for its definition. The lens that best provides this is romantic love. One of the motifs, if not the central motif of marriage in the west in the twenty-first century is romantic love. Empirical studies bear this out. The longitudinal study conducted by Relationships Australia consistently reports that love is either the top reason, or one of the top reasons people give for marrying. (Other factors include companionship and wanting to signify a life-long commitment.) In 2008, a staggering 91 per cent of respondents said it was the reason they married.[60] Alison Diduck and Felicity Kaganas argue that, when all is said and done, marriage is still seen as 'the ultimate commitment one can make to a sexual or emotional partner',[61] and while it is undeniable that there may be many motivations for marriage, Bix claims, they are almost always framed within the language of love.[62]

The coming together of love and marriage has been documented by Stephanie Coontz in her book *Marriage, a History: How Love Conquered Marriage*.[63] Coontz shows that the idea of marrying for love was a highly radical idea, which came to be accepted in the west by the end of the seventeenth century. Before this time, marriage served a variety of social, economic and political purposes. As Coontz puts it, it did much of the work of markets and governments and it 'orchestrated people's personal rights and obligations in everything from sexual relations to the inheritance of property'.[64]

However, she says that by the end of the seventeenth century marriage came to be seen as a private affair, and its success was based upon how well it met the emotional needs of its members. This developed in the eighteenth century, when marriage was elevated to new sentimental heights:

> The Victorians were the first people in history to try to make marriage the pivotal experience in people's lives and married love the principal focus of their emotions, obligations and satisfactions ... Victorian

---

59   Wilcox & Dew, 'Is Love a Flimsy Foundation?: Soulmate Versus Institutional Models of Marriage' (2010) 39 *Social Science Research* 687–699.
60   See Relationships Australia, 'Relationships Indicator Survey' http://www.relationships.org.au/what-we-do/research/australian-relationships-indicators acessed 16/01/2013. See also A Diduck & F Kaganas, *Family Law Gender and the State: Text, Cases and Materials* (Hart, Oxford 2006) 35–36; P R Amato, 'Institutional, Companionate, and Individualistic Marriages: Change Over Time and Implications for Marital Quality' in Garrison & Scott (eds), *Marriage at the Crossroads* 107–125.
61   Diduck & Kaganas, *Family Law, Gender and the State* 36.
62   B Bix, 'Bargaining in the Shadow of Love: The Enforcement of Premarital Agreements and How We Think About Marriage' (1998–1999) 40 *William & Mary Law Review* 145–208.
63   S Coontz, *Marriage: A History — How Love Conquered Marriage* (Penguin Books, New York 2005).
64   Coontz, *Marriage: A History* 9.

marriage harboured all the hopes of romantic love, intimacy, personal fulfilment, and mutual happiness that were to be expressed more openly and urgently during the twentieth century.[65]

Coontz argues that by the middle of the nineteenth century there was unanimity in the middle and upper classes in Europe and North America that 'the love-based marriage, in which the wife stayed at home protected and supported by her husband, was a recipe for heaven on earth'.[66]

According to Marilyn Yaloum, there is now a consensus that 'love has become synonymous with marriage in the western world'.[67] In her book, *A History of the Wife*, Yaloum documents a letter to a 'Dear Abby' advice column in which the writer seeks advice regarding whether she should marry a man who would be 'a wonderful husband and father' but whom she does not love. The letter-writer asks: 'he is all a woman could ask for in a husband, but is that enough to replace love?' The answer comes back decidedly from Abby: 'If you marry this man, knowing in your heart you do not love him, you will be doing yourself and him a great disservice.'[68] This view is widespread. Lawrence Stone, for example, argues that there is a clear distinction in modern western societies between a marriage of interest and a marriage of love, with the former considered 'morally reprehensible'.[69]

Even among the aristocracy, where there is still an understanding that marriages are dynastic rather than love unions, the rhetoric cannot be escaped. When the engagement between Prince Charles and Diana Spencer was announced in 1981, it was well understood that Charles had to marry, and that considerable work had been done to find him a wife who would fulfil all of the necessary requirements of being a princess and future queen. In a pre-wedding television interview, Prince Charles was asked whether he loved Diana. There was a moment of visible discomfort before he replied that it is hard to know what love is.[70] As Mary Evans explains, he could not answer truthfully that the marriage had been a result of 'dynastic pressures' and the best he hoped from the marriage was an 'amicable relationship'.[71] As Evans claims, 'To admit openly that it is possible to enter a marriage and not be in love is tantamount to a refusal of Western culture and a distancing from one of the crucial tenets of popular culture.'[72] It must also be

---

65 Coontz, *Marriage: A History* 177–78.

66 Coontz, *Marriage: A History* 162.

67 M Yaloum, *A History of the Wife* (Perennial, New York 2001) xv.

68 'Dear Abby Advice Column' July 3 1998 *San Francisco Chronicle* in Yaloum *History of the Wife* xi.

69 Stone ,*The Family, Sex and Marriage in England 1500–1800* 86.

70 A Carthew, interview with Prince Charles and Lady Diana ITN 24 Feb 1981 http://news.bbc.co.uk/onthisday/hi/dates/stories/february/24/newsid_2516000/2516759.stm accessed 1/12/2010.

71 M Evans, 'Falling in Love is Falling for Make Believe: Ideologies of Romance in Post-Enlightenment Culture' (1998) 15 *Theory Culture and Society* 269.

72 Evans, 'Falling in Love is Falling for Make Believe' 269.

noted here that the idea of love based marriages has spread beyond western and English-speaking societies.[73] Furthermore, as will be shown in chapter four, the popularity of same-sex marriage doesn't make much sense unless we understand marriage as an institution grounded in romantic love.

Consequences of the Love Marriage (The Feminist Critique of Love)

The connection of love and marriage is not without its problems. Romantic love, from the very beginning, was considered a dangerous idea. Its connection with liberty and freedom, its disconnection from family, class, social and religious duty, make it an obvious target for criticism. Its association, no matter how misconceived, with free love and sexual freedom made it a threat to traditional family structures and to life-long monogamous marriage. This point has some weight. The association of love with marriage has been shown to make the institution of marriage a less stable and more fickle one.[74] Many point to the casualties of romantic love. These casualties are said to be high divorce rates, loneliness, poverty and social instability. As Solomon puts it:

Most of the world looks upon our romantic fantasies as a source of social chaos and irresponsibility … [o]ur emphasis on romance encourages vanity instead of camaraderie, seclusion instead of community, whimsicality instead of responsibility, emotional excitement instead of social stability. The result seems to be a culture that is fragmented, frustrated and lonely just as much as (and because) it is romantic.[75]

Beck and Beck-Gersheim, echoing some of the feminist's arguments we will see below, claim that modern love can turn into a destructive force. The meaning of love, they suggest, is always open for negotiation and always at risk. Love can

---

73   See R Goodwin, *Personal Relationships Across Cultures* (Routledge, USA 1999).

74   Empirical studies do show that marriages based on love are flimsy and much more likely to end in conflict and divorce than those based on values of permanency embedded in religious institutions. See W B Wilcox & J Dew, 'Is Love a Flimsy Foundation?: Soulmate Versus Institutional Models of Marriage' *Social Science Research* 39 (2010) 687–699.

75   Solomon, *About Love* 54. Even more than this, romantic love, along with romanticism in general, is seen as containing within it a deathly streak because it portrays true love as something that must be not only indifferent to, but even welcoming to death. Passionate love is not only the basis for a meaningful life but can also form the basis for a meaningful death. As West puts it, '[i]n reality the relationship of lovers is always vulnerable to frustration either by a hostile society or as a result of the waywardness of human emotion. Romantic extremism responds by showing its willingness to sacrifice reason, social order and, if necessary, life itself for the sake of its absolute commitment to love "even unto death". The impossibility of love in this world becomes the reason for its pursuit in another. A preoccupation with death was, indeed a recurrent feature of romantic thought.' D West, *Reason and Sexuality in Western Thought* (Polity Press, Cambridge 2005) 112.

end on one person's say-so at any time; there is no right of appeal. Love is the opposite of instrumental and rational behaviour, it makes its own rules 'out of sexual desire unhampered by moral or legal obligations'.[76] They argue:

> For individuals who have to invent their own social settings, love becomes the central pivot giving meaning to their lives. In this world where no one demands obedience or respect for old habits, love is exclusively in the first person singular, and so are truth, morality, salvation, transcendence and authenticity ... Growing out of itself and its own subjective views, it easily turns totalitarian; rejecting any outside authority, and agreeing to take over responsibility, to compromise and be fair only for emotional reasons.[77]

However, the most sustained critique of romantic love (not just marriage) comes from feminism. While both Solomon and Giddens have argued that the connection of love with freedom and equality can be liberating and empowering for women,[78] this assertion has been hotly contested by some feminists. Shulamith Firestone described romantic love as the pivot of oppression for women, describing love as a holocaust, a hell and a sacrifice.[79] In this, she echoed Simone de Beauvoir, who argued that given the unequal position of men and women, love becomes 'a curse that lies heavily upon a woman confined in the feminine universe, woman mutilated, insufficient unto herself. The innumerable martyrs to love bear witness against the injustice of a fate that offers a sterile hell as ultimate salvation.'[80] These views have been reiterated by later feminists. As Carol Smart puts it, feminists have identified love as an aspect of 'patriarchy's ideological armament through which women became hooked into dependent relationships with men, entered into an unfavourable legal contract (namely marriage) and ultimately ended up with care of the children'.[81] Here Smart points to one of

---

76   Beck & Beck-Gernsheim, *The Normal Chaos of Love* 194.

77   Beck & Beck-Gernsheim, *The Normal Chaos of Love* 171.

78   See R C Solomon, 'Love and Feminism' in R B Baker K J Wininger & F A Elliston (eds), *Philosophy and Sex*, third edition (Prometheus Books, New York 1998) and A Giddens, *The Transformation of Intimacy: Sexuality Love and Eroticism in Modern Societies* (Polity Press, Cambridge 1992).

79   S Firestone, *The Dialectic of Sex: The Case for Feminist Revolution* (Bantam Books, New York 1970).

80   S de Beauvoir, *The Second Sex* trans H M Parshley (Alfred A Knopf, New York 1953) 669. See also Mary Woolstencraft and Harriet Taylor as discussed in S Mendus, *Feminism and Emotion: Readings in Moral and Political Philosophy* (MacMillan Press Ltd, GB 2000).

81   Smart, *Personal Life* (Polity Press, Cambridge 2007) 60.

the central underpinnings of the feminist critiques. Love is not itself oppressive but becomes so because of the social context in which it is conducted, namely patriarchy[82] and the public and private divide.[83]

This feminist critique of love, sex (and marriage) is developed by Eva Illouz in her latest book, *Why Love Hurts*. Illouz remains committed to love as a central idea of modernity and champions its egalitarian optimism and its ability to subvert patriarchy.[84] However, she also recognises that love is also the source of much misery, stemming from the 'institutional arrangements' around it. Love is played out in 'the marketplace of unequal competing actors' where some people, mostly men, are able to 'command a greater capacity to define the terms in which they are loved by others'.[85] Control is exercised by the ways in which choice, freedom, autonomy and commitment are differently played out between men and women. Within all of these structures, Illouz argues, there is a mismatch of goals and expectations, and 'a set of conundrums'.[86] In relation to commitment, for example, men are less likely to want marriage and a family because these are no longer sites of control and domination, men now measure success not according to a successful commitment, but rather, success on the sexual market. As such, men wish to remain uncommitted for as long as possible. Women on the other hand, see the sexual market as a marriage market and are in it for a shorter period of time because of career goals, and because of the prevalence of the categories of sexiness and beauty closely tied to age.[87]

These feminist critiques are rooted in the social and cultural context that marriage is practiced in. However, feminists have also found love's internal ideology to be problematic. While acknowledging the power of patriarchy and the division of spheres as problematic, Marilyn Freidman considers the central problem of love to stem from its long association with the idea of merger.[88] Friedman argues that the features of merger experienced within romantic love are that: the needs and

---

82   Mary Evans has described love as a 'plot by men to sugar the evil pill of patriarchal domesticity'. 'Falling in Love is Falling for Make Believe: Ideologies of Romance in Post-Enlightenment Culture' (1998) 15 *Theory Culture and Society* 273. For Stevi Jackson, the feminist critique of love is epitomised by the popular saying, 'it starts when you sink into his arms and ends with your arms into his sink'. S Jackson, 'Even Sociologists Fall in Love: An Exploration in the Sociology of Emotions' (1993) 27(2) *Sociology* 204.

83   Elena Pulcini has argued the main prism through which love oppresses is the private sphere. Love she argues not only ties women to the private sphere but reduces them to being guardians of sentiments and privacy. It is true that this embodies some power but it is a hidden power which not only creates inequality but also masks it. E Pulcini, 'Modernity, Love and Hidden Inequality' trans L Fraser in *Love and Law in Europe: Complex Interrelations* (EUI Working papers, European University Institute 2000/2) 41–42.

84   Illouz, *Why Love Hurts* 5.

85   Illouz, *Why Love Hurts* 6.

86   Illouz, *Why Love Hurts* 241–44.

87   See Illouz, *Why Love Hurts: A Sociological Explanation* (Polity, Cambridge 2012) chapter three. See also A Jonasdottir's ideas around love power in 'What Kind of Power is Love Power?' in A Jonasdottir *et al* (eds), *Sexuality, Gender and Power* (Routledge, London 2011).

88   Aristophanes, followed by courtly and romantic love, make the idea of unification between two bodies and souls central to romantic love.

interests of each person become entwined or pooled together; couples feel each other's highs and lows; there is mutual consideration and awareness; couples care for and protect each other; couples can communicate with each other efficiently; couples make joint decisions and long term plans; there is a division of labour; couples desire to be seen as good by each other, and want to be valued by their partners in a way that they value themselves.[89] Friedman does not necessarily see these features as negative in themselves, but they can represent a significant reduction in personal autonomy, and this is more dangerous for women than for men for a number of reasons. First, she argues, when seen in a social context, love 'is guided by norms and stereotypes. Foremost among these are gender norms and ideals of romantic heterosexual love.'[90] One such ideal, for example, is that women should marry 'up'; that a woman should marry someone who is 'taller, stronger, older, richer, smarter and higher up on the social scale'[91] than she is. The result of this is that women will always be seen as bringing less to the relationship than the men, and it is this, Freedman claims, which makes the romantic merger of identities more risky for women than for men.[92] But even overall, she argues that the concept of merger is risky:

> Lovers may be very different from each other in their resources, capacities, and commitments they bring to their love. These differences can create imbalances of power, authority, and status within a romantic relationship. When two lovers become one, the one they become may very well be more than the other. Or the merger might take place within one lover alone, so to speak.[93]

Wendy Langford also disputes the ideology of love itself as being positive. Love is not the great ideal that it is claimed to be. She argues that while the idea that love has spread principles of justice and fairness widely is an attractive and optimistic view, it is empirically unsustainable and conceptually misguided. Along with others,[94] Langord is a strong critic of Giddens' view of contemporary love as outlined above. Langford says that, while our society has come to 'venerate deliverance' through love, with promises of 'liberty, equality and togetherness', romantic love is in fact a 'process by which restrictions, inequality and dissatisfaction are merely obscured'.[95] She argues that the rhetoric that love takes us higher and allows us to develop is wrong, rather, '[l]ove does not merely fail to give us what we desire but in so doing compounds painful

89   Friedman, 'Romantic Love and Personal Autonomy' 169. See also M Friedman, *Autonomy, Gender, Politics* (Oxford University Press, New York 2003) 167–68.
90   Friedman, 'Romantic Love and Personal Autonomy' 173.
91   Friedman, 'Romantic Love and Personal Autonomy' 173.
92   Friedman, 'Romantic Love and Personal Autonomy' 178.
93   Friedman, 'Romantic Love and Personal Autonomy' 169.
94   See also Jamieson, 'Intimacy Transformed?'.
95   Langford, *Revolutions of the Heart: Gender, Power and the Delusions of Love* (Routledge, London 1999) 21.

feelings of dissatisfaction and low self-esteem'.[96] Its effects are not positive, not even neutral, they are largely negative.[97] While love promises happiness and freedom from social constraint, it in fact delivers the opposite.[98] Echoing some of Friedman's arguments, the problem according to Langford is that the success of romantic love depends upon a particular abstract individual type and model of rational behaviour that is seldom found in reality. The individual required is 'self aware and operates on the basis of reason'. Not only is this individual rarely found in society at large, she is rarely found among women, and even more rarely found in the context of love.[99]

What emerges from the above critique is that love, far from being the liberating and egalitarian idea which many claim it is, is instead oppressive and degrading to women. This critique is further strengthened when we consider it alongside the feminist critiques of sex (as we must, given the earlier discussed slippage that occurs between sex and love).

Illouz has argued that the contemporary sexual market is dominated by ideas of freedom and choice, and is motivated by a desire to accumulate as much sexual capital as possible. This model of sexual behaviour, 'promoted by modern masculinity and too often endorsed and imitated by women',[100] does not meet any larger social and ethical goals, nor does it 'build ethical and emotional models congruent with the social experience of women'.[101] Feminists have long argued about sex and its impact on the position of women in society.[102] Two of the strongest voices in the feminist debate over the oppressive nature of heterosexual sex have been Catherine McKinnon and Andrea Dworkin. The view that sex (meaning heterosexual sex) is the 'linchpin of gender inequality', and that heterosexuality institutionalises 'male sexual dominance and female submission', is central to MacKinnon's arguments against sex.[103] She argues that women are defined by male dominance and female subordination. Women's sexuality is defined according to male desire and as such it is not possible to speak of women's pleasure or agency in a sexual relationship with a man.[104] Similarly, according to Dworkin, 'because women are exploited as a sex class

---

96   Langford, *Revolutions of the Heart* 50.

97   Langford, *Revolutions of the Heart* 50.

98   Langford, *Revolutions of the Heart* 4. Echoing this, Mary Evans argues that 'accumulated evidence of the last centuries suggest that people in the West have suffered more in their personal lives from 'love' than any other single ideology.' Evans links romantic love with rape and violence against women, claiming that those 'cultures which condone romance are also beset with the misreadings of it'. Evans 'Falling in Love with Love is Falling for Make Believe' 273.

99   Langford, *Revolutions of the Heart* 152.

100   Illouz, *Why Love Hurts* 247.

101   Illouz, *Why Love Hurts* 247.

102   See S Seidman, *Embattled Eros: Sexual Politics and Ethics in Contemporary America* (Routledge, New York 1992) chapter 3 'Defining the Moral Boundaries of Eros: The Feminist Sexuality Debates'.

103   C MacKinnon, 'Feminism, Marxism, Method and the State: An Agenda for Theory' (1982) 7 *Signs* 533.

104   MacKinnnon, *Feminism Unmodified* 135.

for sex, it is impossible to talk about women's sexuality outside the context of forced sex'.[105] Women cannot be equal to men if they are used as a tool for men's desires: 'What is lost by the woman when she becomes a sexual object, and when she is confirmed in that status by being fucked, is not recoverable.'[106] This is a contentious view. Simone de Beauvoir, for example, said that women needed to invent new 'non-oppressive' ways of understanding heterosexual sex, and not just accept established ideas.[107] Carole Vance claims that '[f]eminism must increase women's pleasure and joy, not just decrease our misery'.[108] Amber Hollibaugh points out that 'sex is not the same for all of us', and that by denying these differences feminism risks alienating many women. She asks, 'are we creating a political movement that we can no longer belong to if we don't feel our desires fit a model of proper feminist sex?'.[109] Camille Paglia and Naomi Wolf have argued that to reduce female sexual existence to sexual oppression completely obscures female sexual pleasure and agency.[110] Furthermore, some feminists have argued that to deny pleasure and agency is to risk a new era of puritanism.[111]

The discussion so far has shown that love has been and continues to be a problematic concept for many feminists. We must be careful not to overstate this. Some feminists dismiss the idea of romance as a site of women's oppression and complicity in patriarchal structures and instead see love as a site of resistance, transformation and agency. As already stated, Illouz sees love as egalitarian and subversive, and she is not alone in this regard. Pearce and Stacey, like Radway before them, argue that love retains its ability to liberate women from patriarchy because of its 'narrativity'. They argue that an engagement with the narrative of romance enables women to facilitate the 'rescripting of other areas of life'.[112] Langhamer has also shown how in everyday courtship behaviour young women in twentieth century Britain have been able to act as 'architects of their own lives and as active agents of social change'.[113]

---

105 A Dworkin, 'Renouncing Sexual Equality' cited in C A Douglas, *Love and Politics* 180.

106 A Dworkin, *Intercourse* (The Free Press, New York 1987) 16.

107 A Schwarzer, *After the Second Sex: Conversations with Simone De Beauvoir* (Pathenon Books, New York 1984) 36.

108 C Vance, 'Pleasure and Danger: Towards a Politics of Sexuality' in C Vance (ed), *Pleasure and Danger: Exploring Female Sexuality* (Routledge Kegan Paul, Boston 1984) 24.

109 A Hollibaugh, 'Desire for the Future: Radical Hope' in Vance (ed), *Pleasure and Danger* 403–04.

110 See C Paglia, *Sex, Art, American Culture* (Vintage Books, New York 1992); N Wolf, *Fire with Fire: The New Female Power and How it Will Change the 21st Century* (Random House, New York 1993); N Wolf, 'The Porn Myth' *New York News and Features* http://nymag.com/nymetro/news/trends/n_9437/ accessed 29/06/10.

111 K Abrams, 'Sex Wars Redux: Agency and Coercion in Feminist Legal Theory' (1995) 95 *Columbia Law Review* 311.

112 L Pearce & J Stacey (eds), *Romance Revisited* (Lawrence & Wishart, London 1995) 13. See also J A Radway, *Reading the Romance: Women, Patriarchy and Popular Literature*, (University of Carolina Press, Chapel Hill 1991).

113 C Langhamer, 'Love and Courtship in Mid-Twentieth-Century England' (2007) 50 *The Historical Journal* 196.

Conclusion

Legally, marriage has moved away from traditional meanings that associated it with religion and patriarchy. It is now more loosely considered a relationship that can be determined according to the parties themselves, especially when there are no children involved. Marriage is now more closely tied to love than ever before. This is evident in the social and cultural discourse of marriage, and in empirical studies on why people marry. If marriage is tied to love, the next important question is: to what extent does this connection impact upon both of these institutions? This inquiry must be aware that love has two predominant readings, one negative and one positive. We have seen that love is disassociated with duty and social boundaries, and is instead associated with ideas of freedom, equality, agency, choice and progress. This reading of love says that it represents a relationship whose content is negotiated between lovers themselves free of any external rules, it is an 'empty canvass, a subjective and mutual invention', capable of many permutations: a relationship that requires free and autonomous beings. It is these features of love that, at least in part, have made it the desirable existential goal it has become. But love has another side, it is closely linked with patriarchy and, as we will see in later discussion, with heterosexuality. This reading claims that the dominant scripts of love are tied up with procreation, family, marriage and domesticity, with monogamy and fidelity. As such, for women, love too readily translates into becoming a wife and mother.[114] This reading of love negates the ideas that love is free from rules and barriers, and renders it less likely to deliver its promises of freedom and equality. In any conversation about love both of these readings must be acknowledged.

The situation is further complicated by the fact that marriage is also a contested idea. There are multiple readings of marriage and multiple reasons people marry. Any discussion on the impact that love and marriage have on each other must consider these multiple meanings.

---

114   This resonates with the queer critique of love, which will be discussed later in the book.

2. The Diminishing Significance of Sexual Intercourse

Damn it, when you get married, you kind of expect you're going to get a little sex.[1]

Introduction

Traditionally, sexual intercourse was considered central to the legal definition of marriage. A marriage could be annulled and legally revoked if it had not been consummated. The law also made is clear that upon marriage a husband had unlimited sexual access to his wife. Neither of these principles are true any longer. This chapter documents the shift in the narrative of the relationship between marriage and sex from one of duty and procreation, to one of mutuality and pleasure, and in doing so examines the process in order to determine what role, if any, romantic love plays in this narrative.

The legal connection between sex[2] and marriage in law is not explicitly stated. The association of sex with immorality and licentiousness make it an uneasy topic for marriage and law. Courts are careful to avoid language that casts sex as a duty and could be interpreted as reducing wives to prostitutes. However it would not be accurate, or even desirable, to separate sex from marriage. Some old laws of marriage accept that sex is part of marriage, but dance around questions of consent, obligation and rights. Others, such as the marital immunity against rape, are unequivocal about both its centrality and the husband's right to demand it.[3] Modern laws have overturned these principles. The 1991 case of *R v L*,[4] asserted that a husband could be found guilty of raping his wife, and established that the crime of rape could exist in marriage, that men could not demand, and women did not have to submit to sex just because they were married. The revolutionary nature of the case cannot be overstated; it redefined the relationship between sex and marriage and helped to recreate the meaning

---

1   Attributed to Senator Jeremiah Denton, Republican, Alabama 1981 http://marriage.about.com/cs/maritalrape.htm accessed 8/04/10.

2   There is often slippage in the meaning of the word sex. This is especially so between the meaning of the word when used to indicate sexual activity and the word used to identify sexual identification. Where there is likely to be confusion, I refer to sexual identity and sexual activity in order to distinguish between the two. Otherwise, I follow the conventions of using the word to mean the two different things according to the context as is the case in everyday Australian English.

3   *R v Clarence* (1888) QB 23.

4   *R v L* (1991) 174 CLR 379.

of marriage. Some ten years later, the centrality of sex in marriage was further eroded with the case of *Re Kevin* which went on to assert that sex (sexual capacity and sexual intercourse) is not the central, defining characteristic of marriage.

Quite a shift has occurred between the old laws and the new laws, but what is the role of love within this new narrative? This chapter will demonstrate that love has come to be considered more important in the discourse of sex and marriage, albeit in a small way. *R v L* changed the perception that sex was an inevitable part of marriage, and instead linked sex with marriage only in the context of a mutually consensual and loving environment. *Re Kevin* also severed marriage from sex altogether and left a silence about the meaning of marriage which, I argue, can be filled with love. Despite the insinuation of love into sex and marriage, and despite the association of love with liberty and progress (as discussed in chapter one), sex and sexual access remain a delicate issue, and this is especially true in marriage.

The Old Discourse of Sex and Marriage

The extent to which law once saw sex as part of marriage requires a discussion of several different common law principles and legislation.

Consortium vitae[5]

According to Thornton, 'there is no precise legal definition of consortium and its elusive nature has permitted the judiciary to place its own gloss on the concept from time to time'.[6] In so far as we can define it, *Crabtree v Crabtree (No 2)* claims that consortium is a raft of things, including sexual intercourse, which together unite a husband and wife.[7] Consortium is defined as a partnership or association that involves a sharing of the good and the bad of the two lives involved: 'In its fullest sense it implies a companionship between each of them, entertainment of mutual friends, sexual intercourse — all those elements which when combined, justify the old common law dictum that a man and his wife are one person.'[8] In the *Marriage of Todd (No 2)*, the Court itemised the elements that make up consortium as 'dwelling under the same roof, sexual intercourse, mutual society and protection, [and] recognition of the existence of the marriage

---

5   Prior to the 1980s, this action was only recognised in common law as belonging to a husband. For a discussion of this see M Thornton, 'Loss of Consortium: Inequality Before the Law' (1984) 10 *The Sydney Law Review*; A Risely, 'Sex, Housework and the Law' (1980–81) 7 *Adelaide Law Review* 421–456. Since then, reform has taken place. The action has been abolished in New South Wales, Tasmania and Western Australia. South Australia has kept the action but allows wives to pursue the action equally with husbands.

6   Thornton, 'Loss of Consortium' 265.

7   *Crabtree v Crabtree* (No 2) [1964] ALR 820.

8   *Crabtree v Crabtree* (No 2) [1964] ALR 820 in Thornton, 'Loss of Consortium' 264–65.

by both spouses in public and private relationships'.[9] The Court stated that these elements need not all be present in every marriage.[10] While sexual intercourse is listed as an element of consortium in both *Crabtree v Crabtree* and in the *Marriage of Todd (No 2)*, most of the cases involving loss of consortium tend to focus on loss of services in relation to domestic work. However, there has also been some discussion on loss of sexual capacity. It is on this issue that I will focus my discussion.

In *Kealley v Jones*[11] Justice Samuels described sexual intercourse as a comfort of the most material kind (for the husband) but avoided the issue of value by saying that you cannot put a replacement/monetary value on something which is as unique as a wife's society. As Thornton puts it, the discomfort shown by Samuels J is understandable, as placing a monetary value on sexual services would 'ineluctably lead to the idea of the wife as a prostitute'.[12]

In *Birch v Taubmans Ltd*,[13] the Court distinguished between losses that were of a temporal nature and recoverable, and those losses that were of a spiritual nature which were not recoverable. Sexual intercourse was considered to be of a temporal nature. This classification was possible, however, because the Court discussed sexual intercourse in terms of loss of opportunity to have children rather than loss of sexual pleasure. In the end, the principle is carefully outlined. The judges said:

> We are of the opinion that where, as in this case, the opportunity ... [to procreate] has been taken away absolutely, such a deprivation transcends matters which might well be said to be within the terms of the limitation above referred to and is a loss which is temporal rather than spiritual.[14]

Subsequent cases, however, have acknowledged that the loss can also be of sexual pleasure. In *Meadows and Meadows v Maloney*,[15] Judge Walters was guided by the High Court's acceptance of the principle as outlined in *Birmingham Southern Railway Co v Lintner* where CJ McClellan accepted that loss of 'the society of a wife' and 'marital companionship' can be different from mere services, and thus can be recoverable. This principle is contained in the statement below by CJ McClellan.

> The husband, also, of course, has a legal right to the society of the wife, involving all the amenities and conjugal incidents of the relation.

---

9   *In the Marriage of Todd* (No 2) (1976) 1 Fam LR 11,188 (Watson J).
10   *In the Marriage of Todd* (No 2) (1976) 1 Fam LR 11,188 (Watson J).
11   *Kealley v Jones* [1979] 1 NSWLR 723 cited in Thornton 'Loss of Consortium' 266.
12   Thornton, 'Loss of Consortium' 268.
13   *Birch v Taubmans Ltd* [1956] 57 SR (NSW) 93.
14   A C Risely, 'Sex, Housework and the Law' (1980–81) 7 *Adelaide Law Review* 434–35.
15   *Meadows v Maloney* [1973] 4 SASR 567.

> This right of society may be invaded by an act which while leaving to the husband the presence of the wife, yet incapacitates her for the marital companionship and fellowship, and such incapacity may be the deprivation of her society differing in degree only from total deprivation by her death. For such impairment, so to say, of the wife's society, of his right of consortium, such deprivation of the aid and comfort which the wife's society, as a thing different from mere services, is supposed to involve, he is entitled to recover.[16]

This right to recover for loss of sexual pleasure within an action for loss of consortium was also recognised in *Hasaganic v Minister for Education*.[17] In this case, the parties were older, already had three children, and there was no question of further procreation. The Court accepted that the husband could claim for loss of services of his wife in relation to housework and to also claim for loss of ability to have sexual intercourse.

Justice Bright in *Fisher v Smithson*[18] welcomed the widening of the concept away from services and towards companionship and affection, claiming that this was more in keeping with the changing marriage relationship:

> [T]he cases seem to me to demonstrate a broadening of the approach, a greater emphasis on loss of companionship and affection, a somewhat reduced emphasis on loss of 'services'. If the law is as I hope, moving in this direction, it is merely reflecting, in my view, changing attitudes towards the matrimonial relationship.[19]

From this small sample of cases we can say that sexual intercourse is considered to be a part of the *consortium vitae*, but that a wife's 'society' is considered unique and is therefore difficult to place a value upon. In so far as courts have placed a value upon it, that value has been restricted to seeing sexual intercourse as an opportunity to procreate. There is some small evidence from the cases of *Hasaganic v Minister for Education* and *Fisher v Smithson* that this view is shifting, with courts showing a willingness to see sex as not only valuable for procreation but for fulfilling other emotional functions.

---

16 McClellan CJ in *Birmingham Southern Railway Co v Lintner* (1904) 141 ALA 427 quoted by Walters J in *Meadows v Maloney* [1973] 4 SASR 577–78.

17 *Hasaganic v Minister for Education* [1973] 5 SARS 554.

18 *Fisher v Smithson* (1977) 17 SASR 223.

19 *Fisher v Smithson* (1977) 17 SASR 227 (Bright J).

Conjugal Rights

Another perspective on the historical picture of the law's view on the relationship between marriage and sex can be gleaned by looking at the old action of conjugal rights.

Section 60 of the Matrimonial Causes Act 1959 (Cth) enabled a party to the marriage to petition the court for a restitution of conjugal rights. In order to succeed, a petitioner had to show, among other things, that the respondent's refusal is without just cause and excuse, and that the petitioner sincerely desires conjugal rights. Some legal dictionaries include sexual activity as an aspect of conjugal rights,[20] but it is important to note that the term remains largely undefined in either legislation or case law.

Cases show that sexual intercourse is an irrelevant factor in deciding whether one spouse has refused to render conjugal rights. In *Fielding v Fielding*,[21] Salmond J categorically asserted that refusal to have sex is not a ground which can be used to petition the court for a restitution of conjugal rights, that action being about co-habitation and not sexual relations. He stated the principle as follows:

> [T]he jurisdiction in restitution of conjugal rights is an old ecclesiastical jurisdiction, and is by the law that was in force in the Ecclesiastical Courts. Conjugal rights in those courts meant the right of co-habitation and nothing more, and that is what it still means.[22]

Similarly, in *Tew v Tew*[23] and *Orme v Orme*,[24] the Court dismissed a petition for restitution of conjugal rights where the applicants relied upon their spouse's refusal to have sexual intercourse.

Other cases, however, have taken an opposite view. *Synge v Synge*[25] was a case where the wife agreed to live with her husband only on the condition that there was no sexual intercourse between them. The husband, on the other hand, agreed to live with her only on the condition that there was. The Court found that refusal to have sexual intercourse is not actionable, but a partner to the marriage is entitled to leave it if the other does not consent to sexual relations. Sir Francis Jeune P said that the law could not condone a situation in which the husband is 'bound continually to expose himself to such mortification and

---

20 *Webster's New World Law Dictionary* defines conjugal rights as 'the mutual rights and privileges between two individuals that arise from the state of being married. These include, among other things, affection, companionship, co-habitation, joint property rights, and sexual gratification.' (Wiley Publishing, Hoboken New Jersey 2010).

21 *Fielding v Fielding* (1921) NZLR 1069.

22 *Fielding v Fielding* (1921) NZLR 1071 (Salmond J).

23 *Tew v Tew* (1921) NZLR 1071.

24 *Orme v Orme* (1824) 2 Add 382.

25 *Synge v Synge* [1900–03] All ER Rep 452.

misery as is necessarily involved' in such a marriage.[26] He went on to say that sex was an inevitable part of co-habitation. For Sir Francis Jeune P the two could not be distinguished:

> The objects of married life are as expressed in the marriage service and are not the less true because they are utterances of a more plain spoken age than the present, and, while human nature remains what it is, I think a husband has a right to decline to submit to a groundless demand of his wife that he should live with her as a husband in name only. Neither party to a marriage can, I think insist on cohabitation unless she or he is willing to perform a marital duty inseparable from it.[27]

A similar view was held by Justice Hill in *Wily v Wily*,[28] who, clearly referring to sex, rejected the view that just because you live in the same house you have performed your duty to your spouse. Both *Wily* and *Synge,* interestingly, refer to sex as a marital duty.

In *Bartlett v Bartlett*[29] Justice Evatt specifically considered whether sex was integrated in an action for restitution of conjugal rights and found that there was authority to support both sides of the question. He concluded that the question of sexual intercourse or 'mutual society' cannot be said to be irrelevant to the question of conjugal rights:

> [I]n the marriage service the woman promises 'to obey him, and serve him, love honour, and keep him in sickness and in health'. The man's promise is to 'love her comfort her, honour, and keep her in sickness and in health'. Revision or elision of some of the promises has been attempted, and with or without authority, been made. But the prayer book's third stated purpose for which marriage was ordained — 'mutual society, help and comfort', is of the essence of the marriage relationship.[30]

Bartlett thus stands for the proposition that sex is a part of marriage; it is not necessarily the most important part, but it is without doubt a part of it. Justice Evatt goes on to extend this relationship and, like Justice Brennan in *R v L*, as we will see, threw love into the mix. In deciding the case before him, he concluded that the relationship could not be saved: conjugality, including sexual relations, cannot be restored. He stated, 'it is difficult to see how, upon

---

26   *Synge v Synge* [1900–03] All ER Rep 461.
27   *Synge v Synge* [1900–03] All ER Rep 461.
28   *Wily v Wily* (1918) P1.
29   *Bartlett v Bartlett* (1933) 50 CLR 3.
30   *Bartlett v Bartlett* (1933) 50 CLR 23 (Evatt J).

the assumption that all love and affection have disappeared this fundamental purpose can be carried out'.[31] For Evatt J, then, it is not only marriage and sex that are connected but marriage, sex and love.

Matrimonial Causes Act (1959)

This Act mirrored the position that English law does not seek to enforce matrimonial sexual intercourse, and that the refusal to engage in sexual intercourse by either husband or wife does not amount to a matrimonial offence.[32] However, sex remains an important subtext to the relationship of marriage in the Act in a number of ways. For example, section 21 states that a marriage may be voidable if one or both parties are incapable of consummating the marriage. Furthermore, 'wilfully and persistently' refusing to consummate the marriage was a ground for divorce under section 28(c), and refusal to engage in sex could also be taken as evidence of desertion and thereby give rise to desertion as a ground for divorce under section 28(b).

In the above discussion we have seen all of the ways that sex was 'supported' as a legal part of marriage. The common law in relation to *consortium vitae* and conjugal rights saw sex as an important part of marriage, but stopped short of imposing it as a duty or even elevating it above any other element of marriage. In the context of cases seeking damages for loss of *consortium vitae* we have also seen a shift in seeing loss of sexual capacity as a loss measurable only in the context of inability to procreate to a widening of the concept to at least allow the possibility of counting loss of sexual pleasure.[33] This is in keeping with the shift that has occurred whereby sex in marriage has come to be seen as being more about pleasure than duty. According to Honore,[34] the old law points to three requirements of the law in relation to sex and marriage: that a husband and a wife have a duty to consummate the marriage; that they develop and maintain a mutually tolerable sexual relationship; and that they are faithful to each other.[35] But the old laws, in fact, go much further than that and assert that sex is an exclusive right of the parties to the marriage, in particular that it is the exclusive right of the husband. This position can be argued by looking at laws in relation to criminal conversation and adultery, which give parties to a marriage a legal right to sue for compensation or for divorce if sex occurs with a third party outside of the marriage. The fact that both of these rights were either exclusively available to men (criminal conversation) and much more readily available to husbands than

---

31   *Bartlett v Bartlett* (1933) 50 CLR 23 (Evatt J).

32   P E Joske, *Joske's Marriage and Divorce* vol 2: Matrimonial Causes, fourth edition (Butterworths, Sydney 1961) 312.

33   There are no cases that have explicitly recognised this, but there are cases that welcome the widening of the concept.

34   T Honore, *Sex and Law* (Duckworth, London 1978).

35   Honore, *Sex and Law* 17–34.

to wives (divorce double standard), supports the argument that exclusive sex was a right a husband could demand of his wife. But nothing asserts a husband's right to have sex with his wife more than the immunity that he enjoyed against marital rape. In this context, a picture emerges of sex being not only inseparable from marriage, but also being a right that a husband enjoyed over his wife. This casts marriage as oppressive and exploitative, a picture that justifies the feminist critiques of both sex and marriage.

Rape in Marriage

In *History of the Pleas of the Crown* (1736), Sir Matthew Hale stated that a husband cannot be guilty of 'a rape committed by himself upon his lawful wife, for by their mutual matrimonial consent and contract the wife hath given herself in this kind unto her husband which she cannot retract'.[36] This was asserted for hundreds of years as the common law of Britain and its colonies. Subsequently, both the legitimacy and the legality of this statement have been questioned.[37] Barton, however, argues that what Hale wrote appears to have been a reflection of established belief at the time, traceable to the thirteenth century.[38]

The idea that a man could not be guilty of raping his wife is founded upon three possible theories.[39] The first is that which emerges from Mathew Hale's statement, that is, that upon marriage a wife has given her consent to sexual relations. This is known as the implied consent theory. Immunity can, however, also be justified under the unity of person theory which views marriage as a unity of two people, or, more precisely, an incorporation of a woman's entity into that of her husband. In this conception of marriage, a woman ceased to be an independent legal entity during marriage and the question of consent therefore becomes irrelevant. As noted earlier, this is the view that was voiced by Blackstone about marriage in general.[40] The third theory is the property theory: upon marriage a woman becomes the property of her husband of which he can 'make appropriate use'.[41]

---

36   Sir Matthew Hale, *History of the Pleas of the Crown 1736* vol 1 629.

37   C Glasman has argued that the marital rape immunity never had any grounding in common law. 'Women Judge the Courts' (1991) 141 *New Law Journal* 395. Brennan J in *R v L* also said it was never part of the common law. The High Court of Australia had cause to visit this question in *PGA v The Queen* (2012) 245 CLR 355. In this case, rather controversially, the majority (5:2) held that even if the marital immunity had at some time existed it had ceased to do so by 1935 at the latest as a result of state legislation. For a discussion of the implications of this case see W Larcombe and M Heath, 'Case Note Developing the Common Law and Rewriting the History of Rape in Marriage in Australia: *PGA v The Queen*' (2012) 34 *Sydney Law Review* 785–807.

38   J L Barton, 'The Story of Marital Rape' (1992) 108 *Law Quarterly Review* 260–271.

39   For discussion of these three theories see S A Adamo, 'The Injustice of the Marital Rape Exemption: A Survey of Common Law Countries' (1989) 4 *American University Journal of International Law & Policy* 555–590.

40   See chapter one.

41   Adamo, 'The Injustice of the Marital Rape Exemption' 560.

The marital rape exemption has over time been justified on the ground that rape in marriage would be difficult to prove, could be misused by a vengeful wife, and could lead to 'unrest and discord' in a marriage.[42] It has also been argued that it would constitute an intrusion into the privacy of marriage.[43] Regardless of its origins and legitimacy, the view became law and was reiterated in academic texts[44] and in law cases for over 200 years. It was not until the last half of the twentieth century that this legal principle came to be seen as insupportable.[45] While many countries have now removed the immunity,[46] too many still have not and, as we will see, in the following discussion, this removal was not without its opponents.[47]

R v Clarence

So entrenched was the view that a husband could not be guilty of raping his wife that even when sex resulted in serious harm, the Court was not willing to disturb the immunity. *R v Clarence*[48] has been quoted over time as giving authority for marital rape immunity. In *R v Clarence,* the husband had contracted venereal disease and was aware of his condition, but did not tell his wife, with whom he continued to have sexual intercourse. She subsequently contracted the disease and her husband was charged with rape and assault. The wife argued that she was raped because she had not consented to having sex with a man who was infected. The majority of judges did not agree. While Barton argues that, between them, the judges expressed every possible logical opinion, a number of them relied on the principle that a husband cannot be guilty of raping his wife, pure and simple.[49]

---

42 Adamo, 'The Injustice of the Marital Rape Exemption' 561.

43 M J Anderson, 'Lawful Wife, Unlawful Sex: Examining the Effect of the Criminalization of Marital Rape in England and The Republic of Ireland' (1998) 27 *Georgia Journal of International & Comparative* 148.

44 For example, see P Brett and L Waller, *Criminal Law: Text and Cases* fourth edition, (Butterworths Sydney 1977) 93–94, where the authors argue that the immunity to marital rape should be extended to people living in any intimate relationship and not just marriage. This view is not repeated in subsequent editions.

45 T Fus, 'Criminalizing Marital Rape: A Comparison of Judicial and Legislative Approaches' (2006) 39 *Vanderbilt Journal of Transnational Law* 481–517. According to Anderson, as late as the mid-twentieth century there was no country that viewed a husband as forcing his wife to have sex with him as a crime. Anderson, 'Lawful Wife, Unlawful Sex'.

46 According to *MarriageAbout.com*, marital rape is considered a criminal offence in many countries, including Argentina, Australia, Austria, Barbados, Belize, Bulgaria, Canada, Croatia, Cyprus, Denmark, Ecuador, England, the Fiji Islands, Finland, France, Georgia, Germany, Honduras, Hong Kong, Ireland, Israel, Macedonia, Mexico, Namibia, Nepal, The Netherlands, New Zealand, Norway, The Philippines, Poland, South Africa, Spain, Sri Lanka, Sweden, Taiwan, Trinidad/Tobago, the United States, Uzbekistan, and Zimbabwe. (Country Reports on Human Rights Practices released by the US State Department, Bureau of Democracy, Human Rights and Labor, were used to determine countries' legal status of marital rape.) http://marriage. about.com/cs/maritalrape/f/maritalrape2.htm accessed 29/06/10.

47 J Mertus, 'Human Rights of Women in Central and Eastern Europe' (1998) 6 *American University Journal of Gender & Law* 369–484 listed Albania, Bulgaria, Croatia, Czech Republic, Hungary, Kosovo, Poland, Romania, Russia, Serbia and Ukraine as still providing some immunity for husbands.

48 *R v Clarence* (1888) QB 23.

49 J L Barton, 'The Story of Marital Rape' (1992) 108 *Law Quarterly Review* 260.

Pollock B, relying on Hale's dictum, stood firm on the assertion that the marriage contract means that the wife has no 'right or power' to refuse sex, and that the fact of venereal disease was irrelevant:

> [T]he husband's connection with his wife is not only lawful, but it is in accordance with the ordinary condition of married life. It is done in pursuance of the marital contract and of the status which was created by marriage, and the wife as to the connection itself is in a different position from any other woman, for she has no right or power to refuse her consent.[50]

Similarly, A L Smith relied on the features of the marriage, and argued that the wife consents to sex at the time of marriage. This consent is not confined to when the husband is sound in body. Smith affirmed the principle that consent to sex stands throughout marriage, and affirmed the existence of the immunity in all circumstances:

> [U]ntil the consent given at marriage be revoked, how can it be said that the husband in exercising his marital right has assaulted his wife? In the present case at the time the incriminated act was committed, the consent given at marriage stood unrevoked. Then how is it assault? ... In my judgement in this case, the consent given at marriage still existing and unrevoked, the prisoner has not assaulted his wife.[51]

Even those judges who thought Mr Clarence was guilty of rape did not wish to disrupt the marital immunity. They simply argued that his suffering a communicable disease created an exception to the rule. Sex was a marital privilege, but with some exceptions.[52] This view continued. Over the years, before *R v L*, courts showed a general unwillingness to water down the marital exemption. Cases show that the presumption that a man cannot be guilty of raping his wife could be displaced by a separation order,[53] a separation agreement,[54] or a *decree nisi*.[55] Until very recently, and even in extreme circumstances, cases show that courts were more willing to develop exceptions to the rule rather than to eliminate the rule altogether. For example, in *R v McMinn*[56] the husband broke into his wife's home and physically and sexually abused her in the presence of their small child. Even then, Starke J did not question the existence of the

---

50   *R v Clarence* (1888) QB 63–64 (Pollock B).
51   *R v Clarence* (1888) QB 37 (Smith AL).
52   *R v Clarence* (1888) QB 51 (Hawkins J).
53   *R v Clarke* [1949] 2 All ER 448.
54   *R v Miller* [1954] 2 QB 282.
55   *R v O'Brien* [1974] 2 All ER 663.
56   *R v McMinn* [1982] VR 53.

rule but instead focussed on the fact that there was a Family Law Court order existing at the time which restrained her husband from molesting her, thus constituting a revocation of consent to sex by the wife.

The Changing Discourse of Sex and Marriage

As previously discussed, the legal discourse of marriage in Australia has been significantly altered by the passing of the FLA. In relation to sexual intercourse, this piece of legislation is silent. Some of the ways that sex was present in the Matrimonial Causes Act (adultery, refusal to consummate a marriage) were removed. The single ground of 'irretrievable break down' evidenced by a 12-month separation removes questions about the nature of the parties' involvement with each other, sexual or otherwise. Furthermore, the discourse of sex in marriage has been significantly altered in Australian common law. This can be illustrated by two leading cases. *R v L* overturned centuries of common law that had protected husbands against the crime of raping their wives. Ten years later, the case of *Re Kevin* recognised a transsexual marriage and along the way asserted that sex (sexual identity as well as sexual intercourse) was no longer a central defining characteristic of marriage.

R v L and the Removal of the Marital Immunity for Rape

In 1991, *R v R* the UK Court of Appeal said the rule that protected husbands against a conviction of raping their wives was 'anachronistic and offensive'.[57] In *R v L* in the same year, the High Court of Australia said that the notion 'was out of keeping with the view society now takes of the relationship between the parties to a marriage'.[58] It is important to note here that, by then, every State legislature had passed laws which removed the distinction between married and unmarried women in relation to intimate partner rape.

Amazingly, given the length of time the rule had operated and the tenacity with which the courts had enforced it, Justice Brennan questioned the legal validity of the principle altogether. He claimed that there was little evidence for it in either the law of marriage or any other doctrine of common law:

> Hale's and Hume's reason for the common law rule that a husband could not be guilty as a principal in the first degree of raping his wife was

---

57   *R v R* [1991] 2 WLR 1065.
58   *R v L* (1991) 174 CLR 390 (Mason CJ, Deane & Toohey JJ).

extremely dubious ... Hale's reason for the rule is not supported by the law of marriage. Nor is that reason supported by any other doctrine of common law.[59]

This question was revived decades later in the 2012 case of *PGA v The Queen*[60] in which the majority of the High Court decided that, even if the rule ever existed, it no longer did so by the middle of the twentieth century. Nevertheless, the idea was certainly entrenched enough that even in the 1990s some were not only defending it but calling for its retention. In a two-part article in the *New Law Journal*,[61] Professor Glanville Williams argued that if a husband did force his wife to have sex with him, this was not rape but rather a sign that the relationship was broken. Williams argued that rape is too serious an offence to apply to the relationship that exists within marriage:

> We are speaking of a biological activity, strongly baited by nature, which is regularly and pleasurably performed on a consensual basis by mankind ... Occasionally some husband continues to exercise what he regards as his when his wife refused him ... What is wrong with his demand is not so much the act requested but his timing, or the manner of his demand. The fearsome stigma of rape is too great a punishment for husbands who use their strength in these circumstances.[62]

A report by UK Criminal Law Revision Committee in 1984 into marital rape took a similar view, arguing that marital rape was more of a problem for social workers than for the criminal law.[63]

In *R v L*, Justice Brennan argued that the law of marriage is to be found in the ecclesiastical courts rather than the common law courts. He claims that a review of those relevant cases shows that connubial rights are an essential part of marriage but 'do not exhaust, the legal incidents of marriage'.[64] Furthermore, he adds that the law has always been that sexual intercourse must be performed

---

59   *R v L* (1991) 174 CLR 401 (Brennan J). See also Glasman, 'Women Judge Courts'.

60   *PGA v The Queen (2012) 245 CLR 355.*

61   G Williams, 'The Problem of Domestic Rape: Part I' (1991) 141 New Law Journal 205–06; 'Problem of Domestic Rape: Part II' (1991) 141 New Law Journal 246–247.

62   Williams, 'The Problem of Domestic Rape: Part I' 206. It is important to note that Professor Williams has argued in other writings that, when it comes to rape, men need the law's protection more than women. In his *Textbook of Criminal Law*, he talks of consent as a 'hazy concept'. He says that women are prone to changing their minds, 'enjoy fantasies of being raped' and therefore welcome a 'masterful advance while putting up a token of resistance'. He goes on to say that girls often lie in relation to sexual consent out of shame or guilt or 'for obscure psychological reasons'. G Williams, *Textbook of Criminal Law* second edition (Stevens and Sons, London 1983) 238. These views are by no means unique. Naffine has shown their predominance in a number of criminal law textbooks. N Naffine 'Windows on the Legal Mind: Evocation of Rape in Legal Writings' (1991–1992) *Melbourne University Law Review* 744–751.

63   UK Report by the Law Reform Commission (law com No 205) CMND 9213 cited in N Naffine, 'Possession: Erotic Love in the Law of Rape' (1994) 57 *Modern Law Review* 22.

64   *R v L* (1991) 174 CLR 392 (Brennan J).

voluntarily.[65] Justice Brennan says that the ecclesiastical approach can be found in Sir William Scott's judgement in *Forster v Forster*[66] which stated that 'the duty of matrimonial intercourse cannot be compelled by this court though matrimonial cohabitation may'.[67] However, he went on to say that it is not a 'matter perfectly light' if a spouse has withdrawn themselves 'from the discharge of duties that belong to the very institution of marriage',[68] thus creating some confusion.

Despite this, Justice Brennan argues that to admit that sexual intercourse is part of marriage is not the same thing as asserting that a man can never be guilty of raping his wife. A wife, he argues, is not upon marriage relegated to the status of sexual chattel. To accept Hale's principle would relegate a married woman to the rank of concubine and reduce her to a mere object of desire and sexual gratification:

> Far from relegating a wife to the position of a sexual chattel, the status of wife created by marriage confers on a wife a right … to live with her husband, to have him listen and talk to her, to be cherished, to be entertained at bed and board and treated with respect. These are not rights that can be enforced by decree but they are rights attached to the status of husband and wife.[69]

He goes on to say that 'marriage is an institution which casts upon a husband an obligation to respect a wife's personal integrity and dignity; it does not give the husband a power to violate her personal integrity and destroy her dignity'.[70]

For Justice Brennan, while sex is part of marriage, it is not the only part of it. Moreover, to say that it is part of marriage does not mean that a spouse must engage in sex at all times. There is a sense in which there is an obligation upon a spouse not to persistently and wilfully refuse sexual intercourse, but this is to acknowledge that consent is necessary for sex during marriage and not evidence for the view that a general consent is granted upon marriage:

> The ecclesiastical courts never embraced the notion of a general consent to sexual intercourse given once and for all on marriage by either spouse. The doctrine of ecclesiastical courts was quite different, namely, that each spouse has a mutual right to sexual intercourse provided the right is exercised reasonably, subject to the health of the spouses and the

65 *R v L* (1991) 174 CLR 392 (Brennan J).
66 *Forster v Forster* (1790) 161 ER 505 (Sir Willam Scott).
67 *Forster v Forster* (1790) 161 ER 508 (Sir Willam Scott).
68 *Forster v Forster* (1790) 161 ER 508 (Sir Willam Scott).
69 *R v L* (1991) 174 CLR 396 (Brennan J).
70 *R v L* (1991) 174 CLR 396 (Brennan J).

exigencies of family life. It is a right to be exercised by consent. It is a right the exercise of which is intended to foster and maintain connubial love, not to be the occasion of abuse and degradation.[71]

Sex in marriage is therefore subject to many factors, consent foremost among them. Brennan's opinion, quoted above, is extremely important because it acknowledges that there is a connection between sex and marriage, but it goes further and asserts that both are also connected to love.

In the Shadow of *R v L*

The decision in *R v L* cannot, however, be taken as evidence that the connection between marriage and sex, and as sex being the right of a husband, has been completely severed in legal discourse. Both in England and in Australia, courts have shown a tendency to treat 'relationship rape' as a less serious offence than rape involving strangers. In England, for example, Warner shows that courts have developed a principle that a pre-existing sexual relationship between the rapist and his victim should operate as a mitigating factor.[72] Mustill LJ in the leading case of *Berry* stated that rape of a former sexual partner makes it a less serious offence. He justified this principle on the ground that the 'violation' and 'defilement' are less of a feature in such cases. He argues that relationship rape cases show that 'in some instances the violation of the person and the defilement that are inevitable features where a stranger rapes a woman are not always present to the same degree when the offender and the victim had previously had a long-standing sexual relationship'.[73]

This view exists also in Australia. For example, in *R v Spencer*, the Court said '[g]enerally I would expect that if the parties were cohabiting at the time of the rape, this would go in mitigation of sentence, recognising the very special relationship between husband and wife'.[74] The special relationship between husband and wife would require, it seems, a lower level of consent to sexual intercourse than in other relationships. And then there was the now infamous 'rougher than usual handling' case, in which Judge Bollen sitting on the case of *R v Johns* in which a husband was tried for six counts of rape, said:

> There is of course, nothing wrong with a husband faced with his wife's initial refusal to engage in intercourse in attempting in an acceptable

---

71   *R v L* (1991) 174 CLR 396 (Brennan J).
72   K Warner, 'Sentencing in Cases of Marital Rape: Towards Changing the Male Imagination' (2000) 20(4) *Legal Studies* 593–94.
73   *Berry* 1988 10 Cr App R (S) 15.
74   *R v Spencer* Queensland Court of Criminal Appeal CA no 80 unreported 1991.

way to persuade her to change her mind and that may involve a measure of rougher than usual handling. It may be, in the end, that handling and persuasion will persuade the wife to agree.[75]

There also exist other situations where courts have displayed attitudes towards the meaning of consensual sex that sound alarm bells. Take, for example, cases of mistaken identity which appear to suggest not only that sex is an implied part of any intimate relationship but also that it requires a much lower level of negotiation and consent than sex in other situations.

In the case *R v George Allan Pryor*,[76] the victim thought she was having sex with her partner but found instead that a stranger had broken into her apartment, led her out of bed and had sex with her in the corridor. The victim realised her mistake when she reached up to touch his face and realised that the features were not those of her partner. She argued that it was rape as she had only consented to having sex on the mistaken belief that she was having sex with her partner. The man was charged with rape but appealed on the ground that she had consented. The Court reviewed a number of old authorities with similar facts, notably *R v Jackson*[77] and *R v Saunders*.[78] In both cases, the wife was asleep and submitted to advances made by a man that each woman believed to be her husband. In both cases, the Court held that it could not be rape as the women had consented to the act of sexual penetration. While in *R v Allan Pryor* the appeal against rape was not successful, one of the judges did adhere to the authorities above, claiming that rape rests upon the essential enquiry of whether there has been consent as to the nature and character of the act of sexual intercourse.[79]

This view is evidence of the assumed ease with which sex is assumed in marriage and marriage-like relationships. Consent, in these cases, did not need any words. In fact it seems that consciousness itself was not required for consent to occur. To accept this state of affairs one must view marriage as a relationship where sex occurs often and with little or no negotiation needed between the partners. The low threshold of consent that the law requires for such cases is questionable, even if it can be argued that it is merely reflecting social attitudes when it does so.[80]

---

75   *R v Johns* South Australia Supreme Court unreported 26 August 1992, quoted in P Easteal, 'Marital Rape Conflicting Constructions of Reality' (1997) 3 *Women Against Violence an Australian Feminist Journal* 26. Judge Bollen's comments caused significant controversy in Australia, leading to a Senate Committee on Gender Bias and the Judiciary. See Graycar & Morgan, *Hidden Gender of Law* 361–62; Kaspiew, 'Rape Lore: Legal Narrative and Sexual Violence'.

76   *R v George Allan Pryor* BC200105198 Supreme Court of Queensland unreported Aug 2001.

77   *R v Jackson* [1822] 8 Car & P 266.

78   *R v Saunders* [1838] 8 Car & P 266.

79   See Byrne J in R v George Allen Pryor.

80   Empirical studies suggest that a woman who has been forced to have sex with a partner might not see herself as a victim of rape with recourse to legal remedies. See N Naffine, 'Windows on the Legal Mind'

The above discussion makes one careful about how to characterise the law's position in relation to sex in marriage and other intimate relationships. Some of the old common law principles (*consortium vitae* and conjugal rights) danced around the issue, while others (rape immunity) were brutally clear that it was to be considered as a duty by the wife to have sex with her husband. While *R v L* was a definite statement against this principle, some surrounding principles involving sex and relationships (lesser thresholds of consent cases), makes one cautious. The case of *Re Kevin*, however, adds some much needed clarity to the relationship between marriage and sex.

The Case of *Re Kevin*

The case of *Re Kevin* saw sexual identity, sexual intercourse and procreation rejected as the central defining characteristics of modern marriage.

Kevin was born a female. At birth her gonads, genitalia and chromosomes were identified as female, but as far back as she could remember she felt herself to be male. Since 1994, she dressed and presented herself as male in all situations. In 1995 she began hormone treatment, in 1997 she underwent breast removal surgery, and in 1998 she underwent sex reassignment surgery, involving a total hysterectomy and a bilateral oophorectomy. In 1996 Kevin met her partner Jennifer. Jennifer fully supported Kevin's transition from female to male. In August 1999 Kevin and Jennifer married and in November 1999 Jennifer, who had become pregnant on an assisted fertility program, had a child. In 2003, during the appeal, Jennifer was pregnant with their second child. Kevin's gender identity history was revealed to all official parties involved in the marriage and the conception of their child. Kevin applied to the Family Court in 2001 to have the marriage between himself and Jennifer validated. The Attorney General intervened in the proceedings arguing that the marriage could not be valid because it was not a marriage between a man

---

741; 'Possession'; *Feminism and Criminology* (Polity Press, Cambridge 1997). Patricia Easteal, in an empirical study, also found that some married women do not see their husbands wanting to have sex against their will as rape. See Easteal, 'Marital Rape Conflicting Constructions of Reality'. Barton and Painter report that a survey conducted in the early 1990s in England, Wales and Scotland designed by the Middlesex Centre for Criminology showed that one in seven women thought it was their duty to have sex with their husbands even when they did not feel like it. C Barton & K Painter, 'Rights and Wrongs of Marital Sex' (1991) 141 *New Law Journal* 394. One can certainly find evidence of this view in the press. For example, in March 2009, prominent Australian sex therapist Bettina Arndt urged women to say yes more often as a key to keeping marriages/relationships alive. In an article entitled 'Women Need to Say Yes to Sex', Bettina Arndt advises women to 'just do it'. Apparently suggesting that women need not be bothered about desire when considering sex, she says: 'Once the canoe is in the water, everyone starts happily paddling. For couples to experience regular, pleasurable sex and sustain loving relationships women must get over that ideological roadblock of assumptions about desire and "just do it". The results will be both men and women will enjoy more, better sex.' Canberra Times 2/03/09 http://www.canberratimes.com.au/news/opinion/editorial/general/women-need-to-say-yes-to-sex/1447294.aspx#.

and a woman. The Family Court ruled that for the purposes of the Marriage Act Kevin was a male and his marriage to Jennifer was therefore valid. This decision was affirmed on appeal in 2003 before a Full Court of the Family Law Court.

Neither Kevin nor the Court argued against the idea that marriage must be between a man and woman. For Kevin, the point to prove was not that love and marriage could exist among same-sex couples, but rather that he was a man. The same-sex marriage issue was not considered in any way relevant to this case. Parliamentary debates on the 2004 amendment to the Marriage Act, however, showed that some MPs did read the decision as a threat to the 'traditional' definition of marriage as being between a man and a woman, and feared that the Court's liberal reading of marriage for the purpose of recognising transgender marriage might be read as a sign for a possible liberal attitude toward same-sex marriage.[81]

The argument for the Court in this case was whether Kevin was a man, but along the way much was said about the meaning of marriage in modern Australia. While the focus was on sex as sexual identity, the arguments led to discussion on the centrality of procreation and sexual intercourse in marriage.

The Legal Arguments and the Decision

The Attorney General in *Re Kevin*[82] argued the following propositions in relation to the meaning of marriage:

- That marriage was to be given the meaning embodied in the Marriage Act of 1961 which implied that marriage was a union for life between a man and a woman.

- The meaning of marriage was to be given the meaning it held in 1961 when the Act was passed, and not, according to current cultural and social factors.

- That marriage was understood to embody Judeo-Christian teachings and, as such, was closely tied with the procreation and care of children.

Assent to all of these propositions would therefore rule out the recognition of the relationship between Kevin and Jennifer as well as the future recognition of 'other' relationships such as same-sex marriages.

The Full Court of the Family Law Court rejected all of the above arguments. In relation to the Marriage Act being a code for the meaning of marriage (as well as

---

81   Liberal Party Senator, Guy Barnett said that 'the issue of marriage has been raised in Australia recently in a number of ways, including in the Family Court case of Kevin and Jennifer. The Full Court said that the words "marriage" and "man" in the Marriage Act have a contemporary everyday meaning. Are we going to allow the longstanding definition of marriage to be interpreted out of the context in which it was written?' Commonwealth, Parliamentary Debates Senate June 17 2004 (Guy Barnett) http://parlinfoweb.aph.gov.au/piweb/view_document.aspx?ID=2014889 accessed 15/05/2008.

82   *Re Kevin (Validity of Marriage of Transsexual) (No2)* [2203] Fam CA 94.

'man' and 'woman') the Court said that it could not be so. Given that the terms had not been defined in the Act, the Court claimed therefore that it had a duty to interpret these terms in relation to 'contemporary', 'normal' and 'everyday' meanings. Furthermore, the Court did not see any use in the argument that marriage is a concept whose meaning is fixed in time:

> We think it plain that the social and legal institution of marriage as it pertains to Australia has undergone transformations that are referable to the environment and period in which the particular changes occurred. The concept of marriage therefore cannot in our view, be correctly said to be one that is ever frozen in time ... There is no historical justification to support Mr Burnmester's contention that the meaning of marriage should be understood by reference to a particular point in time in the past such as 1961. To the contrary, it lends support to the arguments ... that the meaning of the term should be given its contemporary meaning in the context of the Marriage Act.

This argument is further strengthened by an examination of the Court's approach to the interpretation of the constitutional marriage power. The Full Court examined the different approaches taken by the High Court in the interpretation of the marriage power and found that while there were conservative approaches expressed by Brennan J in *Fisher v Fisher*[83] and *R v L*,[84] there were also more liberal approaches such as the view of McHugh J in *Re Wakin; exparte McNally* where, quite coincidentally, McHugh J uses the very example of same-sex marriage to argue for an expansive approach to the constitutional interpretation of the marriage power:

> in 1901 'marriage' was seen as meaning a voluntary union of life between one man and one woman to the exclusion of all others. If that level of abstraction was now accepted, it would deny the parliament of the Commonwealth power to legislate for same sex marriages, although arguably marriage now means, or in the near future may mean, a voluntary union for life between two people to the exclusion of others.[85]

The Full Court accepted that the constitutional power of marriage should be given a broader interpretation:

> [I]t seems to us that we should not in this case adopt the narrow interpretation of marriage ... it seems to be inconsistent with the approach of the High Court to the interpretation of other heads of Commonwealth power to place marriage in a special category, frozen

---

83 *Fisher v Fisher (1986) 161 CLR 438.*
84 *R v L (1991) 174 CLR 379.*
85 McHugh in *Re Wakin; exparte McNally* (1999) 198 CLR 511, Re Kevin no 2 para 96.

in time to 1901. We therefore approach the matter on the basis that it is within the power of parliament to regulate marriages in Australia that are outside the monogamistic Christian tradition.[86]

In the above statement, we see not only approval for a broad legal interpretation of what constitutes marriage but also a rejection of the idea that marriage is to be considered primarily as a Christian institution. The Court said that, while there has been an undoubted relationship between Christianity and marriage, the relationship in contemporary law is such that we cannot see marriage only in a religious context. The Court points out that it is the role of the State rather than the Church that is paramount in the legal regulation of marriage. One can get married without the church, for example, but not without the state. Furthermore, it is accepted as legitimate that the state regulates marriage in ways that have over the years redefined the institution. As discussed elsewhere, the status of women in marriage has been radically altered by legal reforms such as the recognition of women's economic capacity and their human rights against violence and rape. The state has similarly altered the idea of marriage as a life-long relationship by facilitating divorce, and has removed the privileged position of marriage by legitimating de facto relationships and children born out of wedlock.

The Court also considered and rejected the idea that procreation was the underpinning of modern marriage. In the first of the *Re Kevin*[87] cases the trial judge accepted that there is a general sense in which marriage is connected to the generation of children, but he was prepared to accept the different ways that one could do this in a modern society. He was prepared to accept, for example, that the generation of children was not limited to the traditional model of biological parents conceiving and giving birth without the assistance of reproductive technologies, adoption and surrogacy agreements. In fact, Jennifer and Kevin were testimony to this fact, as they were bringing up children. Justice Chisholm stated:

> Given that marriage is a social and legal institution which includes people who are infertile or by reason of illness or otherwise are unable to engage in genital penetrative intercourse, it seems to me odd, rather than self evident, to treat capacity for genital intercourse as 'the essential' role of a woman (or man) in marriage.[88]

In *Re Kevin No 2* the Full Court said:

> We accept as did the trial Judge, that marriage has a particular status. Like the trial Judge, we reject the argument that one of the principal

---

86 *Re Kevin (Validity of Marriage of Transsexual) (No 2)* [2203] Fam CA 94 para 99–100.
87 *Re Kevin (Validity of Marriage of Transsexual)* [2001] Fam CA 1074.
88 *Re Kevin (Validity of Marriage of Transsexual)* [2001] Fam CA 1074 para 95.

purposes of marriage is procreation. Many people procreate outside of marriage and many people who are married neither procreate, nor contemplate doing so. A significant number of married persons cannot procreate either at the time of marriage or subsequently — an obvious example being a post-menopausal woman. Similarly, it is inappropriate and incorrect to suggest that consummation is in any way a requirement to the creation of a valid marriage.[89]

In its argument, the Family Court also considered the English decision of *Corbett v Corbett*[90] where a marriage between a male to female transsexual and a male did not receive legal validation. Whilst the Corbett case was finally overwritten by legislation in the UK in 2004,[91] at the time of the *Re Kevin* decision it was still the authoritative case in the UK concerning transsexual marriage and the Attorney General in *Re Kevin* had been adamant that it should be followed here in Australia.[92]

Justice Ormrod in the *Corbett* case said that sex is determined at birth according to genitalia, gonads and chromosomes. The construction of an artificial vagina through surgery and the growth of breasts as a result of hormone treatment could not alter one's 'true sex'. For Ormrod J, marriage must be dependent upon one's 'true sex' because it is only then that the true function of marriage, procreation, can be realised. In this way Justice Ormond is not only centralising sexual identity in marriage but also heterosexual sexual intercourse, because it alone can lead to conception and birth. It is worth quoting his reasoning at length to show precisely how he arrives at this position:

> [S]ex is clearly an essential determinant of the relationship called marriage, because it is and always has been recognised as the union of man and woman. It is the institution on which the family is built, and in which the capacity for natural heterosexual intercourse is an essential element. It has of course, many other characteristics, for which companionship and mutual support is an important one, but the characteristics which distinguish it from all other relationships can only be met by two people of opposite sex ... since marriage is essentially a relationship between a man and a woman, the validity of the marriage in this case depends, in my judgement, on whether the respondent is or

---

89   *Re Kevin (Validity of Marriage of Transsexual) (No 2)* [2203] Fam CA 94 para 153.
90   *Corbett v Corbett (otherwise Ashley)* [1970] 2 All ER 33.
91   The Corbett case received affirmation in *Bellinger v Bellinger* [2001] EWCA Civ 1140, however, both cases were subsequently overridden by the passing of the Gender Recognition Act UK 2004, which was passed as a response to the decision by the European Court of Human Rights in Christine Goodwin and I v United Kingdom (28957/1995).
92   Its status in Australian law had up to that point been equivocal. Andrew Neville Sharp has described the *Corbett* decision as an undercurrent in Australian law. 'The Transsexual Marriage: Law's Contradictory Desires' (1997) 7 *Australasian Gay and Lesbian Law Journal* 4.

is not a woman ... the question then becomes what is meant by 'woman' in the context of a marriage, for I am not concerned to determine the 'legal sex' of the respondent at large. Having regard to the essentially heterosexual character of the relationship which is called marriage, the criteria must, in my judgement, be biological, for even the most extreme degree of transsexualism in a male or the most severe hormonal imbalance which can exist in a person with male chromosomes, male gonads and male genitalia cannot reproduce a person who is capable of performing the essential role of woman in marriage.[93]

Justice Ormond here not only argues that one's sex is determined permanently at birth, but also that marriage relies upon the heterosexual sex act for its legitimacy, as that act alone has the potential to lead to procreation. The Court thus spent a considerable period of time establishing whether the couple had had sex, and what the nature of the sexual act had been between them. The Court was concerned to establish not only whether penetration had occurred but also whether there had been orgasm. But the Family Court was not convinced by the reasoning in *Corbett*.

Sex and Marriage and Love

In both the first and the second *Re Kevin* cases, the Family Court rejected *Corbett* and its essentialising of sexual identity and the capacity for sexual intercourse and procreation. In fact, Justice Chisholm was critical of Justice Ormrod's approach in the case, saying that in his opinion it presents a 'remarkable focus on the mechanics of genital sexual activity'.[94] He goes on to question the approach more specifically and asks:

'[W]hat is the essential role of a woman in marriage'? Does it require a capacity for sexual activities? If so, precisely which activities? Is a woman who is unable to have genital intercourse because of illness or disability unable to perform her 'essential role'? Further, why should it be assumed that 'the essential role of a woman' in marriage is concerned merely with matters of sex and biological sexual constitution?

He quotes with approval Gordon Samuels's criticism of Justice Ormrod's approach:

[T]here is no reason to suppose that she could not provide the companionship and support which one spouse ordinarily renders to the other. She could not conceive and bear children. But it is not the law that marriage is not consummated unless children are procreated

---

93 Ormond J in *Corbett v Corbett (otherwise Ashley)* [1970] 2 All ER 33.
94 *Re Kevin (Validity of Marriage of Transsexual)* [2001] Fam CA 1074 para 94.

or that procreation of children is the principal end of marriage. Hence the female spouse's ability or willingness to produce children is not a necessary incident of a valid marriage.[95]

Samuels' reasoning was similarly quoted with approval by the Full Court in the second *Re Kevin* case, where the Court said that it represented the modern approach to marriage.[96]

In rejecting *Corbett*, the Family Court in *Re Kevin* argued that procreation and sex are only aspects of marriage and are not necessarily the defining characteristics of the relationship. The Court claimed that there has been a considerable shift in the community away from 'purely sexual aspects of marriage in the direction of defining it in terms of companionship'.[97] This is evident in the FLA reforms discussed earlier.

The Full Court also draws upon the *R v L* decision by the High Court and quotes with approval Mason CJ Deane and Toohey JJ's position which similarly disengages marriage from sex:

> [W]hatever the scope of the power of the parliament to make laws with respect to marriage, it is apparent that the Commonwealth Act does not attempt comprehensively to regulate the rights and obligations to consent to sexual intercourse by a party to a marriage. Refusal to consummate a marriage is no longer a ground for dissolution. In one of the early decisions on the Commonwealth Act, the Family Court accepted that sexual intercourse between the parties to a marriage may have ceased without the marriage having broken down irretrievably.[98]

Re Kevin therefore represents a significant statement by an Australian court in relation to the significance of sexual activity and its (dis)connection to marriage. But what does it say about love?

Re Kevin is an important case for the legal recognition of love in marriage, not because of its assertions but because of its silences. The case told us that marriage does not have to be about procreation and it does not have to be about having sex. It told us that marriage can have multiple meanings. The Court acknowledged that marriage varies according to age (menopausal women unable to procreate, for example), and to disposition (not wishing to procreate, for example). In all of these ways, the Court removed traditional meanings of marriage and left a silence around its meaning, a silence which, given the strength of the love rhetoric that exists in other discourses of marriage, can be readily implied here.

---

95   G Samuels, 'Transsexualism' (1983) 16 *Australian Journal of Forensic Sciences* 62.
96   *Re Kevin (Validity of Marriage of Transsexual) (No 2)* [2203] Fam CA 94 78128.
97   *Re Kevin (Validity of Marriage of Transsexual) (No 2)* [2203] Fam CA 94 para 38.
98   Mason et al *R v L* quoted in *Re Kevin (Validity of Marriage of Transsexual) (No2)* [2203] Fam CA 94 para 294.

Conclusion

There has been a shift in the law in relation to sex and marriage. Old legal principles clearly asserted that sex is an essential part of marriage. In describing sex, judges have used phrases such as 'the society of the wife'[99] or, more inclusively, 'mutual society'.[100] However, when it comes to describing the importance of sex in marriage judges have said that it is a 'marital duty inseparable from it',[101] 'the essence of the marriage relationship',[102] and a 'duty that belongs to the very institution of marriage'.[103] In one instance, a Court described a situation where there was no sexual intercourse as a relationship in which a husband would be 'a husband in name only'.[104] These decisions imply that sexual intercourse not only defines marriage but also the very identity of 'husband'. When we take these views alongside the marital rape immunity, the only reading of the old law that makes sense is that a husband had an unlimited right to have sex with his wife. The law enforced the power of men and the subordination of women, and sex was simply one expression of that reality.[105]

But these principles have been beaten back by more recent cases. The decision of *R v L* unequivocally removed the right of a husband to have sex at his pleasure and *Re Kevin* asserted that neither sex (identity and intercourse), nor procreation form the essential part of modern Australian marriage. To some extent, these cases reflect the changes that have occurred in society to the institution of sex. As discussed in the introduction, sex has come to be seen as a legitimate activity engaged in for pleasure. It is disconnected from marriage and from procreation, and forms its own distinct narrative.[106] But where is the love? So far I have argued that there is both a distinction and a connection between love and sex and, in turn, marriage. The relationship between love and sex has undergone various permutations. In Ancient Greece, sex could be an expression of love, but love was primarily seen as the attainment of knowledge and goodness. In contrast, Christianity saw sex as largely negative, barely tolerated even in marriage and then only for procreation. Courtly love and romantic love legitimated sexual pleasure *per se*, a project that (despite its problems) reached its fruition with the sexual revolution of the 1960s. The link between marriage and procreation inevitably makes sex an essential part of marriage. This connection is still

---

99   *Birmingham Southern Railway Co v Lintner* (1904) 141 ALA 420.
100   *Bartlett v Bartlett* (1933) 50 CLR 23.
101   *Synge v Synge* [1900–03] All ER Rep 461.
102   *Bartlett v Bartlett* (1933) 50 CLR 23.
103   *Forster v Forster* (1790) 1 Hag Con 144.
104   *Synge v Synge* [1900–03] All ER Rep 461.
105   See Kathryn MacKinnon, discussed earlier.
106   It can also be argued that, as a result of the sexual revolution and the gay liberation movements, sex has become disconnected from gender and sexuality.

strong,[107] but, as we have seen in legal judgements considered in this chapter, mutual sexual pleasure, rather than the mere act of copulation has come, over time, to be seen as an essential feature of a successful marriage. Sex has been transformed from a duty of marriage undergone for the sake of procreation and as a service of the wife to the husband, to something which is negotiated and consensual, at the heart of which lies, to use Justice Brennan's words, 'connubial love'.[108] These cases are not enough to assert that sex is no longer a part of marriage, but rather that it alone cannot be so central. Sex can be linked to procreation, to consent, to personal satisfaction, but Justice Brennan also links it to love, and this is important for the central argument of the book.

Love is reflected in the new discourse of sex and marriage in a number of explicit and implicit ways. Above we saw that love is explicitly mentioned in the two cases of *R v L* and *Bartlett v Bartlett*. These cases reflect the romantic discourse that sex is an expression of love; as love is a mutual feeling so too must sex be mutual and consensual and pleasurable. It can be argued that love also emerges implicitly in the *Re Kevin* case. By rejecting some traditional meanings of marriage this case left a silence about the meaning of marriage. Given the strength of the rhetoric of romantic love in the popular discourse of marriage documented earlier in the book, it is a legitimate conclusion that *Re Kevin* left open the idea that marriage is about love more than anything else.

The introduction of love to both marriage and sex would suggest that a liberating and more equal relationship between men and women is now the model of marriage before us. However, more legal evidence is needed before we can say that sex in marriage has become imbued with the ideology of love and is seen as an expression of love, delivering mutual satisfaction, negotiated under equal conditions. The two cases of *R v L* and *Re Kevin* discussed in this chapter certainly come close to asserting this to be the case. Their history and context, however, make one cautious. Before jumping to this conclusion one must also remember the feminist critique of love and the oppressive reading of love that emerges from it. We need to be cognisant of the fact that the removal of sex and insertion of love in the legal discourse of marriage might not necessarily have the desired effect, it may simply be a new form of oppression.

---

107   This is especially the case in the same-sex marriage debates.

108   *R v L* (1991) 174 CLR 396 (Brennan J).

3. The Continuing Importance of Economic Factors

I see you are open for business so let's to church[1]

Introduction

In the previous chapter, I analysed the legal discourse of marriage in relation to what has been one of its most fundamental defining aspects — sexual intercourse — and argued that there has been a very significant change in the discourse of marriage, with love beginning to be insinuated. This chapter will turn to the equally important association of marriage with economic and financial considerations. Marriage has traditionally been connected to wealth, property and economic welfare, and has represented the economic union of two parties. This chapter asks what role love plays in the law when we consider it alongside the economic, commercial and financial aspects of marriage, and shows that, despite the acknowledgement of romantic love in this discourse, traditional meanings remain strong.

Despite the many obvious economic, financial and business aspects of marriage, the law is careful to retain a distinction between the market place and the home. The economic exchanges that occur between intimates can neither be completely commercialised nor completely ignored. This chapter examines the case of *Garcia v the National Australia Bank*, which is much discussed in Australian legal literature. This case represents the struggle that the law can face in this context. The case reaffirmed a principle, established in *Yerkey v Jones*,[2] that a married woman who had signed a guarantee for her husband's business and who did not know its full effect at the time, could avoid the guarantee. In reaffirming the principle, the majority of the full Court of the High Court of Australia rejected calls to remove an 'archaic' and 'discriminatory' principle in favour of what they saw as protecting a married woman who found herself in a position of disadvantage because she had placed 'trust and confidence' in her husband.

The case received much attention for the ways in which it changed banking practices, extended the principle of unconscionability in Australian law, and affirmed the role of Equity in commercial law, as well as the extent to which it replicated an outdated mode of gender relations in a modern Australian

---

1   John Madden, *Shakespeare in Love* (Universal Studios, 2004).
2   *Yerkey v Jones* (1939) 63 CLR 649.

marriage.[3] It is this final point that makes this case central to the analysis in this book. Discussion here will focus on the case's representation of marriage, and will question the role it affords to love within marriage. While the case does not mention love specifically, I will argue that love forms part of the meaning of marriage via the elements of trust and confidence which were considered crucial to marriage by the Court in the case.

The rhetoric of modern romantic love and marriage, as discussed in chapter one, is rarely associated with practical considerations such as compatibility due to economic circumstances, class and education. Indeed, as previously discussed, romantic love is conceived as a liberation from such considerations.[4] The extent to which this represents reality is debatable.[5] Nevertheless, the rhetoric is that love is above all such considerations. The case of *Garcia* represents more than a recognition that marriage is of economic consequence, it also represents an example of how economic and business dealings become entangled with emotional issues in a marriage; how incompatible they can be with each other, and what disadvantage they can cause. In this way, the case recognises both of the faces of love that I identified earlier: the liberating and the oppressive.

The Economic Discourse of Marriage and the Law

Marriage needs to be understood within an economic paradigm. Stone[6] argues that the legal requirement that marriage should be registered and performed publicly was initially motivated by a desire by wealthy families to prevent their children from making unsuitable matches with members of the lower classes,

---

3   Among the 60 or more articles written on *Garcia*, see G Williams, 'Equitable Principles for the Protection of Vulnerable Guarantors: Is the Principle in Yerkey v Jones Still Needed?' (1994) 8 *Journal of Contract Law* 67–83; B Fehlberg, 'The Husband, the Bank, the Wife and her Signature' (1994) 57 *Modern Law Review* 467–75 and 'The Husband, the Bank, the Wife and her Signature the Sequel' (1996) 59 *Modern Law Review* 675–694; B Collier, 'The Rule in Yerkey v Jones: Fundamental Principles and Fundamental Problems' (1996) 4 *Australian Property Law Journal* 181–222; Su-King Hii, 'From Yerkey to Garcia: 60 years on and Still as Confused as Ever!' (1997) 7 *Australian Property Law Journal* 47–75; K Green & H Lim, 'Weaving Along the Borders: Public and Private, Women and Banks' in S Scott-Hunt & H Lim (eds), *Feminist Perspectives on Equity and Trusts* (Cavendish, London 2001) 85–109; E Stone, 'Infants, Lunatics and Married Women: Equitable Protection in Garcia v National Australia Bank' (1999) 62 *Modern Law Review* 604–613; R Haigh & S Hepburn, 'Bank Manager Always Rings Twice: Stereotyping in Equity After Garcia' (2000) 26 *Monash University Law Review* 275–311; K Dunn, 'Yakking Giants': Equality Discourse in the High Court' (2000) 24 *Melbourne University Law Review* 427–461; J Pascoe, 'Women Who Guarantee Company Debts: Wife or Director?' (2003) 8 *Deakin Law Review* 13–48; T Wright, 'The Special Wives' Equity and the Struggle for Women's Equality' (2006) 31(2) *Alternative Law Journal* 66– 69, 87.

4   See discussion on the meaning of love in the introduction.

5   See Illouz, *Consuming the Romantic Utopia: Love and the Cultural Contradictions of Capitalism* (University of California Press, Berkeley 1997), Bix, 'Bargaining in the Shadow of Love: The Enforcement of Premarital Agreements and How We Think About Marriage' (1998–1999) 40 *William & Mary Law Review* 145–208.

6   See L Stone, *Uncertain Unions: Marriage in England, 1660–1753* (Oxford University Press, Oxford 1992).

thus diminishing the economic value of the family's accumulated wealth.[7] Economic considerations remain a large part of making marriage decisions. Bix argues, that despite the rhetoric, economic security is still a factor in people's decision of who to marry, even if it is framed in terms of who to fall in love with rather than who to marry. He suggests that whether acknowledged or not, most marriages have elements of both love and economic utility: 'that a partner can offer security may be part of his or her romantic allure'.[8]

Eva Illouz makes a similar argument, drawing from empirical studies in America. She shows that marriage is still considered to be a strategy of investment, embodying issues of economics and class:[9]

> Under capitalism, social relations are characterized by class stratification and individual competition; marriage bonds are formed in this context and sustain rather than disrupt it ... Marriage is often still a search for a partner with the 'best available assets', and the affectionate marriage has paradoxically enough instituted a 'market point of view' in romantic relationships.[10]

There are many obvious examples, both historical and current, where the courts are forced to confront the economic value of marriage. In the past, courts placed a monetary value on marriage in cases of loss of consortium and breach of promise to marry.[11] Furthermore, the economic value of marriage is implied in many other less visible ways; for example, in the 'marriage discount' used to calculate damages in tort cases based on the chance of a woman remarrying.[12] The increasing recognition of prenuptial agreements is a further example of the 'economic thinking' that takes place between prospective marriage partners. Yet, despite these many examples, the dominant approach in law is to retain a distinction between the market and the home. The most illustrative example of this is the contract law presumption of intention against the legality of agreements arising in the domestic social sphere, which is still quoted with authority almost 100 years after it received its first judicial utterance. The case of *Balfour v Balfour*[13] established a presumption that promises made between husbands and wives, even when they pertain to the economic arrangements between them, have no legal weight as they are promises made only in consideration of love. The leading judgement of Lord Justice Aitken relies on the arguments that a contract cannot exist between a husband and a wife because there is no

---

7 Stone, *Uncertain Unions* 32–34. See also Coontz, *Marriage: A History* 177–178.

8 Bix, 'Bargaining in the Shadow of Love' 162.

9 See P Johnson & S Lawler, 'Coming Home to Love and Class' Sociological Research Online (2005) 10(3) www.socresonline.org.uk/10/3/johnson.html accessed 16/10/2009.

10 Illouz, *Consuming the Romantic Utopia* 197.

11 M Thornton has looked at these issues in 'Loss of Consortium'. See also M Thornton, 'Historicising Citizenship: Remembering Broken Promises' (1995–1996) 20 *Melbourne University Law Review* 1072–1086.

12 See M Thornton, 'Rapunzel and the Lure of Equal Citizenship' (2004) 8 *Law Text Culture* 231–262.

13 *Balfour v Balfour* [1919] 2 KB 571.

intention between the parties to be legally bound.[14] He argued that it was not within the parties' contemplation to have their agreement litigated because of the nature of their relationship. He said that the common law 'does not regulate the form of agreements between spouses. Their promises are not sealed with seals and wax. The consideration that really obtains for them is that natural love and affection which counts so little in these cold courts.'[15] This distinction is justified on the ground that behaviour in the home is motivated by different values than behaviour in the market. The philosophical underpinnings of commercial activity, and therefore commercial law, can be found in a number of principles that emphasise self-interest. Peason and Fisher, for example, list the following as the principles of commercial law: party autonomy, predictability, flexibility, good faith, the encouragement of self-help, the facilitation of security interests, and the protection of vested interests. The protection of vulnerable parties is also listed, but as an equitable principle rather than a common law one.[16] These are in turn visible in more specific guiding legal principles such as the 'freedom to contract' principle that assumes that contracting individuals are free and rational, and motivated only by a wish to maximise their interest. Another is the principle 'caveat emptor' (buyer beware), which imposes upon buyers a responsibility to look after their own interest. Another is the principle that the law will not interfere in cases of mistake, generally letting the loss lay where it falls.[17]

All of these principles are generally considered to be out of place in an intimate family relationship. Frances Olsen, for example, argues that marriage and family are founded upon an ethic of altruism. 'Neither husband nor wife are expected to pursue selfish interests over the other'.[18] Sharing and self-sacrifice are considered appropriate behaviour. That this is, in reality, what happens has been well documented by Belinda Fehlberg, who found that, overwhelmingly, women in family businesses saw themselves as playing a support role, and that the justification for that role came from the love and affection they felt for their husbands. A typical articulation of this was from one subject in the Fehlberg study, Ms Fenwick, who said 'when you love someone, you just do what they

---

14   Ironically, at the same time as arguing that married couples never contemplate litigation to enforce agreements between them, the second reason for denying the existence of a contract is the floodgates argument. Aitken LJ argued that without such a presumption the number of small courts in the country would have to be 'multiplied by one hundredfold', thus appearing to contradict his first argument. The final argument Aitken relies on for the presumption is the old private sphere chestnut. As he famously stated, 'each house is a domain into which the King's writ does not seek to run, into which his officers do not seek to be admitted'. *Balfour v Balfour* 579.

15   *Balfour v Balfour* [1919] 2 KB 579 (Aitken LJ).

16   G Pearson and S Fisher, *Commercial Law: Commentary and Material* (LawBook Company, NSW 2009) 7–14.

17   See *non est factum* case *Gallie v Lee* [1971] AC 1004 and unilateral mistake case *Taylor v Johnson* (1983) 151 CLR 422.

18   F Olsen, 'The Family and the Market a Study of Ideology and Legal Reform' (1983) 96 *Harvard Law Review* 131.

ask you to do',[19] adding that 'loyalty is the main thing, isn't it? ... it would be totally disloyal not to [sign]'.[20] Other wives in the study were motivated by a desire to sustain the family, avoid conflict, and demonstrate loyalty and trust.[21] For some women this requirement was so strong that they did not see themselves as having any choice but to defer to their husband's requests. Mrs Elliot, for example, said that 'you have a choice whether you're going to stay married or not, and that's really what you're down to, isn't it?'[22]

There is nothing problematic *per se* in a discourse of economic union and altruistic behaviour, were it not for the fact that it is inextricably linked to traditional gender roles patriarchy and unequal power, and thus ends up disadvantaging women. The fact of the matter is that the dominant marriage model places women at home and men at work.[23] The work that they perform is seen as part of the bargain of love and has no political and economic value. Men's work, on the other hand, might just as equally be done for love but it has the added value of bestowing upon the giver economic and political value. As Thornton puts it, 'nurturing and housework have conventionally been perceived as a natural part of cohabitation and the conceptualisation of what women do in the home is deemed to be of no value in economic terms'.[24] To redress this imbalance, feminists have been arguing for a re-evaluation of the 'caring' work that women do,[25] including agitating for placing a dollar value on all of the work done in the 'home' mostly by women, including placing a value on sexual intercourse.[26]

This creates some interesting reflections for the approach law should take in acknowledging and regulating the economic and the emotional aspects of

---

19 Fehlberg, *Sexually Transmitted Debt* 148.

20 Fehlberg, *Sexually Transmitted Debt* 182.

21 Fehlberg, *Sexually Transmitted Debt* 174, 187.

22 Felbergh, *Sexually Transmitted Debt* 182.

23 This model is still mostly true. Even if women participate in the workforce they are still more likely than men to be part-time workers and are more likely than men to spend periods of time away from work while at home caring for children. According to Australian Bureau of Statistics figures published on a NSW government website, in 1966 women made up 31 per cent of the NSW workforce, while in 1995 they constituted just under 43 per cent of the workforce. (ABS Catalogue No. 4107.1) In August 1995, 52.1 per cent of all women in NSW aged over 15 years were participating in the labour force (the national female average was 54 per cent). This was significantly lower than the equivalent male participation rate, which was 72.7 per cent (ABS Catalogue No. 6201.1). Women's levels of participation in the labour market vary during their working lives. The participation rate of married women is lower during the childbearing age range of 25–34 years (ABS Catalogue No. 4107.1). In 1995, just below 40 per cent of employed women in NSW worked on a part-time basis. Women made up about 75 per cent of all part-time employees in NSW (ABS Catalogue No 6201.1). http://www.industrialrelations.nsw.gov.au/About_NSW_IR/Issues_and_policy/Archive/Pay_equity_inquiry/Womens_pay_and_employment_patterns.html accessed 27/07/10.

24 Thornton, 'Intention to Contract Public Act or Private Sentiment' in N Naffine R Owens J Williams (eds), *Intention in Law and Philosophy* (Ashgate, Aldershot 2001) 231.

25 See C Gilligan, *In a Different Voice: Psychological Theory and Women's Development* (Harvard University Press, Cambridge Massachusetts 1982); N Noddings, *Caring: A Feminine Approach to Ethics and Moral Education* (New York Teachers College Press, Berkely 1984); M A Fineman, *The Neutered Mother: The Sexual Family and Other Twentieth Century Tragedies* (Routledge, New York 1995).

26 See L R Hirshman & J E Larson, *Hard Bargains: The Politics of Sex* (Oxford University Press, New York 1999).

intimacy in general, and marriage specifically.[27] Elaine Hasday points to two traditions within the legal system, the first and more prominent is what she terms an anti-commodification stance, which deems that economic exchange between intimates is inappropriate and therefore should not be enforced. This view that is in keeping with the contract law presumptions against contracts entered into between intimates. The second position is termed a 'pro-market' position, which sees the super-imposition of an economic model upon an intimate relationship as a way for law to achieve a more equal relationship between people. Hasday argues that both of these positions underestimate the extent to which law already regulates economic exchanges. In marriage, while careful not to reduce the institution to a corporation, legal precedent tends to recognise agreements that fulfil certain characteristics: those that recognise the joint interests of husband and wife rather than their individual interests, and those that do not take a direct specific exchange model.[28] Hasday claims that in this way the law recognises that intimate relationships are neither wholly spontaneous nor completely free of bargaining.[29] An example of the law's task in this area is the Case of *Garcia*.

The Case of *Garcia*

Jean Garcia was married to Fabio Garcia in 1970. They had two children. Jean Garcia had a diploma in physiotherapy and ran her own practice. Fabio Garcia had a Master of Business Administration from Harvard University and during their marriage ran a range of companies involved in foreign exchange and gold import and export. By the time the case came to Court, the Garcias had divorced. The dispute involved some guarantees and a mortgage over the family home that Jean Garcia had signed with the National Bank of Australia to guarantee some loans for her husband's company, 'Citizen Gold'.

Economic Relationship

Jean and Fabio each conducted their own businesses. While it appears that Fabio had little to do with Jean's physiotherapy practice, Jean was named as a second director in some of Fabio's companies to fulfil formal company law requirements,[30] and was therefore required to have a formal involvement in

---

27   See Viviana Zelizer, 'The Purchase of Intimacy' (2000) 25 *Law and Social Inquiry* 817–848; 'Payments and Social Ties' (1996) 11 *Sociological Forum* 481–495.

28   J E Hasday, 'Intimacy and Economic Exchange' (2005) 119 *Harvard Law Review* 491–530.

29   Hasday, 'Intimacy and Economic Exchange' 459.

30   Corporation laws in the 1990s required companies to have more than one director, in fact, two or three were required depending on the type of company in question. Many small family companies fulfilled this legal requirement by naming a spouse as a director. Corporations Law 1990 s221 (1). This was reformed in the First

Fabio's affairs, this involvement consisting primarily of signing documents, which she mostly did without discussion. In fact, evidence showed that she was so little aware of what she was signing that her signature was forged from time to time, with her knowledge, by Fabio.

In 1984, upon the liquidation of one of Fabio's companies, Jean appeared before the Registrar of the Supreme Court of NSW, who accepted that Jean had little knowledge of, or actual role, in the affairs of her husband's company and cautioned her against signing documents without knowing what they were about in the future. Subsequently, Jean began to take more notice but would still mostly follow her husbands' requests to simply sign documents. Often Fabio asked her to sign documents when she was in a hurry rushing out of the door to meet an appointment with a client and making it difficult for her to make necessary inquiries. On the occasions that Jean tried to ask questions about Fabio's business matters, he would reply that she understood little about how business and markets worked and that she should leave business decisions to him.

Earnings from Fabio's businesses fluctuated. The nature of the business meant that the bank account could be in credit by six figures one day and in debit by a similar amount shortly after. When business was going well, as in 1985, Fabio would contribute more to the family income and expenditure, paying school fees and depositing money into their joint account, but this was not a constant state of affairs. In short, the evidence presented showed that Fabio's companies were the total creation, and in his total control. Fabio and Jean owned a family home. This home was built by the couple on some land that Jean bought in 1971 with the help of her father. Jean transferred half of the interest in the land to Fabio in order to have his name on the title for borrowing purposes, but he paid nothing for this interest. They jointly borrowed the money to build the house upon that land.

Emotional Relationship

The emotional relationship between Fabio and Jean was not close. He would often come home late and eat his dinner while watching television. Fabio seemed moody and was often unkind to Jean, suggesting that she was unsophisticated and ignorant of business affairs. Evidence showed that Fabio had been having an affair for a number of years and he eventually left Jean to live with his lover.

The relationship between husband and wife had been quite strained immediately prior to the signing of the 1987 guarantee that this case hinged upon. Jean had been away on an overseas trip. Upon her return, her husband had been in a rage and hardly spoke to her. Then, quite suddenly, Fabio began to be more

---

Corporate Law Simplification Act 1995.

attentive, coming home early and taking his wife and children out to dinner. On one of these occasions he told her he wanted to increase the overdraft to his business account. She indicated that she was nervous about this course of action but he assured her that there was nothing to worry about because, if the money was not there then the gold would be, and that there was no risk involved. He 'reassured' her by telling her '[y]ou are so conservative just like the rest of your family. One of these days I won't be around and you can be boring all by yourself.'[31] When Jean agreed to go to the bank and sign the necessary documents, Fabio told her to do it that week.

The Legal Argument

In *Garcia v National Australia Bank Ltd*,[32] Justice Young found that Mrs Garcia could avoid her financial responsibilities for the guarantee over her husband's business by relying on a principle which has been termed the 'special equity of wives'. This principle is found in the 1939 High Court case of *Yerkey v Jones*.[33] Dixon J's judgement in this case is taken to be the definitive statement of this rule. Dixon J said that while no presumption of undue influence emerges between husband and wife, there is an equitable presumption of an invalidating tendency where a wife bestows her separate property upon a third party for the benefit of her husband. The rule was stated thus:

> If a married woman's consent to become a surety for her husband's debt is procured by the husband and without understanding its effect in essential respects she executes an instrument of suretyship which the creditor accepts without dealing directly with her personally, she has a prima facie right to have it set aside.[34]

Yerkey v Jones actually dealt with two circumstances involving a wife as surety for a husband, the first being where there is actual undue influence by a husband over a wife, and the second where there is a failure to explain adequately and accurately the suretyship transaction which the husband seeks to have the wife enter for the immediate economic benefit of the husband.

Justice Young said that he did not see why the second circumstance in the *Yerkey v Jones* principle did not apply to Mrs Garcia. Mrs Garcia presented herself as an intelligent woman but she did not take an active part in her husband's business,

---

31   *Garcia v National Australia Bank Ltd* BC 9301944 Supreme Court of NSW Equity Division 1993, 26 (Young J).

32   *Garcia v National Australia Bank Ltd* BC 9301944 Supreme Court of NSW Equity Division 1993.

33   *Yerkey v Jones* (1939) 63 CLR 649 (Dixon J).

34   *Yerkey v Jones* (1939) 63 CLR 683 (Dixon J).

trusting Mr Garcia to make the necessary decisions. For Justice Young, there was nothing unusual in the fact that Mrs Garcia trusted her husband and left business decisions to him:

> Mrs Garcia presented herself as a capable and presentable professional. What she said was in general inherently believable. Despite women's liberation, there are still in the community a large number of women who, especially when their husband is a Master of Business Administration from Harvard and their talents lie in another field, still do trust their husbands to carry out the business from which the family will receive benefit in the way in which the husband thinks best. Furthermore they will act as directors and sign pieces of paper on request ... the general picture of the relationship between FBG and the plaintiff was one where she did trust him to organize business, she did in general what he wanted her to do.[35]

This finding was successfully appealed in *National Australia Bank v Garcia*[36] where the Court said that, while in the past it might have been appropriate to infer or accept that a married woman could not form a sound judgement of a business transaction or that she would be unduly influenced by her husband, this inference could not be made in Australia in the late 1990s. Mahoney P said that:

> [I]n the past, the matrimonial relationship and the experience of married women may have been such that it was proper to infer such matters as facts or even to accept that in principle such was the case. To infer such matters now would so often be contrary to experience that it is wrong to accept them to be so, in principle or as a presumption of fact.[37]

Sheller JA quoted with approval a statement made in 1985 by Justice Rogers, over 10 years earlier, which described the decision in *Yerkey v Jones* as not only out dated but as insulting to married women.[38] In *European Asian of Australia Limited v Kurland* Justice Rogers had criticised *Yerkey v Jones*:

> I feel compelled to say that in the year 1985 it seems anachronistic to be told that being a female and a wife is, by itself, a sufficient qualification

---

35   *Garcia v National Australia Bank Ltd* BC 9301944 Supreme Court of NSW Equity Division 1993, 22 (Young J).

36   *National Australia Bank v Garcia* [1996] NSWSC 253 (Mahoney P) http://www.austlii.edu.au/au/cases/nsw/NSWSC/1996/253.html accessed 1/09/2008.

37   *National Australia Bank v Garcia* [1996] NSWSC 253 (Mahoney P) http://www.austlii.edu.au/au/cases/nsw/NSWSC/1996/253.html accessed 1/09/2008.

38   *National Australia Bank v Garcia* [1996] NSWSC 253 (Sheller JA) http://www.austlii.edu.au/au/cases/nsw/NSWSC/1996/253.html accessed 1/09/2008.

to enrol in the class of persons suffering a special disadvantage ... that being a female spouse should place a person shoulder to shoulder with the sick, the ignorant and the impaired is not to be tolerated.[39]

For Sheller JA this was even truer in 1996 than it had been in 1985.

The two decisions used different approaches. The focus for Mahoney P, Sheller and Meagher JJA, was on Mrs Garcia's capabilities to form sound judgement in her husband's business, whereas for Justice Young the focus had been on whether she was justified in not taking an interest in her husband's business affairs. This is an important distinction that has often been overlooked in commentaries on this case and I will return to the point later in this chapter.

The decision was successfully appealed in the High Court,[40] where the majority upheld *Yerkey v Jones* and successfully applied it to Mrs Garcia. The majority did not accept that *Yerkey v Jones* no longer had any application, rather they argued that it formed part of general equitable principles which have as much application in contemporary Australia as in the 1930s. They argued that while much has changed in Australian society particularly the role of women both in marriage and in general, 'some things remain unchanged'. The majority still thought there are 'a significant number of women in Australia in relationships which are, for many and varied reasons, marked by disparities of economic and other power between the parties'.[41]

The first point made by the High Court majority was that, despite the many changes to the position of married women, protection was still needed, as many married women were still believed to be in a vulnerable economic position. However, the majority argued that this vulnerability does not stem from women being inferior to men, or from marriage being a disadvantage, but rather because a marriage relationship is based upon trust and confidence which implies that each partner to the marriage leaves the other to make decisions without necessarily needing to discuss them.

The second major point made by the majority was that the vulnerability in which married women find themselves stems from the assumption that, once married, some women will leave most if not all business decisions to their husbands because they trust them and have confidence in them to do it well:

> [T]he marriage relationship is such that one, often the woman, may well leave many, perhaps all, business judgements to the other spouse. In that kind of relationship, business decisions may be made with little consultation between the parties and with the most abbreviated

---

39   *European Asian of Australia Limited v Kurland* (1985) 8 NSWLR 200 (Rogers J).
40   *Garcia v National Australia Bank Ltd* [1998] CLR 395.
41   *Garcia v National Australia Bank* [1998] CLR 403–404 (Gaudron, McHugh & Hayne JJ).

explanations of their purport or effect. Sometimes with not the slightest hint of bad faith, the explanation of a particular transaction being given by one to the other will be imperfect and incomplete, if not simply wrong. That that is so is not always attributable to the intended deception, to any imbalance of power between the parties, or, even, the vulnerability of one to exploitation because of emotional involvement. It is, at its core, often a reflection of no more or less than the trust and confidence each has in the other.[42]

In this statement, the majority of the Court made trust and confidence central to the relationship of marriage.

Justice Kirby dissented from the view of the majority.[43] While he favoured protection for vulnerable people in a disadvantageous transaction, he did not support this protection as formulated by *Yerkey v Jones* because it targeted married women and, as such, he saw it as 'anachronistic', 'discriminatory and outmoded':

[W]hy should undergoing the ceremony of marriage make only a female partner to the relationship more needful of protection from equity than an unmarried female partner? ... to select marriage as a criterion of vulnerability also appears inappropriate at this stage of the evolution of personal relationships in this country. Rather than choose the fact of marriage and sex of one party to it as objective indication of vulnerability for legal purposes, it would seem more rational to look at all of the facts of the relationship between the surety and the borrower. So long as married women, as such, are treated as necessarily vulnerable, whatever the facts of their relationships, the focus of the law will remain upon a consideration which, in most cases, is simply irrelevant.[44]

He went on to say that, while the *Yerkey* principle provides protection to vulnerable people, it is expressed in a way that is unacceptable in contemporary Australia.[45]

Justice Kirby asked why married women should need the protection of the law more than anyone else. Why should marriage be seen as a disadvantage for women? What the majority found, however, was that it may well be that the principle applied to all people in publicly declared relationships, but they chose

---

42 *Garcia v National Australia Bank* [1998] CLR 404 (Gaudron, McHugh & Hayne JJ).

43 This was not surprising given that he had been highly critical of the *Yerkey v Jones* decision when he was on the NSW Court of Appeal. See, for example, *Warburton v Whitely* (1989) 5 BPR 97388.

44 *Garcia v National Australia Bank* [1998] CLR 425 (Kirby J).

45 *Garcia v National Australia Bank* [1998] CLR 428 (Kirby J). Many commentators had made the same comment. Su-King Hii, 'From Yerkey to Garcia: 60 Years On and Still as Confused as Ever!'; G Williams, 'Equitable Principles for the Protection of Vulnerable Guarantors: Is the Principle in Yerkey v Jones Still Needed?'; B Collier, 'The Rule in Yerkey v Jones: Fundamental Principles and Fundamental Problems'.

to avoid laying down any principle of law which may incorporate them. Instead they retained the gender and marriage specific principle as outlined in *Yerkey v Jones*:

> It may be that the principles applied in *Yerkey v Jones* will find application to other relationships more common now than was the case in 1939 — to long term and publicly declared relationships short of marriage between members of the same or opposite sex — but that is not a question that falls for decision in this case. It may be that those principles will find application where the husband acts as a surety for the wife but again that is not a problem that falls for decision here.[46]

Subsequent application of *Garcia* has not successfully extended the principle to non-married women. In *Liu v Adamson*[47] Macready M argued that Garcia did apply to a de facto wife if the creditor was aware of the relationship. In that case, however, the de facto wife failed to show that she did not gain a benefit from the guarantee. There are also a number of cases where the possibility of a husband using the *Garcia* defence has been discussed,[48] but to date no actual case with such facts has arisen for determination.

Justice Kirby favoured a principle of protection that was not specific to wives or women only. He saw this as being possible via the adoption of a principle based on the UK case of *Barclays Bank Plc v O'Brien*.[49] Justice Kirby's proposed approach was to rely on a principle which focussed on wrong doing by the principle debtor in the form of undue influence or misrepresentation, and on an approach which focussed on reasonable steps being taken by the credit provider to ensure that wrongdoing had not occurred. The merit of Justice Kirby's approach is threefold: firstly, it is expressed in non-discriminatory terms; secondly, it addresses the real causes of vulnerability; and thirdly, it recognises the credit provider's power to insist on guarantors seeking independent legal advice.[50]

Another aspect of the *O'Brien* approach that appealed to Justice Kirby was that it retains the economic usability of the family home in business affairs. Kirby J wanted to ensure that the law did not develop in such a way as to render the family home economically sterile. This view was also expressed by Justice Callinan. Both judges quoted with approval the statement of this principle in *O'Brien*:

> Wealth is now more widely spread. Moreover a high proportion of privately owned wealth is invested in the matrimonial home. Because of the recognition by society of the equality of the sexes, the majority of

---

46 *Garcia v National Australia Bank* [1998] CLR 404 (Gaudron, McHugh and Hayne JJ).
47 *Liu v Adamson* [2003] NSWSC 74.
48 See *Commonwealth Bank of Australia v Allregal Enterprises Pty Ltd* [1999] WASC 186.
49 *Barclays Bank Plc v O'Brien and another* [1194] 1 AC 180.
50 *Garcia v National Australia Bank* [1998] CLR 431 (Kirby J).

matrimonial homes are now in the joint names of both spouses. Therefore in order to raise finance for the business enterprises of one or other of the spouses … [there] is a need to ensure that the wealth currently tied up in the matrimonial home does not become economically sterile … it is therefore essential that a law designed to protect the vulnerable does not render the matrimonial home unacceptable as security to financial institutions.[51]

This focus on the family home as a measure of economic value is one way in which the case endorses the economic aspects of the marriage relationship. Others are discussed below.

Impact of the Decision

The *Garcia* case sparked much discussion among legal commentators, with some of this discussion uncharacteristically moving away from the legal principles at stake and towards the social and normative implications that emerged from the decision.

Discussion of the case focussed on the decision's implications for women, with many commentators taking Justice Kirby's view that the decision represented a step back for women's equality before the law. This view is founded upon the argument that married women in modern Australia are not, and should not be seen to be, ignorant of the business decisions of their husbands. For many, the decision represents a view of marriage which is founded upon inequality and dependence of a wife upon her husband, and thus represents a denial of the many advances that women have made in the decades since the *Yerkey v Jones* decision. Berna Collier is one of many people who strongly argued against the decision along these lines, stating:

> The advance in the status and education of women, the increasing role of women (including wives) in business and commercial affairs and the variety of personal relationships today all make a principle fashioned in terms of a wife's disadvantageous position vis-à-vis her husband, unsafe when stated as a general rule of universal application. Even as a statement of a *prima facie* position the statement is now unsound and objectionable in principle. It is also of dubious accuracy in practice.[52]

In many ways the decision is perplexing. On the one hand, it says that modern marriage is no longer an institution that oppresses women. However, the majority of judges wanted to retain protection for those women who are in need of it. The Court did not want to remove the special features of that protection that are so

---

51 *Barclays Bank Plc v O'Brien* [1994] 1 AC 188 (Browne-Wilkinson LJ).
52 Collier, 'The Rule in Yerkey v Jones' 79–80.

uniquely applicable to married women. The Court did recognise that the special disadvantage can occur equally for husbands, partners in de facto and same-sex relationships, but they were unwilling to subsume the protection into a broader legal principle such as unconscionability or the principle as stated by *O'Brien*. Why is this so?

I believe that the answer can be found by looking at the decision from a different angle. The majority of the High Court in the *Garcia* case was not interested in a discussion about how much marriage had changed, nor to what extent married women engaged in economic decision making in a modern Australian marriage. Instead, the decision makes more sense if we see it as being foremost about the meaning of marriage. There are three main features of marriage which the *Garcia* decision reinforces: first, that marriage is an economic as well as emotional union; second, that once married a couple's economic interests become united; third, and most obviously, that wives and husbands should have trust and confidence in each other.

What is Marriage According to *Garcia*?

Garcia represents an explicit recognition in law that marriage is as much a relationship about economics and money as it is about anything else. The relationship is presented as inevitably involving business decisions and entanglements. Despite the fact that the Garcias had separate businesses, Mrs Garcia was called upon to assist in the business affairs of her husband in different ways. The Court does not examine these actions through the lens of business dealings but, rather, as the economic aspects of a marriage relationship. This implies different values from those we usually associate with economic activity/ interest that occurs in the marketplace. In a marriage this 'work' is associated with the ethics of altruism, care and love.

An explicit recognition of the economics of marriage in the case can be found in its discussion of the family home. The family home,[53] while imbued with so much emotional significance, is recognised as an economic asset that must be protected. Justices Kirby and Callinan in *Garcia*, and Lord Browne-Wilkinson in *O'Brien*,[54] were concerned that a decision based on the special equity of

---

53   D N Benjamin, *The Home: Words, Interpretations, Meanings and Environments* (Avery, Aldershot 1995); L Fox, *Conceptualising Home* (Hart, Oxford 2007); S Bright & J Dewar (eds), *Land Law Themes and Perspectives* (Oxford University Press, Oxford 1998).
54   *Barclays Bank PLC v O'Brien and another* [1994] 1 AC 180.

wives would jeopardise the economic utility of the family home. However, the economic discourse of marriage in *Garcia* goes further. It is more than a recognition, it is an economic unification of a married couple's interests.[55]

The *Garcia* case reinforces the idea that, once married, a couple's economic interests become unified. As we saw previously, what this actually meant in the past was that, upon marriage, women ceased to have an independent economic/commercial existence.[56] While this is no longer the law, the unity of economic interests between a husband and a wife remains.

In *Garcia* we saw that the wife played an important role in assisting her husband fulfil formal business requirements, with the family home used to assist in his business requirements. The judgement takes this as a perfectly normal state of affairs. There was nothing wrong with a woman supporting her husband in his business affairs without necessarily having any direct involvement, knowledge or authority in those affairs.

In all three *Garcia* cases, there is no suggestion that a wife should not help her husband out in his business and financial affairs, even when she knows nothing about them. There is amazing tolerance for the fact that she was completely unaware of the business dealings of the companies of which she was a director. There is also tolerance for the fact that her husband forged her signature. The fact that she was passively involved was not seen as a problem. As Janine Pascoe puts it, the special equity cases do not require wives to act with care and diligence. It requires them not to act at all.[57] *Garcia* is not concerned with changing this, focussing instead on how to protect a wife when the trust she has placed in her husband turns out to be illusory. *Garcia* assumes economic unification in marriage such that self-interest, usually considered to be the necessary driver for economic activity in the marketplace, is suspended when considering economic activity in marriage.

The other aspect of marriage that emerges from *Garcia* is the idea that marriage embodies trust and confidence between a husband and wife. The Court never explained what trust and confidence meant, but it is my view that these can be read as love, or at the very least, as elements of love. Trust and confidence can of course exist in relationships other than romantic ones. One can speak of trusting a business partner or an advisor, for example. Similarly, one can have confidence in another person's ability without loving them. However, can there be love without trust and confidence? While this is arguable, we can say with more certainty that trust and confidence *may* constitute elements of

---

55   This has limits. For example, when it comes to property division under the Family Law Act there is no assumption that all assets are equally owned.

56   See chapter one's discussion on coverture.

57   J Pascoe, 'Women Who Guarantee Company Debts: Wife or Director?' [2003] 2 *Deakin Law Review* 12.

love.[58] A telling point is the fact there have not been any cases where trust and confidence outside of a romantic relationship have been successful in giving rise to the defence in *Garcia*.[59]

A plausible interpretation of the majority in the High Court decision of *Garcia* is that, once you are married, you have to trust your husband/wife and have confidence that the economic decisions they are making are right. What the majority want to enforce is the idea that it is not outmoded for a woman to trust her husband and leave him to conduct business matters if that is what she chooses. Laws should not erode this principle of trust and confidence in marriage but rather protect it by supporting those (more commonly women) who find themselves disadvantaged when that trust and confidence has been abused. *Garcia* avoids any legal development that places a married woman in a position where she must distrust her husband, where marriage is seen, to use Justice Kirby's phrase, as a 'suspect relationship'.[60]

Despite his dissent, Justice Kirby actually has a similar argument, although he arrives at it in a slightly different way. He rejects any suggestion that we should interpret marriage in any way that entrenches it as anything less than an embodiment of trust and confidence. In arguing against seeing marriage as giving rise to undue influence, he asks, 'Is that what marriage has come to in this day and age, that from being a relationship of complete trust and devotion, it has become a suspect relationship?'[61] In his judgement, Justice Kirby, like the majority, was interested in preserving marriage as a special 'space'. Kirby J fails to see that the majority had the same objective.

That *Garcia* did not want to deny or minimise trust and confidence (or love) in the marriage relationship is a point recognised by Elizabeth Stone,[62] who has argued that the distinctiveness of the *Garcia* principle lies in its recognition of the unique feature of the marriage relationship. She says, 'the High Court has taken judicial notice of a feature of the marital relationship which is highly unusual: a fully competent adult may choose to remain ignorant of her legal affairs without being careless, and this fact is notorious'.[63]

---

58   Trust is discussed as an element of romantic love for another purpose in Delaney, 'Love and Loving Commitment' 342.

59   To date the defence has been very limited, although it has been applied to a child-parent relationship in *State Bank of NSW v Layoun* [2001] NSWSC 113; Higgins CJ in *Watt v State Bank of New South Wales* [2003] ACTCA 7 was very strong in his opinion that it should not apply to parent child relationships.

60   Transcript of Proceedings Garcia v National Australia Bank (High Court of Australia S18/1997 March 1998) (Kirby J).

61   Transcript of Proceedings Garcia v National Australia Bank (High Court of Australia S18/1997 March 1998) (Kirby J).

62   E Stone, 'The Distinctiveness of Garcia' (2006) 22 *Journal of Contract Law* 170–193.

63   Stone, 'The Distinctiveness of Garcia' 178.

To be successfully applied, therefore, *Garcia* requires a fact situation which 'hinges not on wrongdoing but on excusable ignorance' and where that excusable ignorance is a 'notorious feature of the relationship',[64] a 'normal and unremarkable incident'[65] of the relationship. Stone says that to succeed using *Garcia* 'it must be established that it [the relationship] is of such unusual trust and confidence that ignorance of one's own affairs is an outcome both likely and defensible'.[66] This, she claims, can only be found in marriage, maybe in de facto relationships, and possibly in same-sex relationships, but further than this it is unlikely to go. She says it is simply not 'a normal feature of other relationships to cede total control of one's affairs':[67]

> *Garcia* should be limited to circumstances where a choice to remain ignorant of one's own financial and legal affairs is not merely possible but normal; not merely understandable but excusable. Beyond marriage, de jure or de facto, such relationships are unlikely to be found.[68]

Recognising this aspect of the relationship explains why the decision has been limited in its application in subsequent cases. It also makes sense of a decision that otherwise appears to be at odds with other central legal principles which apply in commercial dealings. The *Garcia* approach makes sense if we return to the interpretation that the High Court wanted to retain marriage first and foremost as an emotional relationship:

> [T]he fact that protection is given in such circumstances must be understood to be quite anomalous. It is submitted that the protection extended to mistaken wives is justified, but that the intimacy of the relationship and the social desirability of encouraging such intimacy, which provide the justification for that protection are unique.[69]

In *Garcia* the High Court was recognising that there is a conflict between having love — as manifested in trust and confidence — and economic dependence in a relationship, and that this situation may lead one to a disadvantaged position. The Court was mindful of the fact that the disadvantage was more often than not experienced by wives and therefore wanted to highlight that special protection for them. This reading of the case implies that the High Court's view is in harmony with the feminist critiques of both love and marriage, and the *Garcia* decision can be read as an attempt to accommodate those critiques. The Court was also, however, attempting to reconcile the conflicting paradigms of economics and love, of the market and the home. The decision is an indication of the conflict

---

64 Stone, 'The Distinctiveness of Garcia' 178.
65 Stone, 'The Distinctiveness of Garcia' 186.
66 Stone, 'The Distinctiveness of Garcia' 180.
67 Stone, 'The Distinctiveness of Garcia' 180.
68 Stone, 'The Distinctiveness of Garcia' 188.
69 Stone, 'The Distinctiveness of Garcia' 180.

(discussed earlier) that law faces between giving voice to people's economic rights and interests that coincide with their personal intimate relationships, of retaining the distinctiveness of marriage and marriage like relationships while enforcing their economic and commercial rights.

Conclusion

The *Garcia* case incorporates an economic as well as a romantic discourse of marriage. The romantic discourse of marriage emerges from the High Court's focus on marriage as a relationship of trust and confidence, which I have argued can be read as elements of love. As well as reflecting these two discourses in their judgement, the High Court in *Garcia* goes further and recognises that they may be the cause of conflict and disadvantage. The Court's reasoning reflects the idea that loving someone, acting altruistically, and trusting their spouse totally, including in business affairs, may leave one of the partners to a marriage at a disadvantage. Even in modern Australia, with its many social changes to gender roles and the institution of marriage, the Court believed this was more likely to impact upon a wife than upon a husband. In recognising this, the judgement of the majority could be interpreted as reflecting the feminist critiques of love and marriage outlined earlier: that patriarchy renders women vulnerable in love. By continuing the *Yerkey v Jones* principle in *Garcia*, the Court is accommodating this critique but is not disrupting the established discourse of love and marriage.

The romantic discourse that remains, and is even nurtured after *Garcia*, is that upon marriage a couple should trust and have confidence in each other, and be free to act altruistically rather than self-interestedly. Married couples should not be suspicious of each other's motives. Such behaviour would be at odds with the emotional aspects of the marriage relationship. Whether we use the word love or not, this is a message that emerges unmistakeably from the case. Trust and confidence (or love) are part of marriage and should be part of marriage. This ought to be not only recognised but also nurtured and dealt with when it creates problems. Nevertheless, despite the acknowledgement of the emotional aspects of marriage, the reality is that, as evidenced in the *Garcia* case, economic and romantic discourses can conflict with each other. The case, therefore, represents the dilemma discussed at the beginning of this chapter, of how to reconcile romantic love with the economic and financial aspects of the marriage relationship. The rules of love and the rules of business and economics are not the same. The *Garcia* case attempts to reconcile this by alleviating against the economic disadvantages that can arise when love and marriage fail.

The importance of this case for this book lies with what it claims about love and marriage. When read in this context, *Garcia* establishes that marriage in modern Australia cannot be read independently of economic or romantic discourses, and that while these can conflict they are both to be accommodated rather than eroded by legal principles. The case shows the difficulty that the law has had in reconciling the economic realities of an intimate relationship. The law has wanted to retain the distinctiveness of the marriage relationship, and has not wanted to reduce marriage to a business — wives to housemaids and sex workers, and men to financial providers — and therefore selectively chooses which economic aspects of the relationship to honour. In *Garcia*, the Court focussed on the economic value of the home. This is in keeping with the Hasday's argument that the law only acknowledges those aspects that fit into a paradigm of a unified set of interests, the family home more than any other property is loaded with emotional meaning. Whether this selective honouring of economic agreements reflects the modern understanding of marriage as a relationship based on love which lasts for as long as the love does, is debatable.

4. The Foregrounding of Love in the Same-Sex Marriage Debate

Love Does not Discriminate[1]

Introduction

Previous chapters have outlined a number of legal challenges to the traditional meanings of marriage. In relation to the connection between marriage, sex and procreation, *Re Kevin* asserted that sexual intercourse and procreation alone do not define marriage. In relation to the idea that marriage is about economic unity and support, *Garcia* reasserted this connection and continued the law's attempt at balancing the tensions between the home and the market that are so clearly manifest in the marriage relationship. In previous chapters, the small ways in which love is explicit and implicit in the legal discourse of marriage have been shown. When we turn to consider the same-sex marriage debate, however, love takes centre stage. This debate has specifically demanded that marriage be understood as a relationship ruled by love and that the law be altered to reflect this.

This argument can be traced by examining two key legal episodes in the same-sex marriage debate in Australia: the changes made to the Marriage Act in 2004, and the passing and subsequent disallowance of the Civil Union Act in the Australian Capital Territory in 2006. In examining these two episodes, this chapter shows how the debate became one about whether we understand marriage to be about procreation or love, as well as demonstrating how the connection between marriage and procreation is flawed and Christian underpinnings of this connection are open to debate. Finally, the chapter turns to the question of what the same-sex marriage debate will do, not only for the meaning of marriage, but also for the meaning of love. We know that marriage is a conservative institution fighting to break free from its oppressive past. What is less well understood is that love also can be read conservatively. As we have seen from some feminist critiques of love, it is closely connected to patriarchy and traditional gender roles, and, as we will see from the queer critique in this chapter, it replicates heteronormativity. The recognition of same-sex marriage, however, has the potential to imbue both institutions with a more progressive and radical meaning.

---

1   Slogan on placard at protest march in Canberra to support marriage for same-sex, intersex and transgender couples. 2/08/2009 *Sunday Canberra Times* 4.

The Same-Sex Marriage Debate

Support for same-sex marriage is not universal in the Australian gay and lesbian community. The gay marriage debate is often depicted as a struggle between the LGBTI[2] community and political progressives against right wing conservatives and the Christian right. However, there is also considerable opposition to gay marriage from within the LGBTI and progressive traditions. This opposition stems from a number of inter-related factors. Marriage is too 'loaded' an institution, its association with patriarchy and the oppression of women make it an unviable institution for many progressively minded people, regardless of their sexuality. Judith Butler's view of gay marriage is indicative of this position:

> For a progressive sexual movement, even one that may want to produce marriage as an option for non heterosexuals, the proposition that marriage should become the only way to sanction or legitimate sexuality is unacceptably conservative … What does this do to the community of the non married, the single, the divorced, the uninterested, the non monogamous, and how does the sexual field become reduced, in its very legibility, once we extend marriage as a norm?[3]

Furthermore, the acceptance of marriage as a form for same-sex relationships is seen as a risky strategy. Michael Warner argues that agitating for same-sex marriage replicates and privileges heterosexuality and 'authorizes the state to make one form of life — already normative — even more privileged'.[4] This may lead to those relationships being erased because they don't fit the legal model of marriage.[5]

Opposing gay marriage is not the same as stating that equality of rights between heterosexual and same-sex relationships is not desirable. However, it is argued

---

2   Lesbian, Gay, Bi-sexual, Transsexual and Intersex. I have used the term LGBTI to be as inclusive as possible, but this inclusivity at times can appear to be insensitive to the diversities that exist between the groups these initials denote. In particular, when it comes to marriage, it must be made clear that the issues facing transsexual people are quite different from those facing same-sex couples. I only discuss them together because a liberal reading of transsexual marriage in the case of *Re Kevin* was understood by many as implying a liberal attitude towards same-sex marriage.

3   J Butler, 'Is Kinship Always Already Heterosexual?' (2002) 13 *Differences* 21–44. See also N D Polikoff, 'We Will Get What We Ask For: Why Legalising Gay and Lesbian Marriage Will Not "Dismantle the Legal Structure of Gender in Every Marriage"' (1993) 79 *Virginia Law Review* 1535–1875. This article articulates very clearly the argument against the idea that same-sex marriage will transform the institution of marriage for the better.

4   M Warner, *The Trouble With Normal: Sex, Politics, and the Ethics of Queer Life* (Free Press, New York 1999) 112.

5   For example, Katherine Franke's comparison of the campaign for gay marriage with the campaign for the right to marry for African-Americans following their emancipation as slaves leads her to worry that it might have some of the same outcomes. She shows how the right to marry was used as a weapon to 'civilise' African Americans and get them to adopt the domestic patterns of elite white Americans. She argues that, in that period, a right to marry collapsed into an obligation to do so, a negation of other relationships they once enjoyed, and a punitive approach toward those who broke the rules and duties of marriage. She warns that these same outcomes could emerge from the legal recognition of same-sex marriage. K Franke, 'The Curious Relationship of Marriage and Freedom' in Garrison & Scott (eds), *Marriage at the Crossroads* 87–106.

by some that, in so far as marriage itself is capable of delivering such a goal,[6] it is not the only way to achieve it. Jenni Millbank has argued that marriage ought not to be the only 'yardstick for legal equality',[7] that reform should proceed according to what is needed to remove discrimination in specific contexts rather than the 'one-stop comprehensive' formal equality that would be achieved through marriage. She says, 'relationship recognition for lesbian and gay families should proceed on the basis of what is needed by such families rather than by simply assuming that formal equality is the only, or most desirable goal'.[8]

Despite opposition to gay marriage within the community, the amendments to the Marriage Act to legislate the meaning of marriage as a union between one man and one woman forced many to take a more entrenched position than otherwise would have been the case,[9] and, within a short space of time, same-sex marriage increasingly came to be seen as an important 'equality goal' in Australia. Surveys show that support for gay marriage doubled between 2001 and 2005,[10] but its popularity cannot be reduced simply to a capricious stand against conservatism. Marriage remains a goal because it is a means by which legal rights and status are allocated to people in society, and the state's denial of this to one group is seen as a means of reinforcing inequality. In large part, therefore, the arguments for same-sex marriage are articulated in the language of liberalism, with a focus on rights, justice and equality.[11] As Tamara Metz puts, it while the institution of marriage is problematic, the fact is that, 'a commitment to equal treatment before the law demands it. Period.'[12] But even more than this, the debate has shown us that what we thought was becoming an obsolete institution, in fact, still carries with it a meaning many crave. Marriage 'elicits *ethical recognition*',[13] provides 'moral approval' and embodies the 'complex normative account of the

---

6   Many argue that it isn't. See J Josephson, 'Romantic Weddings, Diverse Families' (2010) 6(1) *Politics and Gender* 130.

7   J Millbank, 'Recognition of Lesbian and Gay Families in Australian Law: Part One — Couples' (2006) 34(1) *Federal Law Review* 9.

8   Millbank, 'Recognition of Lesbian and Gay Families in Australian Law: Part One — Couples' 8–9; R Graycar & J Millbank, 'From Functional Family to Spinster Sisters: Australia's Distinctive Path to Relationship Recognition' (2007) 24 *Journal of Law and Policy* 122.

9   Nicola Roxon MP claimed that 'it was not until this bill was proposed by the government that calls were made more widely for marriage to be broadened to encompass same-sex couples'. Commonwealth, Parliamentary Debates House of Representatives June 16 2004 (Nicola Roxon) http://parlinfoweb.aph.gov. au/piweb/view_document.aspx?ID=2262589 accessed 13/05/2008. The same point is made by Graycar & Millbank, 'From Functional Family to Spinster Sisters' 161.

10   Graycar & Millbank, 'From Functional Family to Spinster Sisters' 161. See also Pink News 'Australian Territory Legalises Gay Civil Partnership Ceremonies' http://www.pinknews.co.uk/2009/11/11/australian-territory-legalises-gay-civil-partnership-ceremonies/ accessed 13/11/2009. Carol Smart, in her studies on same-sex weddings, found that the political nature of choosing same-sex marriage is well understood by those couples that are getting married. See C Smart, 'Can I Be Bridesmaid?: Combining the Personal and Political in Same-Sex Weddings' (2008) 11(6) *Sexualities* 763–778.

11   A Wilson, 'Feminism and Same-Sex Marriage: Who Cares?' (2010) 6(1) *Politics and Gender* 134.

12   T Metz, 'Demands of Care and Dilemmas of Freedom: What We Really Ought to be Worried About' (2010) 6(1) *Politics and Gender* 120.

13   Metz, 'Demands of Care and Dilemmas of Freedom' 123.

relationship it names'.[14] It is an 'idealised' rite of passage for couples, signifying the 'successful transition into adulthood', responsibility and social legitimacy.[15] As such, it is desired by 'couples who have long been outside the boundaries of legitimacy'.[16] For example, see how the following comment from a prominent sex advice columnist makes the connection between marriage, respectability and 'real love':

> Once our relationships were only respected if we had remained together for a long, long time. Only longevity earned us some modicum of respect. Straight couples could always rush that validity by getting married. Now ... some gay kids, desperate to have their gay love taken seriously, will wield their new marriage licenses and say: 'See how real our love is? ... You better respect us now!'[17]

It appears that despite the very many legal changes to the institution which, many have argued, have moved the relationship away from one of status, and despite the many negative associations especially for women, marriage retains a significant degree of status and respectability. The continuing popularity of marriage as a goal can be explained by its legal and social meanings, and by the practical benefits it bestows on couples. Where it continues to be popular, some of this popularity must also be attributed to its connection with romantic love.

Legal Episodes in the Debate

Amending the Marriage Act (1961)

In May 2004, then Attorney General Phillip Ruddock presented the Marriage Legislation Amendment Bill 2004 to the Federal Parliament. In the second reading speech, the Attorney General explained that the Bill was needed because there was considerable community concern about the erosion of the institution of marriage. He explained that

> the government has consistently reiterated the fundamental importance of the place of marriage in our society ... It is a central and fundamental

---

14   Metz, 'Demands of Care and Dilemmas of Freedom' 123.

15   Diduck & Kaganas, *Family Law, Gender and The State* 34.

16   L J Marso, 'Marriage and Bourgeois Respectability' (2010) 6(1) *Politics and Gender* 152.

17   Dan Savage, sex advice quoted in 'Young, Gay & Married (And Divorced)' *Out Now Global* http://joemygod.blogspot.com/2008/04/young-gay-married-and-divorced.html accessed 10/06/2010.

institution. It is vital to the stability of our society and provides the best environment for the raising of children. The government has taken steps to reinforce the basis of this fundamental institution.[18]

The Bill did three things: firstly, it provided a definition of marriage as a voluntary union between a man and a woman; secondly, it prevented Australian courts from recognising same-sex marriages that had taken place in other countries; thirdly, it prevented same-sex couples from adopting children from overseas.

On the issue of definition, while the 1961 Marriage Act did not provide a definition of marriage, section 46 required a marriage celebrant to state that 'marriage according to Australian law, is the union of a man and a woman to the exclusion of others, voluntarily entered into for life'.[19] Significantly, during the passing of the original Marriage Act, a proposed amendment to specifically define marriage had been defeated in the Senate. It had then been argued by Liberal Senator John Gorton (who later became Prime Minister from 1968–1971) that the definition of marriage was best left to the common law.[20]

The Howard government's desire to legislate the definition was motivated by significant concern among some Liberal MPs that the courts were moving away from a traditional meaning of marriage. The decision to validate a transsexual marriage in *Re Kevin* was clearly a matter of concern for some MPs, as were comments made out of court by members of the judiciary which showed a leaning towards a 'contemporary meaning' of marriage.[21] These concerns led to a delegation of 30 members of parliament concerned about the recognition of same-sex relationships in overseas jurisdictions and the impact that this was likely to have on Australia approaching the Prime Minister, John Howard. Alby Shultz later identified himself as one of these MPs and openly disclosed the role that religious organisations played in the debate:

> it is my belief that moving away from the traditional definition of marriage would be to the detriment of our society. Marriage provides

---

18 Second Reading Speech, Commonwealth, Parliamentary Debates House of Representatives May 27 2004 (Phillip Ruddock) http://parlinfoweb.aph.gov.au/piweb/view_document.aspx?ID=2259205 accessed 14/04/2008.

19 Marriage Act (1961) section 46. The definition of marriage in section 46 derives from the UK case of *Hyde v Hyde and Woodmansee* [1861–1873] All ER Rep 175. For an analysis of this definition and its relevance for a modern society see S Poulter, 'The Definition of Marriage in English Law' (1979) 42(4) *The Modern Law Review* 409–429. The article was written in the 1970s and makes some interesting comments about same-sex marriage being accepted in the future.

20 Sen John Gorton in the Senate debates on the passing of the original Marriage Act (1961) quoted in Commonwealth, Parliamentary Debates House of Representatives June 16 2004 (Arch Bevis) http://parlinfoweb.aph.gov.au/piweb/view_document.aspx?ID=2262773 accessed 13/05/2008.

21 See, for example, comments made by Sen Guy Barnett, Commonwealth, Parliamentary Debates Senate June 17 2004 (Guy Barnett) http://parlinfoweb.aph.gov.au/piweb/view_document.aspx?ID=2014889 accessed 15/05/2008.

stability and is a solidly-built roof under which children can grow and be nurtured. The Australian Family Association has strongly supported this view, as has the Australian Christian Lobby.[22]

It is also worth noting that 2004 was a big year for the meaning of marriage in the US. The US House of Representatives passed the Marriage Protection Act, and many states held referenda to consider amendments to the Constitution concerning the definition of marriage.[23] This activity reverberated in Australia.

It was suggested by Graycar and Millbank, however, that the definition of marriage was seized upon as a cynical political exercise by the Howard government, designed to act as a wedge issue leading up to an election.[24] Its effect, according to Graycar and Millbank, was to reaffirm the 'special-ness of marriage' and to single out 'lesbians and gay men as objects of exclusion'.[25] It was indeed the case that gay marriage did become, and still is, a wedge issue in Australian politics. This aspect of the debate is illustrated most clearly by the Australian Capital Territory's thwarted attempts to pass legislation that came closer than ever before to legislating gay marriage.

Civil Union Bill ACT (2006)

When the ACT Government began consulting with the LGBTI community in Canberra on the best model to adopt in the ACT for the recognition of same-sex relationships, the community favoured a model which closely resembled a marriage.[26] As such, on 28 March 2006, then Labor Chief Minister, Jon Stanhope, introduced into the ACT legislative assembly the Civil Union Bill 2006. He explained the content of the Bill in the following way:

> A civil union will be treated in the same way as marriage under territory law. A civil union is not a marriage but, will, so far as the law of the ACT is concerned, to be treated in the same way. The government is of the view that this is preferable to providing an alternative form of marriage that would not have equal recognition to commonwealth marriage. The

---

22 Commonwealth, Parliamentary Debates House of Representatives June 17 2004 (Alby Shultz) http:// parlinfoweb.aph.gov.au/piweb/view_document.aspx?ID=2263265 accessed 13/05/2008.

23 A Bernstein, 'Questioning Marriage' in A Bernstein (ed), *Marriage Proposals Questioning a Legal Status* (New York University Press, New York 2006) 1–29.

24 Graycar & Millbank, 'From Functional Family to Spinster Sisters' 160–61.

25 Graycar & Millbank, 'From Functional Family to Spinster Sisters' 160.

26 'Our consultation made it very clear that the community would prefer the legislation include a formal ceremony and that that was important to couples both personally and more broadly in tackling discrimination against same-sex couples.' Heidi Yates, representative for gay lobby group Good Process, in Ross Peake, 'Angry Corbell Abandons Gay Plan' 5/5/2008 *Canberra Times*http://www.canberra.yourguide.com.au/ printerFreindlypage.asp?story_id+1237202 accessed 5/05/2008.

civil union is a new concept that can be used by anybody, regardless of gender. It will give couples functional equality under the ACT law with married couples but does not replace or duplicate marriage.[27]

This Bill was quickly met with opposition. On May 3 2006, the Liberal leader, Bill Stephaniak, introduced into parliament an alternative Bill based on the Tasmanian registration model, the Registration of Relationships Bill 2006, which, he argued, did not undermine the values of marriage. Just over one week later Stephaniak tabled in parliament a petition gathered by the Australian Christian Lobby and signed by 1,710 people who opposed the Civil Union Bill. The petitioners said: 'We the undersigned believe that this creates a marriage like relationship which so mimics marriage as to confuse and diminish it.'[28]

Extensive debate followed regarding the extent to which a civil union under this legislation mimicked marriage. Zanghellini explains that under the Bill a civil union resembled marriage because 'a ceremony was required for it to be brought into existence and because a validly contracted civil union was to be treated like marriage for the purposes of all ACT laws'.[29] However, civil unions were different to marriage not only in name but also because they would always be regarded differently to marriage in other jurisdictions, including the federal one.

The Federal Liberal Government was vehemently opposed to the Bill for two main reasons. They argued firstly that the ACT Government did not have the constitutional power to legislate for marriage, and secondly that marriage as an institution should be preserved as a union between one man and one woman. The ACT Civil Unions Bill was seen to be creating a relationship between same-sex couples which was too close to that marriage model, and therefore eroded the idea that it takes a man and woman to have a marriage.

The Civil Union Bill became the Civil Union Act (2006) (ACT) but it never came into effect. On 13 June 2006, Governor-General Michael Jeffery, on the advice of the Federal Government, disallowed the Civil Union Act (2006) under section 35 of the Australian Capital Territory (Self-Government) Act (1988). The Federal Government disallowance was described as 'autocratic'[30] as 'very unusual',[31] and, by one Greens Senator, as 'homophobia dressed up as an argument about state rights'.[32]

---

27 Australian Capital Territory, Parliamentary Debates Legislative Assembly 28 March 2006, 657 (Jon Stanhope).
28 Australian Capital Territory, Parliamentary Debates Legislative Assembly May 11 2006, 1519 (Bill Stephaniak).
29 A Zanghellini 'Marriage and Civil Union: Legal and Moral Questions' (2007) 35(2) *Federal Law Review* 265.
30 Australian Capital Territory, Parliamentary Debates Legislative Assembly Dec 12 2006, 3953 (Simon Corbell).
31 George Williams described the act as 'very unusual' in Farah Farouque, 'Why or Why Can't I Have a Civil Union' 10/06/2006 *The Age* http://wwwtheage.com.au/news/in-depth/why-oh-why-cant-I-have-a-civil-union/2006 accessed 22/05/2008.
32 Sen Rachel Siewart Commonwealth, Parliamentary Debates Senate June 15 2006 http://parlinfoweb.aph.gov.au/piweb/view_document.aspx?ID=2345461 accessed 13/05/2008.

The ACT Government persevered. On 12 December 2006 the ACT Government presented into the ACT Parliament the Civil Partnership Bill 2006. This new Bill made the following changes in the hope of addressing the concerns of the federal government:

- The new Bill did not use the word 'union'. This would remove any confusion, as the word is more closely associated with marriage because it is used to describe marriage in the Marriage Act 1961;
- The new Bill did not specify that a civil partnership is to be treated like a marriage;
- A civil partnership could be entered into by any two people whether they were same-sex or not; and
- The ceremony associated with a civil partnership would not be performed by marriage celebrants, but rather by civil partnership notaries.

The new Bill was still not considered acceptable to the Federal Government and the Federal Attorney-General announced that his government would not rule out again using the Governor-General's disallowance power to override the Act.[33] The ACT government left the Bill on the books, but waited until after the coming federal election to stage their next move. In November 2007, the Rudd Labor Government was elected and the ACT announced it would revive the legislation.[34] By now, however, the Federal Labor Party and its socially conservative Christian leader, Kevin Rudd, had eagerly succumbed to conservative pressure and declared its own commitment to the principle that marriage is between a man and a woman. Negotiations between the ACT Government and the Federal Government came to a conclusion in May 2008 with a clear understanding that the Federal Government would not allow the ACT to pass legislation which in any way mimics marriage. An angry ACT Government had no choice but to scrap all previous plans and introduce legislation that instead mimics the Tasmanian registration model.[35]

On 11 November 2009, the ACT legislature once again opened up the issue by passing the Civil Partnerships Amendment Bill 2009. This Bill, introduced by the ACT Greens and supported by the ACT Labor Party, introduced the right of parties to declare their relationship before a civil partnership notary, and thus introduced the much sought after ceremony that had been attempted by past

---

33   Phillip Ruddock MP Attorney-General 'ACT Civil Partnerships Bill Does Not Remove Concerns' (Press Release, 6 Feb 2007).

34   Cathy Alexander, 'Corbell to Revive Gay Union Act' 30/11/2007 *Canberra Times*http://canberra. yourguide.com.au/news/local/news/general/corbell-to-revive-gay-union accessed 13/05/2008.

35   Ross Peake, 'Angry Corbell Abandons Gay Plan' 5/5/2008 *Canberra Times*http://www.canberra. yourguide.com.au/printerFreindlypage.asp?story_id+1237202 accessed 5/05/2008.

versions of the legislation.[36] The first 'partnership' under the new law took place on 25 November 2009.[37] After initial concerns that the Federal Government would override this amendment, it has remained untouched. However, the issue of gay marriage has not gone away. In 2013, three countries — Uruguay, New Zealand and France — passed legislation that legalises gay marriage, bringing the total of countries to do so to 14.[38] A Bill recognising gay marriage has passed the House of Commons in England,[39] and US President Obama is now supporting gay marriage and has stated:

> Our journey is not complete until our gay brothers and sisters are treated like anyone else under the law — for if we are truly created equal, then surely the love we commit to one another must be equal as well.[40]

In Australia too there is a shift in the mood. Kevin Rudd recently announced that he had changed his position on the issue and was now a supporter of gay marriage and the Lobor Party has agreed to allow a conscience vote in parliament on the issue.

Sensing a possible change of mood, the ACT once more introduced legislation. The Marriage Equality (Same Sex) Act 2013 passed the legislative assembly in October 2013, but its fate was short lived. The Act was successfully challenged in the High Court on the constitutional ground of inconsistency with a federal law (section 109). The ACT therefore remains without gay marriage legislation and the rest of Australia spasmodically argues the issue.

The Struggle for the Meaning of Marriage

Procreation v Love

In large part, the same-sex marriage debate in the ACT became an argument about whether we understand marriage as an institution whose *raison d'etre* is procreation or love. For Labor and the Greens, the goal became not only to recognise same-sex relationships but also to recognise them as love relationships.

---

36 The Bill also facilitates the creation of civil partnership notaries and the recognition of civil partnerships made in other jurisdictions. It avoids the issue of mimicking marriage by being for the exclusive use of same-sex couples.

37 http://actgay.e-p.net.au/news/280-first-ceremony-takes-place-in-canberra accessed 2/12/09.

38 B Miller, 'Joy, Anger as France Legalises Same-Sex Marriage' http://www.abc.net.au/news/2013-04-24/joy-anger-as-france-legalises-same-sex-marriage Accessed 24/04/2013.

39 'Gay Marriage Bill Passes Britain's House of Commons' http://www.abc.net.au/news/2013-05-22/britains-gay-marriage-bill-passes-major-hurdle/4704878 accessed 14/06/2013.

40 'Obama's Evolution On Gay Marriage' http://abcnews.go.com/Politics/obamas-evolution-gay-marriage/story?id=19150614 accessed 14/06/2013.

Love had been raised in the federal parliamentary debates around the changing of the Marriage Act,[41] but it became more central in debates about the ACT's Civil Unions Bill. Andrew Barr MLA said that the Civil Union Bill is about,

> supporting loving, caring relationships regardless of the sexuality of those involved. ... Saying no to civil unions is to say that some relationships are more legitimate than others; that some loving, committed long-term relationships are; for some inexplicable reason, of lesser value.[42]

Jon Stanhope said that '[t]hose of us who enjoy rich and enduring marriages might ask ourselves how we would feel if we were to be suddenly and rudely informed that our love was a lesser love'.[43]

In the Senate, Greens Senator Kerry Nettle told a story of a lesbian couple in the ACT who had been planning their civil union when the legislation was struck down. When the news had reached their daughter that her mothers could no longer have a civil union she had declared that it was not the Prime Minister's business who can fall in love. Senator Nettle went on to say:

> I reckon that the 12-year-old has a better handle on what this debate is about than a lot of parliamentarians do. She understands that this debate is about love. It is about who can love each other and who can have their relationship recognised.[44]

Senator Bob Brown also thought it was a debate about love: 'What is it about these gentlemen that they cannot recognise thousands of Australia's loving relationships'.[45] Senator Christine Milne also saw the debate as being about love, arguing that: 'it is about recognising love and commitment — and isn't that the very definition of the marital ideal, of what marriage, of what civil union is fundamentally about; love and commitment?'[46]

The fact that, for many, the argument for same-sex marriage is about the recognition of same-sex love is also evident in the way the struggle is being conceived by

---

41 Arch Bevis, in the debate about the changes to the Marriage Act, said that 'the thing that establishes ... loving relationships is not gender and is not sexuality. Love, respect and tolerance for one another and honesty with one another are keys to that lasting loving partnership. I know a number of people, people I have worked with and people who are friends of mine, who are gays and lesbians in longstanding relationships who I believe have that same love and respect and tolerance and open honesty with one another that I identify in my relationship with my wife.' Commonwealth, Parliamentary Debates House of Representatives June 16 2004 (Arch Bevis) http://parlinfoweb.aph.gov.au/piweb/view_document.aspx?ID=2262773 accessed 13/05/2008.
42 Australian Capital Territory, Parliamentary Debates Legislative Assembly May 11 2006, 1602 (Andrew Barr).
43 Australian Capital Territory, Parliamentary Debates Legislative Assembly May 11 2006, 1623 (Jon Stanhope).
44 Commonwealth, Parliamentary Debates Senate June 15 2006 (Kerry Nettle) http://parlinfoweb.aph.gov.au/piweb/view_document.aspx?ID=2345413 accessed 13/05/2008.
45 Commonwealth, Parliamentary Debates Senate June 15 2006 (Bob Brown) http://parlinfoweb.aph.gov.au/piweb/view_document.aspx?ID=2345425 accessed 13/05/2008.
46 Commonwealth, Parliamentary Debates Senate June 15 2006 (Christine Milne) http://parlinfoweb.aph.gov.au/piweb/view_document.aspx?ID=2345449 accessed 13/05/2008.

activists. For example, the Victorian Gay and Lesbian Rights Lobby's campaign for relationship recognition is called 'Equal Love'.[47] Recently the Mayor of the NSW town of Byron Bay moved a motion to recognise gay marriage and establish a 'Love Park' in town as a symbol of recognition and acceptance of gay and lesbian relationships. That this is a love park rather than a 'tolerance', 'acceptance', 'inclusion', 'justice', 'equality' or 'rights' park, is telling.

The same-sex marriage debate is very much about making romantic love visible outside of heterosexual relationships. It is quantitatively about breaking down the disassociation that exists between same-sex couples and love, because love as much as marriage carries with it the badges of legitimacy and respectability. In Senator Milne's speech, however, we get to the crux of the matter. What we are seeing here is a debate not just about who can love, but also about whether love and marriage go together. What we see in this debate is the argument that, on the one hand, marriage is about love and nothing else — this being the modern romantic love rhetoric of marriage —, and, on the other, the argument that marriage is not only about love, but also about procreation. The central debate and issue is very clearly stated by ACT Liberal MLA, Vicki Dunne, in the following lengthy quotation. Here she argues that heterosexual relationships are different to homosexual ones because they are 'ordered towards reproduction, towards having children'and, as such, she argues, are fundamentally different and more valuable to society than homosexual relationships:

> Heterosexual relationships, particularly marriage, have the potential to produce a material benefit to society in the form of new members, something separate from and external to the relationship. Homosexual relationships on the other hand, are simply not like that. The partners might be just as affectionate and they may be just as sincere as those in a heterosexual relationship, but that does not alter the simple fact ... that their relationship is formed for a different purpose ... The fundamental *raison d'etre* for society's recognition of heterosexual relationships through the legal institution of marriage is not the recognition of the love and affection ... Love and affection are enormously important qualities but ultimately they are the ones which are superimposed on the fundamental rationale for the legal institution of marriage which is reproduction.[48]

---

47 See http://www.vglrl.org.au/campaigns/equal-love/index.php.

48 Australian Capital Territory, Parliamentary Debates Legislative Assembly May 11 2006, 1619 (Vicki Dunne). See also Senator Stephen Fielding (Family First): 'The major difference between marriages and same-sex relationships is that marriages can produce children' Commonwealth, Parliamentary Debates Senate June 15 2006 http://parlinfoweb.aph.gov.au/piweb/view_document.aspx?ID=2345445 accessed 13/05/2008; Patrick Farmer (LP): 'The institution of marriage remains the principal basis of our social foundation. We need to promote this view of marriage for what it truly is — a pillar of our society — and it should not be altered.' Commonwealth, Parliamentary Debates House of Representatives June 16 2004 (Patrick Farmer) http://parlinfoweb.aph.gov.au/piweb/view_document.aspx?ID=2263233 accessed 13/05/2008.

This position, that marriage is more about procreation than anything else, relies on another often made argument: that a heterosexual family is the best model for society. This view is typified by the following statement by Peter Jensen, Anglican Archbishop of Sydney:

> We are better off generally speaking, living in families founded by a man and a woman who have made their initial public promises of lifelong fidelity. It is the family so constituted that is the primary source for the love and care without which we cannot survive. It is this family that best meets our relationship needs. It is this family that provides children with the experience of the interaction of human maleness and femaleness. It is children of this family who we may expect will look after their aged, lonely and sick.[49]

The same argument was rehearsed in almost identical terms in the debate on the same-sex adoption Bill introduced into the NSW Parliament in August 2010. Debate on this Bill consisted of, on the one hand, the NSW Council of Churches asserting the importance of a heterosexual relationship in bringing up children, while, on the other hand, supporters of the Bill arguing that the sexuality of parents makes little difference to their ability to provide a loving and secure environment for children to grow up in.[50]

Indeed, the whole debate around same-sex marriage and same-sex families forms part of a much wider debate about how we understand family and relationships and whether such concepts must be constructed around sex, gender and traditional heterosexual forms. The concept of family is problematic for same-sex couples because it has been understood as being framed within these factors. While outward signs point to a change in these perceptions, the understanding of family via biology and nature continue to exercise influence. Many have challenged this understanding. Judith Butler, for example, is one of many who point to the success of non-traditional family forms not only in same-sex families but also in other cultures; African American families in the US and

---

49   Peter Jensen, Anglican Archbishop of Sydney, 'Unique Union' *The Australian* May 8, 2008 http://www.theaustralian.com.au/news/unique-union/story-e6frg73o-1111116275570 accessed 25/07/10. See also Alby Shultz (LP): 'it is in the best interest of children to have a mother and a father' Commonwealth, Parliamentary Debates House of Representatives June 17 2004 (Alby Schultz) http://parlinfoweb.aph.gov.au/piweb/view_document.aspx?ID=2263265 accessed 13/05/2008. See also comments during the 2010 federal election campaign by Family First candidate Wendy Francis, who was quoted as saying: 'Children in homosexual relationships are subject to emotional abuse. Legitimating gay marriage is like legalising child abuse.' Wendy Francis, Family First candidate for 2010 federal election, cited in C Glennie, 'Family First candidate sparks outrage over gay marriage' ABC *PM* 09/07/2010 http://www.abc.net.au/pm/content/2010/s2977960.htm accessed 10/08/2010. Recently, the Australian Christian Lobby released a media alert warning that legalising same-sex marriage would create a 'new stolen generation' because it would be robbing children from their biological parents. See 'Mr Rudd's Change On Marriage Sets Up a New Stolen Generation' ACL media release 21/05/2013 http://www.acl.orf.au/2013/05/mr-rudd%E2%80%99s-change-on-marriage-sets-up-a-new... accessed 1/06/2013.

50   J Macey, 'Same-Sex Adoption bill in NSW Parliament' ABC PM 31/08/2010 http://www.abc.net.au/pm/content/2010/s2998784.htm accessed 1/09/2010.

Na families in China, for example.[51] But a more sustained change needs to occur. John Borneman has called for a general re-evaluation, from seeing descent and affinity as part of marriage and procreation and heterosexuality toward a recognition of the diversity of 'forms of intimacy and sociality' that have existed over time and in different places, and which have fulfilled the essential function of caring and being cared for.[52]

In the meantime, in relation to the same-sex debate, two fallacies must be challenged; first, that procreation can only occur as a result of sex and heterosexuality; and second, that it is this context that creates the best environment to bring up children. The reality is that children are born to couples via a variety of means, such as artificial insemination, donors and surrogacy agreements. The reality, we also know, is that many people marry without ever intending to have children, because they already have them, because they are infertile, or simply because they do not want to. All of these points were made in *Re Kevin*. In relation to heterosexual parents being the best parenting model, as Labor MP Anthony Albanese suggested, it might be the case that same-sex couples actually make better parents. He argued: 'I have seen a lot of bad parents. I have not seen bad same-sex parents. I do not know very many, but every same-sex couple I know really wants their child and loves their child. That should be respected'.[53] Furthermore, leaving aside the parents, empirical studies consistently show that growing up in a same-sex family either has a neutral or a positive effect on raising children.[54]

Christianity and Marriage

The persistence of the marriage for procreation argument can be attributed to the influence of Christianity on the discourse of marriage. Take for, example, Liberal Party MP Robert Baldwin's position: 'what I am seeking to do is ensure that the Christian values of marriage — being an institution between a man and a woman for the purpose of procreation — remain as the cornerstone of the foundation

---

51   Butler, 'Is Kinship Always Already Heterosexual?' 15–16.
52   J Borneman, 'Caring and Being Cared For: Displacing Marriage, Kinship, Gender, and Sexuality' in J D Faubon (ed), *The Ethics of Kinship Ethnographic Inquiries* (Rowan & Little Field Publishers, Boston 2001) 30, 43.
53   Commonwealth, Parliamentary Debates House of Representatives June 16 2004 (Anthony Albanese) htpp://parlinfoweb.aph.gov.au/piweb/view_document.aspx?ID+2263289 accessed 13/05/2008.
54   Charlotte Patterson's study on gay and lesbian families for the American Psychological Association found no study that concluded that a parent's sexuality had a negative psychological impact upon the development of their children. Charlotte J Patterson, *Lesbian and Gay Parenting* American Psychological Association 1995 cited in T A Salzman & M G Lawler, 'New Natural Law Theory and Foundational Sexual Ethical Principles: A Critique and a Proposal' (2006) 47 *The Heythrop Journal* 191. Joan Laird in her study found that children of gay and lesbian parents were more tolerant and empathetic than children brought up in heterosexual families. Joan Laird, 'Lesbian and Gay Families' in F Walsh (ed), *Normal Family Processes*, second edition (Guilford Press, New York 1993). See L Nicholson, 'The Myth of The Traditional Family' In H Nelson (ed), *Feminism and Families* (Routledge, New York 1997) 27–42.

of our society'.[55] Leaving aside the question of whether we are to understand marriage in a modern secular society such as ours as a religious institution, it is important to note, without wishing to overstate the case, that one can find support within Christianity for the proposition that marriage is for love. Within the Catholic tradition, Acquinas said that marriage was an institution that relies upon '*societas/amicitia*' a kind of friendship and companionship as well as upon procreation.[56] Erasmus too saw love as part of marriage and in fact goes further in defining love as both sensual and spiritual.[57] Edmund Leites argues, however, that the idea that marriage is about love within Christian theology finds its most prominent expression in Puritan theories of marriage. By looking at the works of leading theologians of the seventeenth century, such as William Gouge, Richard Baxter, Daniel Rogers and Jeremy Taylor, Leites argues that the Puritans saw love as one of the greatest goods in life, as being central to marriage, and as one of the duties of married of life. He says that, according to these writers, 'love is not simply permitted, given the existence of a higher, holier, "spiritual" relation between man and wife, nor is it allowed only to forward the other purposes of marriage, it is required as a constituent and intrinsic element of a good marriage'.[58]

The connection between marriage and love in Christian theology, however, should not be overstated. That marriage is for procreation is still a central view within Christian faith and, even when love is admitted as a part of marriage, it is still the case that the meaning of love itself converges around the heterosexual procreative act. Take, for example, the views of the prominent Catholic and natural law theorist John Finnis. Finnis agrees with Acquinas's conception of marriage as being for both procreation and *amicitia*, however, he says that *amicitia* is a bond that occurs between couples only as a result of a particular sexual act, that is, penile-vaginal penetration. This sexual act, and only this sexual act, is capable of creating unity between two people. This view is reiterated by many: Lee and George say that while oral sex and anal sex constitute body parts coming together, it is not the same thing as penile-vaginal sex because only then is there a biological unification between two people.[59] Germain Grisez says that every animal, whether male or female, is incomplete in relation to reproduction, that each animal is only a potential part of a mated pair. He suggests that '[t]his is true also of men and women: as maters who engage in sexual intercourse suited to initiate new life, they

---

55   Commonwealth, Parliamentary Debates House of Representatives June 17 2004 (Robert Baldwin) http://parlinfoweb.aph.gov.au/piweb/view_document.aspx?ID=2263225 accessed 13/05/2008.

56   J Finnis, 'Law, Morality and "Sexual Orientation"' (1995) 9 *Notre Dame Journal of Law Ethics and Public Policy* 28–29.

57   See Leites, 'The Duty to Desire: Love, Friendship, and Sexuality in Some Puritan Theories of Marriage' (1982) 15 *Journal of Social History* 385–86.

58   Leites, 'The Duty to Desire' 388–89.

59   P Lee & R P George, 'What Sex Can Be: Self Alienation, Illusion or One-Flesh Union' (1997) 42 *American Journal of Jurisprudence* 146.

complete each other and become an organic unit. In doing so, it is literally true that they become one flesh'.[60] In order to realise the good that is in marriage (either procreation and/or love) the couple must achieve unity and complementarity 'so really and so completely that they are two in one flesh'. 'One flesh reality', is achieved via 'marital consent' and 'bodily communion'.[61] Conjugal sex is required to achieve this heightened state of togetherness. But not any sexual contact will do, only the union of the reproductive organs is capable of achieving the required complementarity.

This reliance on the reproductive act for love is not the same as equating marriage with procreation. This is too crude an interpretation. Having children is not required for a marriage to be valid.[62] Having a child is an extrinsic act to marriage and cannot therefore define marriage. Marriage is to be defined by its intrinsic value and this value is to be found in friendship (love) and parenthood. For Finnis then, 'the moral importance of the marital act ... is determined by its intrinsic procreative and unitive meanings, not by any instrumental, that is extrinsic meaning',[63] such as procreation.

The Struggle for the Meaning of Love

What emerges from the new natural law view of marriage and love is the centrality of the idea of complementarity. In the new natural law view, complementarity is understood in different ways: it can be biological, genital, reproductive, parental and affective.[64] Central to it is the idea that there are certain 'realities that belong together in the created order and that together produce a whole which neither produces alone'.[65]

The idea of complementarity to an understanding of love is not unique to new natural law theory. Returning briefly to Plato's *Symposium*, here we find the expression *par excellence* that love is the unification of two halves, the creation of a full being. Aristophanes' myth tells that, long ago, human beings were physically very different. They had four hands, four legs, two heads and two sets of genitalia. They could move forwards and backwards and would move very quickly by cart-wheeling on all eight limbs. In this powerful form, humans were a great threat to the gods and for this reason Zeus decided to cut them

---

60   G Grisez, *The Way of the Lord Jesus* vol 2: Living a Christian Life (Franciscan Press, Quincy University 1993) 146.
61   Grisez, *The Way of the Lord Jesus* 586.
62   Although there is an argument implied here that sex is required.
63   Salzman & Lawler, 'New Natural Law Theory' 185.
64   Salzman & Lawler, 'New Natural Law Theory' 185.
65   Salzman & Lawler, 'New Natural Law Theory' 186.

in half. Humans were miserable in their reduced state and spent their whole time searching for their 'other half'. When they found each other they stayed together, foregoing all other activity in fear of losing each other again.[66]

The history of romantic love continued to build upon this idea of merging. The courtly tradition, known for ennobling love, also saw love as an intense and passionate relationship that established a 'oneness' between the lovers. This idea progressed even further during the eighteenth and nineteenth centuries with the idea that love could involve, to borrow Singer's words, a 'oneness with an alter ego, one's self, a man or woman who would make up one's deficiencies, respond to one's deepest inclinations, and serve as possibly the only person with whom one could communicate fully'.[67] Robert Nozick claimed that the central idea of romantic love is a desire to 'constitute a new entity in the world, what might be called a *we*'.[68] Delaney says that 'perhaps the most important thing people associate with the ideal of romantic love, is this desire to unite with another person in profound psychological and physical ways'.[69] By the end of the twentieth century, Marilyn Friedman described love as having become 'merger mania'.[70]

The idea of a merger does not have to be between a man and a woman *per se*, Aristophanes certainly did not specify that the two halves were of opposing sex. In fact, he specifically said that some would be of the same-sex. The idea has, however, continued to be understood as a man and a woman coming together. Branden, for example, describes romantic love as fulfilling our need to 'encounter, unite with, and live out vicariously our opposite-gender possibilities: The need, in males, to find an embodiment in the world of the internal feminine: The need in females, to find an embodiment in the world of the internal masculine.'[71]

The idea of the male and female coming together to form a unity is a popular idea that we can find expressed in other places. Zanghellini points out that it is a common message in popular culture, evolutionary psychology and can be found also in unexpected places such as the discourse of difference that exists in some strands of feminist theory.[72] Complementarity and merger are, in turn,

---

66   The idea can also be found in other traditions that have nothing to do with love. For example, the concepts of Ying and Yang in Chinese philosophy. See Aristophanes' myth in Plato *Symposium*.

67   Singer, *The Nature of Love* vols 3 & 4.

68   R Norzik, *Examined Life: Philosophical Meditations* (Simon and Shuster, New York 1989) 70.

69   Delaney N, 'Love and Loving Commitment: Articulating a Modern Ideal' (1996) 33(4) *American Philosophical Quarterly* 340.

70   Friedman, *Autonomy, Gender, Politics* (Oxford University Press, New York 2003) chapter 6; 'Romantic Love and Personal Autonomy' 115–139. She is critical of this in relation to the impact it has on women's autonomy.

71   Zanghellini, 'Marriage and Civil Union' 225.

72   Zanghellini, 'Marriage and Civil Union' 290–91.

easily understood within the concepts of nature and procreation that are central tropes in both marriage and love. These elements are evident in the same-sex marriage debate. However, as discussed, romantic love is a contested idea.

In contemporary society, romantic love is considered a radical power capable of breaking down the most entrenched of social cultural and religious barriers. It is associated with freedom, individual satisfaction and equality. Theorists such as Giddens have equated it with the democratisation of the private sphere. It is these features that make it threatening to traditional institutions. At the same time, perhaps paradoxically, romantic love is considered quite conservative and it has been linked with the replication of both patriarchy and heteronormativity.

The Heteronormativity of Law and Love (The Queer Critique of Love)

In *The Straight Mind* Monique Wittig says that to 'live in society is to live in heterosexuality … heterosexuality is always already there within all the mental categories. It has sneaked into dialectical thought (or thought of differences) as its main category.'[73] It is not surprising, therefore, to find profound heterosexual assumptions at work in our understanding of romantic love.

In the long running 1979 Harvey Fierstein play, *Torch Song Trilogy*, Arnold's mother is shocked when Arnold compares the loss of his gay partner, who has been murdered in a homophobic attack, to his mother's loss of her husband. Arnold responds to his mother's admonishment by saying:

> Cause everybody knows that queers don't feel nothin' …

> Cause everybody knows that queers don't matter! Queers don't love![74]

What Arnold exclaims here is the silence of homosexual love within romantic love.[75]

Cheshire Calhoun has argued that romantic love is constructed in our society in a way that excludes 'non-heterosexual' love.[76] Calhoun argues that romantic love, like other emotions, is dependent upon a society's emotional scripts. Such scripts have the function of teaching us those emotions, the proper object of

---

73 M Wittig, *The Straight Mind* (Harvester Wheatsheaf, New York 1992) 40–43.
74 Harvey Fierstein, *Torch Song Trilogy* (Villard Books, New York 1983 c 1979) 144–46.
75 Incidentally, he is also pointing out the silence that exists around homosexual death.
76 C Calhoun, *Feminism, the Family, and the Politics of the Closet: Lesbian and Gay Displacement* (Oxford University Press, New York 2000); 'Sexuality Injustice' (1995) *9 Notre Dame Journal of Law Ethics & Public Policy* 241–274; 'Making Up Emotional People: The Case of Romantic Love' in Bandes (ed), *The Passions of Law* (New York University Press, New York 1999) 217–240; 'Family's Outlaws: Rethinking the Connections Between Feminism, Lesbianism and the Family' in H Nelson (ed), *Feminism and Families* (Routledge, New York 1997) 131–150.

them, how to assess their authenticity and how to perform them.[77] The problem in relation to homosexual and lesbian love is that there are no paradigm scenarios or emotional scripts to follow. Even more importantly, there are actual barriers to the performance of romantic love for gay and lesbian couples, such as the prohibition to marry and to have a family.[78]

Paul Johnson[79] has argued that the heterosexual construction of love is maintained by its association with traditional scripts of marriage and domesticity, (as well as its connection with nature).[80] The link between love and traditional scripts of relationships, domesticity and procreation are so pervasive that they find expression in the gay and lesbian community itself. Sean Slavin's study of sexual practice among gay men found that the men struggled to make sense of their sexual and romantic lives through the binaries of sex and love, and sex and relationships.[81] Slavin found that the men to some extent accepted these traditional binaries, but at the same time were frustrated by the attempt to make sense of their relationships in these ways.[82] As Lauren Berlant has put it, when there is only one plot, and that plot counts as life, then 'those who don't or can't find their way in that story — the queers, the single, the something else — can become so easily unimaginable, even often to themselves'.[83]

Slavin has argued that gay men have to fight for the recognition of the relationships they actually have. Open relationships, casual sex with regular partners, multiple sex partners, can all represent love and must not be categorised as only sex.[84] This view has been voiced by others. Bell and Binnie have argued that love must move away from the couple and include non-monogamy, polyamory and episodic sexuality.[85] The recognition of 'other' relationships is central to the breakdown of the heteronormativity of love. They argue that one of the positive contributions that gay liberation has made is the blurring of the distinction between sex and love, between the categories of friend, lover and partner. This blurring has

---

77   Calhoun, 'Making Up Emotional People' 222.

78   Calhoun, 'Making Up Emotional People' 222.

79   Johnson, *Love, Heterosexuality and Society*.

80   Johnson, *Love, Heterosexuality and Society* 40.

81   S Slavin, 'Instinctively, I'm Not Just a Sexual Beast: The Complexity of Intimacy Among Australian Gay Men' (2009) 12 *Sexualities* 79–96.

82   Slavin, 'Instinctively, I'm Not Just a Sexual Beast' 93.

83   L Berlant (ed), *Intimacy* (University of Chicago Press, Chicago 2000) 6. The same point is made by Judith Butler who says '[i]f you're not real, it can be hard to sustain yourself over time'. J Butler, 'Is Kinship Always Already Heterosexual?' (2002) 13 *Differences* 25.

84   Slavin, 'Instinctively, I'm Not Just a Sexual Beast' 93.

85   D Bell and J Binnie, *The Sexual Citizen: Queer Politics and Beyond* (Polity Press, Cambridge 2000) 128.

introduced an ethic to casual sex that includes 'affection, care, respect, consent and playfulness.'[86] This contribution can be extended to love itself, love can be played out in different kinds of relationships based on new scripts.[87]

The importance of replicating heterosexual love scripts (monogamy, family, parenthood, domesticity)[88] has proven to be important for success in legal disputes in a number of different contexts. In the case of *Re Kevin*, for example, a case can be made that a large part of the success that that couple had in having their relationship recognised as marriage was the extent to which they so successfully replicated the scripts of domesticity and family. Kevin and Jennifer presented themselves very much as the model of a heterosexual couple committed to each other and committed to the romantic ideal. They were in a long-term relationship, had one child and were expecting another. In evidence before the Court, Kevin was described repeatedly as a loving husband and father. Friends gave evidence the couple was, '[j]ust another married couple living their lives with their son'[89] and 'your average mum and dad with a much loved little boy',[90] and described Kevin as 'a fine husband and father to Quentin'.[91] Justice Chisolm described Kevin and Jennifer and their child as a family in 'every sense of the word.'[92]

Contrast these facts with the UK *Corbett v Corbett* case.[93] The couple in *Corbett* could not be more different to the couple in *Re Kevin*, they fitted more readily in the stereotypical bohemian and sexually deviant LGBTI life/sex scripts. April Ashley was a male-to-female transsexual. She worked as an entertainer in the South of France with a well-known troupe of 'transvestites'[94] at the Hotel Carousel. She also worked as a model and had become a minor celebrity following a series of articles in the *News of the World*.

Arthur Corbett was divorced and had four children. He was interested in 'transvestism'. He enjoyed dressing as a woman and had had homosexual experiences with several men. The Court described him as someone who had

---

86   Bell & Binnie, *The Sexual Citizen* 134. See also J Weeks, *Invented Moralities: Sexual Values in an Age of Uncertainty* (Polity Press, Cambridge 1995); S Seidman, *Romantic Longings: Love in America, 1830–1980* (Routledge New York 1991).

87   F Manalansaniv, 'Queer Love in the Time of War and Shopping' in G E Haggerty & M McGarry (eds), *A Companion to Lesbian, Gay, Bisexual, Transgender, and Queer Studies* (Blackwell Publishing, MA 2007) 77–86.

88   See Johnson, *Love, Heterosexuality and Society*.

89   *Re Kevin* 170 (Chisholm J).

90   *Re Kevin* 170 (Chisholm J).

91   *Re Kevin* 170 (Chisholm J).

92   *Re Kevin* 168 (Chisholm J).

93   *Corbett v Corbett (otherwise Ashley)* [1970] 2 All ER 33.

94   The language used in the original case is 'transvestite' and 'transvestism'.

become 'more and more involved in the society of sexual deviants, and interested in sexual deviations of all kinds … He is a man who is extremely prone to all kinds of sexual fantasies and practices.'[95]

Arthur Corbett had sought a meeting with April because he was fascinated by her success as a female; April had gained some fame in 'transvestite' circles. Following their meeting, however, Arthur claimed that he developed an interest in her as 'a man would for a woman'. In other words, he fell in love with her, although such language was not used in the case.

Despite their turbulent relationship, and despite the fact that April found Arthur to be a 'difficult and perplexing person',[96] April eventually agreed to marry him. The marriage lasted only 12 days. The Court could not establish the extent to which the relationship had been sexual, but it was clear that this relationship was not conventional. Their love for each other was not displayed by the couple living together, having sex together, sharing daily life and so on. Unlike Jennifer and Kevin, they did not adhere to the traditional heterosexual scripts of love, relationships and domesticity. The Court described Arthur's feelings for April as an obsession, and described him as living 'in the grip of his fantasies'.[97] Words such as 'commitment', 'affection', 'desire' or 'love' are never used to describe this relationship, and both April and Arthur were judged incapable of such emotions. Instead of love, they were described as feeling 'obsession';[98] instead of desire they were 'prone to sexual fantasies and practices'.[99] Justice Ormond puts it as plainly as can be:

> Listening to each party describing this strange relationship, my principal impression was that it had little or nothing in common with any heterosexual relationship which I could recall hearing about in a fairly extensive experience of this court.[100]

Their fate was sealed, their marriage would never receive the legal recognition April wanted. How could it? Unlike Kevin and Jennifer, their relationship had 'little or nothing in common' with the heterosexual ideal of romantic love.

The heteronormativity of both marriage and love makes many cautious, but while the legal recognition of same-sex marriage has the potential to reinforce the heteronormativity of marriage and of love, it is also capable of strengthening the radical rhetoric of love and has the potential to radicalise marriage.

---

95   *Corbett v Corbett* 37–38 (Ormrod J).
96   *Corbett v Corbett* 38 (Ormrod J).
97   *Corbett v Corbett* 39 (Ormrod J).
98   *Corbett v Corbett* 38 (Ormrod J).
99   *Corbett v Corbett* 38 (Ormrod J).
100   *Corbett v Corbett* 38 (Ormrod J).

Feminists and Queer theorists are right to say that accepting marriage into their political frameworks can be read as a watering down of the radical nature of their love, but it can be equally argued that it will have the opposite effect. The recognition that love can be played out in different kinds of relationships, based on new scripts, is central to the breakdown of the heteronormativity of love and central to a positive reading of love. This could be read as an aspect of queering love.

Just as there are positive feminist readings of love, so too are there positive queer readings of love. Berlant, for example, argues that love is ultimately a site of optimism, change and transformation: 'love approximates a space to which people can return, becoming as different as they can be from themselves without being traumatically shattered; it is a scene of optimism for change, for transformational environment'.[101] Johnson claims that 'whilst romantic love may create the hell of mutual alienation it also retains its primacy as an anti-alienating potential because it offers a way of expressing forms of pleasurable subjective transformation'.[102] To be able to achieve this, however, love must be seen as being connected rather than disconnected to agency, as being connected to but not subordinate to desire, and, importantly, it must be seen as something that exists outside of heterosexual scripts. Berlant says that when queer thought enters the discourse of love, it must not teach 'that we are all alike and compelled to repeat our alikeness intelligibly, but by teaching some of what we've learned about love, under the surface, across the lines, around the scenes, informally'.[103] Queering love for Berlant is achieved when it lives up to its promises of existing outside of established institutions, when it challenges all rules connected with it which presume to establish principles for living.[104] In other words, when love delivers what it promises, intimate relationships that are free of oppressive and traditional forms and rejects established rules and barriers. The project then is to break down a number of associations that define love: to break down the binary of love and sex and see them instead as existing in more fluid combinations; to break down the connection that now exists with, on the one hand, same-sex relationships and sex, and on the other, heterosexual relationships and love;[105] and to break down the connection between love and marriage, family and procreation. Same-sex marriage can assist this project.

Recognition of same-sex marriage does not have to be a recognition of the oppressive and heteronormative love that feminists and queer theorists have warned us against, rather it can be a recognition of the radical and optimistic

---

101   L Berlant, 'Love: A Queer Feeling' in T Dean & C Lane (eds), *Psychoanalysis and Homosexuality* (Chicago University Press, Chicago 2000) 448.
102   Johnson, *Love, Heterosexuality and Society* 83.
103   Berlant, 'Love: A Queer Feeling' 448.
104   Berlant, 'Love: A Queer Feeling' 443.
105   Same-sex relationships are seen as either sexual or platonic but rarely as loving in the romantic sense.

love that breaks down barriers of culture, religion, class and sexuality and values and creates equality. It will recognise a love that is closer to Giddens' idea of a democratic and inclusive love. It will not achieve the broad recognition of all loving relationships that exist in society that many queer theorists want, but it will expand the recognition beyond the narrow heterosexual model and progress us along the road to making love even more radical than we now think it is.

Conclusion

The legal debate over same-sex marriage has exploded not only the meaning of marriage but also of love. In the legal episodes previously discussed, while traditional meanings of marriage were being discarded, little was said about how we are to interpret modern marriage This void can be filled by romantic love. In the same-sex marriage debate, this has become an explicit argument. Here, the argument comes down to whether marriage is about procreation or love. The view that has so far appeared to dominate is that marriage is about procreation. Deconstructing the debate, however, shows that for a significant number of participants in the debate, marriage can also be about love. Just when we appear to have broken down the connection between marriage and procreation, which is considered to be *the* barrier, we discover that the barrier is also love itself. Framing the debate as one in which procreation and love compete for the central place is, in fact, not very helpful at all, because the two institutions appear to be grounded in the same ideas. The central tropes in both marriage and love are biology, nature and procreation.

A less understood aspect of the debate is how we understand love. The idea of love that appears to dominate the debate is one embedded in love as merger and complementarity. Christianity and new natural law see this as being achieved only via the sexual merger of a male and female body. This is not unique to the Christian view of love, however. It has permeated our understanding of love since classical times and has retained currency throughout the history of the western idea of love. Viewing the same-sex marriage debate through this lens, it is difficult not to conclude that the orthodox idea of love does not serve us well. In particular, it makes the idea that romantic love is liberating sound hollow. The way we conceive of romantic love does not mean that *'love does not discriminate'*.[106] It is not the great leveller in society that Solomon and others[107] insist it is. Cinderella might have got her prince and all that came with it, but no matter how much she loved, she would not have got her prize if *she* had been a *he*.

---

106   Quote on a placard at a rally in support of same-sex marriage in the ACT in 2009.
107   See the discussion on romantic love.

This is a pessimistic view of the idea of love that emerges from the debate, and ignores another, more optimistic, reading. The same-sex marriage debate can also be read as enforcing the idealistic ideas of love which many see as revolutionary and capable of breaking down entrenched barriers. Agitating for same-sex marriage on the ground that marriage is about love rather than procreation challenges not only the heteronormativity of marriage but also of love. Two readings of love can come out of the legal recognition of same-sex marriage. One of those readings is that love is indeed steeped in both patriarchy and heterosexuality; the other is that it is a radical and liberating force. I think that the latter reading has more force. Feminism and queer theory have come too far to agitate for the recognition of the rights of women and LGBTI to now enter an institution and simply get subsumed into its dark past. The more likely outcome is that the institution of marriage will change to reflect these new modes of loving and help to reflect the radical reading of romantic love and obscure the other.

5. Conclusion: Law, Love and Marriage

Despite sustained criticism, love has remained a central discourse in western societies. Marriage, despite looking at times like becoming obsolete, has proven itself to be an entrenched and powerful social institution. This book has tested the extent to which these two concepts interact with each other within the ambit of a third powerful institution: law. In the process, this book has said something about law, about love, and about marriage.

Law

This book challenges the understanding we have of law. Thinking about law and love has important consequences for thinking about the relationship between reason and emotion in public life, and, in turn, thinking about the role that emotion plays in law. Law and emotion scholarship asserts that emotions are important for public life and for law, informing both theory and practice. This book has adopted this position and tested it in relation to the legal discourse of marriage, showing how such an analysis can lead to a better understanding of the legal institution of marriage.

The dominant paradigm of law stems from positivism. Positivism removes emotion from law in rejecting morality and rights as irrelevant, embracing a scientific paradigm and exalting and striving for objectivity above all else. However, positivism's view of law has been challenged by critical approaches which have made 'space' for emotion as a result of a number of central assertions about law.

Critical jurisprudence has insinuated emotion in law through a number of challenges. Critical jurisprudence scholarship has challenged the idea that law is and can be objective by claiming instead that law is political (CLS), sexist (feminism), racist (CRT), and heteronormative (queer). Critical jurisprudence has challenged the idea that objectivity is required for the legitimacy of law and has argued instead that objectivity is the law's downfall (CLS). Critical jurisprudence has also legitimated emotion by arguing against the public and private divide (feminism) and by legitimating the subject of law and storytelling (feminism, CRT, queer and post-modern). Finally, emotion is legitimated by critical jurisprudence via its rejection of a unitary and metaphysical paradigm of law (postmodernism, CLS). Despite the achievements of critical jurisprudence and law and emotion scholarship, law is still considered to be separate from emotions generally, and from love even more so. This view impoverishes our understanding of law in general and its specific enterprises, such as the regulation and construction of marriage.

Love

The idea of love has existed at least since classical times. Its importance in everyday life grew under the influence of Christianity, during the courtly period, and the romantic period. Christianity raised the idea of love to something divine. The courtly tradition began a process of equating it with freedom, personal happiness and sexual satisfaction. These ideas were spread to the masses during the romantic period, and today we can speak of love as being a reason for life itself. Equality, freedom, agency, progress, enlightenment and humanism are all words used in this book in association with love. Love has come to symbolise the opposite of power and control; a society based on love is assumed to be a more free and humane one. These features of love make it an interesting partner for marriage, which has more often had the opposite associations. However, love is not without its critics. While many have sung love's praises, it has also been described as a 'modern monster' which 'fails to satisfy' and 'easily turns into a destructive force'.[1] Moreover, the assumption that love will make our society a more humane one is disputed.

Feminists have seen love as oppressive, a vehicle by which women are enslaved in relationships of domesticity and dependence.[2] Love's problem lies in the extrinsic environment in which it is played out: the institution of marriage, patriarchy, the private and public division, and its association with sex all contribute to make love a 'curse' for women.[3] However, to acknowledge these extrinsic factors is not to let love itself off the hook. Intrinsically love's own logic of self-satisfaction and self-government are destructive. Its ideology is circular, chaotic and unruly:[4] love itself is therefore a problem.

For queer theorists, love's extrinsic 'problem' is heterosexuality. Love is understood as embodying heterosexual rituals and scripts of domesticity and, as such, excludes same-sex relationships.[5] In this way, queer theorists are challenging the rhetoric of romantic love which claims that love breaks down barriers. In fact, their critique is that love is not romantic enough because it excludes 'non-heterosexual' love. Furthermore, love itself is mostly understood as a physical and

---

1   Beck & Beck-Gernsheim, cited by C Smart, *Personal Life* (Polity Press, Cambridge 2007) 62.
2   See the arguments made by De Beauvoir, Firestone, Smart, Freidman and Langford discussed earlier.
3   De Beauvoir, *The Second Sex* trans H M Parshley (Alfred A Knopf, New York 1953) 669.
4   See W. Langford, *Revolutions of the Heart: Gender, Power and the Delusions of Love* (Routledge, London 1999).
5   See Calhoun and Johnson, discussed earlier.

natural feeling, as a 'merging' with another, our other half,[6] as a means to attain goodness, or a supernatural, mythical feeling. In these ways it is understood as being embedded in discourses of merger and of nature. This discourse inevitably becomes linked to stereotypical gender roles and to heterosexuality.

The following four statements can be made in relation to our contemporary understanding of romantic love:

- Love has become an existential goal, a means to happiness and fulfilment. It is the central paradigm for ordering intimate relationships between people, including sex and marriage;

- The rhetoric of love asserts that it is above all other social rules, and trumps social, cultural, traditional, economic, family, religious, and, class conventions and expectations. It is its own law;

- The context in which love is played out is oppressive to women and to same-sex couples. These contexts are patriarchy, the private-public division, and heterosexuality; and

- Love is embedded in concepts of nature that inevitably link back to stereotypical gender roles and heterosexuality.

Marriage

Love has become a dominant idea in modern society and has come to dominate much of our social thinking, including how we think about the institution of marriage. This is true despite the fact that, for many, the traditional, religious and patriarchal meanings of marriage remain. For an overwhelming majority, when all other reasons for marrying have largely evaporated, the one that remains is love. While love can exist without marriage, marriage is considered the ultimate expression of two people's love. It is this connection with love that has strengthened the institution of marriage. Despite the various challenges to marriage thrown down in the latter part of the twentieth century, it remains a central goal for many people, and is widely regarded as a good in society.[7] Once marriage became disconnected from economic need, religious and family obligation, realigning itself with romantic love, it found a new audience. Not only has it remained popular for heterosexuals, but, as we have seen, it has become a goal for same-sex couples.

6　This view can be traced all the way back to the myth of Aristophanes, discussed earlier.

7　See Finnis, discussed in chapter four. There is also a discernable pro-marriage movement which has emerged arguing that marriage makes people 'happier, healthier and wealthier', protects the wellbeing of children, and that the whole of society and should therefore be protected and upheld by governments. See, for example, 'The Marriage Movement's Statement of Principles' at http://www.americanvalues.org/pdfs/marriagemovement.pdf accessed 28/10/2010. See also L C McClain, 'What Place for Marriage (E)quality in Marriage Promotion?' in Bernstein (ed), *Marriage Proposals* 106–144.

The cases of *Garcia*, *Re Kevin*, and the same-sex marriage debate have revealed a number of significant themes in relation to the legal discourse of marriage. Marriage is to be understood in conjunction with sexual identity and sexual intercourse, gender and sexuality, procreation and family, and, not least, in conjunction with business, economic and commercial interests.

Historically, sex has been seen as central to marriage. To be valid, a marriage had to be consummated, and procreation was considered its central purpose. With the rise of the romantic marriage, sex has come to be connected with mutual satisfaction and expression of love. This shifting narrative has been shown via analysis of the marital immunity of rape. The narrative came to a decisive point with the case of *Re Kevin*, where the Family Court unequivocally said that sexual intercourse was not a defining feature of marriage. However, I have argued that, given *Re Kevin's* facts and its heteronormative reading of marriage, it must be read cautiously.

To say that sex is no longer relevant in the modern legal discourse of marriage would be misleading. The shadow of the law that stated that a man could never be guilty of raping his wife faintly remains. Courts have continued to see a pre-existing relationship as relevant to the question of consent. Cases continue to show that there is a nexus between being married (or being in a relationship) and a lower threshold of consent. Empirical studies suggest that on this issue the law is merely reflecting a significant social attitude that still connects marriage with a man's right to have sex.

Nevertheless, it cannot be denied that law has shifted ground considerably in relation to sex and marriage. It has gone from saying that a valid marriage requires consummation, and from saying that a husband can never be guilty of raping his wife, to saying that sexual intercourse is irrelevant to the legal status of a marriage either way. Sex is part of marriage only as a result of mutual consent. Justice Brennan in *R v L* alludes to love as the means by which sex is negotiated between a married couple.

Garcia considered the relationship between marriage, business and economics. The economic aspects of marriage have a history as dark as that relating to sex. In the past, marriage reduced women to non-economic actors, incapable of owning and controlling property and, indeed, being seen as property themselves coming completely under the control of their husbands. The *Garcia* case resonated with the bad old days of marriage in the sense that, on the surface, the Court was endorsing the idea that a woman does not and should not necessarily have an informed involvement in her husband's or the family's business affairs.

Critics argued that the Court's decision did not reflect the new narrative of marriage where the wife was a free, autonomous individual capable and willing to act independently of her husband, not only in general ways, but also specifically in the spheres of business and economics. The majority of the judges did not dispute this narrative of marriage but argued that it was incomplete. The majority decision maintained that marriage is an economic union and, importantly, that upon marriage a husband and wife's economic interests are united. However, the judgement also endorses the idea that marriage is an emotional union based on trust and confidence, and the existence of these factors means that marriage justifiably leads to people acting 'ignorantly' as opposed to 'self-interestedly'. While love was never mentioned in the case, I have argued that 'trust and confidence' can be interpreted as aspects of love. The Court refused to create a situation where the trust and confidence that usually exists in a marriage would be replaced with suspicion and self-interest, which would be tantamount to pulling down a central pillar of marriage. In centralising trust and confidence in marriage, the Court in *Garcia* acknowledged both the good and the bad about love. People such as Mrs Garcia do everything for their husbands, for love — people do that, women do that, and when it goes wrong the law will help. But that help was not to be at the expense of eroding the romantic aspects of marriage. The aspects that translate into people behaving in 'non-rational' non 'self-interested' ways. Relief could only be given under the 'special equity of wives' because this principle alone retained and nurtured the special features of marriage as a relationship of trust and confidence as avatars of love. Garcia also points to a broader issue in relation to marriage and economic interests. The law selectively honours individual economic interest in marriage. If marriage is a life-long union then there is some sense in seeing it as an economic union. But if marriage is a love union which only lasts as long as the love does, then the law must learn to acknowledge, measure and allocate individual economic interest.

If *Garcia* alluded to love via trust and confidence, *Re Kevin* can be interpreted as further building the case for love in marriage. *Re Kevin* challenged some central assertions about the meaning of marriage. It refuted that the central reason for the relationship is procreation and asserted that sexual capacity and sexual intercourse are not central to marriage. As such, the decision went further than law had before towards constructing marriage as a love relationship. The decision can be understood as an affirmation of the importance of love in marriage. If the decision in *Re Kevin* looked like liberalising marriage, the federal legislative response against it was swift. In amending the Marriage Act and in overriding the ACT's Civil Union Act the federal government reasserted that marriage is more about procreation than anything else, and, as such, must be between a man and a woman, and cannot be between same-sex couples. Love is important, but not the most important thing in marriage. However, proponents of same-sex marriage are now using love to break down the legal door barring their entrance to marriage.[8]

In the light of the discussion in this book, to what extent can we say that love is part of the legal discourse of modern Australian marriage? We have seen that the popular rhetoric of love has colonised marriage. Even in the most conservative of institutions, such as the monarchy, marriage needs to be presented within the romantic love discourse in order to fulfil social conventions.[9] As such, one would expect to find love within the legal discourse, but it is barely visible there. The legal discourse of modern Australian marriage presented in this book shows that marriage is still understood according to some of its traditional associations: that marriage is, and should be, between a man and a woman (*Re Kevin*, same-sex marriage debate), and that, upon marriage, economic and business/commercial interests become united (*Garcia*). However, some traditional links have also been broken: sexual intercourse and procreation are not the defining characteristics of marriage (*R v L*, *Re Kevin*), and sexual intercourse in marriage is subject to mutual consent (*R v L*). As we have seen, love is explicitly visible in this discourse in the context of the same-sex marriage debate, where it is pitted against procreation as the central defining characteristic of the institution, and it is explicitly visible as a means by which sexual relations are negotiated (*R v L*). At the same time, love can be inferred in the discourse via the assertion that trust and confidence are elements of love (*Garcia*). Moreover, when the legal discourse rejects all traditional meanings of marriage, the silence left behind can implicitly be filled by romantic love (*Re Kevin*). The impact that the presence of love has on marriage is debatable. While its rhetoric of freedom, liberty, equality and agency all inevitably leave a mark, love has not shown itself to completely displace the traditional meanings of marriage.

Over the years covered by the legal episodes explored in this book, the legal discourse of marriage has clearly shifted. There are many reasons for this shift, including the entry of love into the discourse. Given the progressive nature of romantic love, this leads to hope for a redefinition of the institution of marriage along more progressive lines. However, before one can gauge the significance that love might have on the institution of marriage, something needs to be said about the discourse of love that emerges from the analysis in this book.

---

8   For example, one of the major groups agitating for same-sex marriage in Australia is called 'Equal Love'. The emphasis on the idea of love has been evident during the 2010 federal election campaign in Australia. A hypothetical advertisement made for the Greens clearly states that if you are a supporter of same-sex marriage, then you believe that marriage is about love. ABC *Gruen Nation* episode 3, 10/07/2010 'The Pitch: Republic of Everyone' http://www.youtube.com/watch?v=O4jI1atQwp4 accessed 23/08/2010.

9   We saw the impact love had on the royal wedding of Prince Charles and Lady Diana. It was also the only discourse that justified their divorce. The thing that saved Prince Charles from total unpopularity was that he did it all for his love for Camilla.

Love Again

In *Re Kevin* the Family Court of Australia rejected some traditional notions of marriage. The Court rejected the idea that marriage required sexual activity and capacity to be valid, and it rejected procreation as the central defining reason for marriage. In rejecting these traditional aspects of marriage, the case came closer than any other legal act to insinuating love as a reason for marriage. However, the case can also be read as sustaining the traditional association of marriage with heterosexuality, asserting that marriage is fundamentally a heterosexual institution and, even if love is part of it, that love itself is also understood as heterosexual. Kevin and Jennifer were accepted as legally married because they loved each other, and because their love closely replicated normative heterosexual love. The scripts of this love are procreation, family, domesticity and marriage.

The same dynamics are evident in the same-sex marriage debate. The argument over same-sex marriage has become an argument over whether marriage is about procreation or love. Proponents of same-sex marriage believe that a win for love marriage is a win for same-sex marriage, but this denies the heteronormativity of romantic love. The predominant way of understanding romantic love in our society and culture is primarily as a union between two people, a merger of two soul mates, which, as such, is embedded in nature and inevitably heterosexuality.

Re Kevin and the same-sex marriage debate contest the notion that marriage is grounded in biology and procreation, but do not disturb those very same notions where they exist in our understanding of love. There is therefore a great circularity that occurs in the argument that always comes back to heterosexuality as the basis for both marriage and love. The analysis in this book points to an important failure in the way we understand romantic love which goes to the heart of its philosophy and renders it incapable of delivering the great progress, freedom and equality which it promises. As long as the notion of merger continues to be dominant in our understanding of love, love cannot separate itself from nature and therefore from scripts of reproduction, sex difference and heterosexuality. We have seen how this is disadvantageous to same-sex love, which is accepted only when it reproduces the scripts of heterosexuality. Even in the context of trans-sexuality, something more than a physical change in sexual identity is required: domesticity, family, parenthood and marriage are all important aspects in the construction of a loving couple.

While feminist critiques of love have focussed mainly on patriarchy and the private and public divide, a nature paradigm is also significant for their critique. Freeman showed clearly how the merger paradigm of love works against women.[10] If love is to deliver the promises that Solomon and others claim it makes, then it seems that it must reconceptualise itself away from the idea of merger. In this way, it can once and for all sever the connection with nature, biology, reproduction and parenthood. In this way, both heterosexuality and gender roles, which have been so damaging to women and to LGBTI couples, can be disrupted.

The features of love evident in the legal discourse do not match love's rhetoric of liberty, equality and progress. In the legal discourse love is constructed within other constructs such as nature, family, gender and sexuality. Furthermore, romantic love appears to be embedded in a discourse of complementarity and merger that inevitably are tied up with power. For 'non-heterosexuals', therefore, love is yet another barrier that can only be overcome to the extent that one can fool nature and 'act' the part.

Given these conclusions about the meaning of love, we can either work to reduce its hold over the modern imagination or work towards redefining it to accommodate these criticisms. Despite the critiques of love, few are willing to jettison it. Its connection with individual freedom and autonomy makes it a hard idea to reject. Love is part of who we are, and we cannot go back to a time before it. As Langford says, it is neither possible nor desirable to return to a time when personal relationships were not seen within the paradigm of romantic love. 'No remedy', she argues 'is to be found in a reactive return to the regulation of love along traditional lines. Justice and humanity cannot thrive through the imposition of a repressive moral order and the institutionalisation of oppressive practices.'[11] Also, as Illouz argues, we must not forget that the dominance of love has directly correlated with a decline in men's power over women and with an increase in equality between men and women.[12] The many legal changes that have occurred in the laws of marriage have coincided with the period of history where intimate relationships have been influenced by the liberalising egalitarian and radical ideology of love. The answer must therefore lie in reconceptualising love. For Illouz and Langford, the answer lies in a love which reflects women's experiences and desires as much as men's, and a love which embodies a more ethical ideology. For queer theorists, what is needed is a love that moves away from heterosexuality. For both feminists and queer theorists, moving love away from the discourses of nature and biology are beneficial.

---

10   As stated earlier, Freeman says that merger represents a significant reduction in personal autonomy, this impacts much more on women than on men because of the social context that love is played out in. M Freeman, 'Romantic Love and Personal Autonomy' in French P A & H K Wettstein (eds), *Midwest Studies in Philosophy, XXII (1998): The Philosophy of Emotion* (University of Notre Dame Press, Indiana 1998) 169–178.
11   Langford, *Revolutions of the Heart* 151.
12   E Illouz, *Why Love Hurts: A Sociological Explanation* (Polity, Cambridge 2012) 5.

Earlier, I alluded to the possibility that the formulation of love offered by Giddens might help to fulfil some of these promises. Giddens has formulated love as an emotional tie that can be independent of extrinsic factors, including sexuality. This is a love that is entered into and structured along individual lines, disconnected from marriage or even monogamy. This formulation of love moves away from nature and is democratic and inclusive. However, it also leaves itself wide open to the criticism that it is potentially exploitative and unethical. In the discourse we have seen, it appears to be difficult therefore to reconcile a freer and open love with a more caring and ethical one, and yet this seems to be what is needed.

Feminism and queer critique have identified many problems with love, but they have also provided insights that will help to recover and fulfil its radical and liberating potential. Feminists have identified the liberating potential of romantic love. Illouz, Radway, Pearce, Stacey and Langhamer, among others, have shown how women use love exactly to achieve what Solomon and Giddens have argued can be the case. Love provides a means by which women can subvert patriarchy.

Queer theorists who have retained love at the same time as opposing its heteronormativity are also a big part of this project. Warner, Berlant, Johnson, Slavin, Binnie and Bell, all cited in this book, have argued that relationships, described by Berlant as being on the 'edges', can all be described as love.

It might well be that law can also help to create this new discourse of love. *Garcia*, for example, reflected a view of marriage that was built upon love and mutuality, and which nurtured both. *Garcia* accepted that love is anarchical but refused to either jettison it or to leave its wounded victims unprotected. *Re Kevin* must also be part of this re-reading of love. While I have argued that the social construction of love as heterosexual — embedded in concepts of family and domesticity — are paramount in the reading of this case, it must not be forgotten that the case breaks the connection between love and nature. Kevin 'becomes' a man, is not 'born' one, he falls in love and marries and defies the 'nature' connection that exists in both love and marriage.

The eventual recognition of same-sex marriage could also achieve this aim, and can be read as a decisive breaking down of marriage as a heterosexual institution. Same-sex couples will bring to the institution an understanding of love that is not necessarily steeped in scripts of family, procreation and domesticity. Indeed, they will join heterosexual couples who are also interested in breaking down these connections. There are feminists (both men and women) who marry, there are people who do not have children who marry, there are couples who reject and act against gender stereotypes who marry. Same-sex married couples and non-traditional heterosexual couples will join forces to reflect a different meaning to love and marriage.

The way we read *Re Kevin* and the legal recognition of same-sex marriage is crucial. According to the reading that they replicate heterosexual scripts, love's radical potential is diminished; but if we read them as validations of 'other', less traditional expressions of love then they recover and reinforce love's radical meaning.

Love and Marriage

Considering the relationship between love and marriage is not an easy task. At first, it would appear that the two are opposites: love is freedom, marriage is oppression; love is anarchical, marriage is ordered and rule bound; love is individualistic, marriage is a unity of a man and a woman; love is selfish, marriage is altruistic; love is about pursuing personal satisfaction, marriage is about giving and caring for others; love lasts for as long as it does, marriage is a life-long institution.

But this is too simplistic a reading of both institutions. Neither love nor marriage are static concepts. This book has shown that there are at least two readings of both love and of marriage. Love, we have seen, is a discourse of both freedom and of oppression. One breaks down social barriers while the other reinforces them. Marriage can be read both according to its traditional, patriarchal, religious and — we need to acknowledge — old common law meanings, as well as along its more modern feminist and queer equality/difference meanings. The influence that love has on marriage depends upon the readings we take for both of the institutions.

If we take the radical reading of love, then its association with marriage can be a sign of the marriage institution also becoming radicalised, more equal, more able to deliver satisfaction to each of its parties, more open to individual negotiation, less embedded in rules and expectations, more free, less tied to gender stereotypes, less focussed on biological and natural readings, less heterosexual, less family, less monogamous.

If we take the oppressive reading of love, that it simply mirrors heterosexuality, and in turn domesticity and family, that it is structured along conservative views of 'nature' gender and sexuality, and that it is still largely religious and patriarchal, then the connection of love and marriage does very little to change the traditional meanings of marriage. Love simply reinforces marriage as a life-long union, whose primary role is procreation, the reinforcement of the heterosexual family, the economic union of two people, and arguably the reinforcement of stereotypical gender roles and of patriarchy.

The same question must also be asked in reverse: what does marriage do for love? Again, the question depends on the interpretation of marriage. Staying with the traditional meanings, if we connect marriage to love, it diminishes its radical potential. This is the very concern that has been shown by feminists and queer scholars who have opposed same-sex marriage. Marriage is too conservative an institution, its past is too dark and too oppressive for those who have a radical outlook and radical aspirations in their own love lives to be aligned to it. What this suggests is that the radical potential of love will be lost when it is aligned to marriage. But what if we see marriage in the modern guise many want it to assume, as an equal relationship where personal freedom and satisfaction are obtainable? In this model, marriage and love simply reinforce each other's radical potential.

The legal analysis undertaken in this book reflects the careful manouvering that is occurring in society in relation to the meaning of marriage. The law has stomped on some of the worst aspects of the legal effect of marriage (sex, marital rape), but it tiptoes around others (same-sex marriage). It also reflects the tensions that exist in relation to the meaning of love. Yes, love is great, yes we all can have it (*Re Kevin*), but it can have consequences that are not so great (*Garcia* and same-sex marriage). This might mean that love is not all we need to make marriage a progressive institution.

Law Again

Going back to our starting point, and knowing what we know about the dominance of the positivist rhetoric of law, it would have been surprising to find a more open discussion of love in the legal discourse of marriage. For the courts to have engaged openly with love would have been to depart from 'objective' reasoning and application of law. Critical jurisprudence has done quite a good job of challenging the positivist view of law which excludes emotion. What remains is for that work to penetrate the many layers of law more deeply and more convincingly.

If we are serious about fostering an engagement between law and emotion, we must also consider how that engagement can take place. Returning to the law and emotion scholarship with which this book began, we can identify several trends. We see scholarship that describes emotions that exist in different legal processes. We also see scholarship that calls for the inclusion of emotion in legal processes such as judging. Very little is said in these works about how this could actually occur. We see methodologies of law, such as therapeutic jurisprudence and restorative justice, that attempt to use emotions to achieve justice as an alternative to the adversarial system. Finally, we see work that takes the lens of love to challenge not what law does but how law thinks. This has been the approach taken here.

Law that is understood in an emotional vacuum is the poorer for it. Law as a social discourse needs to be viewed through an emotional lens as much as any other. This book has shown the dynamic that exists in the legal discourse between love and marriage, arguing that the impact of love on marriage can help to move the institution away from its oppressive nature and help to create a more equal relationship based upon mutual needs and wants. Love can be associated with mutuality rather than individuality. When it comes to same-sex marriage, an analysis of the issue through the lens of romantic love helped to show a side which has hitherto been little discussed, and has helped to clarify aspects of the argument. To show the role love plays in defining marriage, and to show the features of that love, will make a contribution to the same-sex marriage debate. Such an insight will enable law reformers to more clearly articulate their demands, and their opponents to more clearly frame their opposition. The debate is thus enriched by the inclusion of emotional analysis.

We have come to accept that political, historical, sociological, and philosophical perspectives are all important to law. We need to add emotions to that perspective. To show why it is so, and to indicate something of how it can be done, has been the contribution of this book. Thinking about law within an emotional framework makes law more engaged with the community it serves and, as such, better able to understand it, and deliver it justice. Understanding the emotions involved in human institutions such as marriage enables law-makers and law reformers to more clearly articulate their claims and demands. Understanding legal issues through an emotional paradigm increases understanding of the issues themselves, and consequently leads to better legal decision-making at all levels. Including emotion in law dramatically changes for the better the perception we have of law. To believe that emotions can be divorced from law isolates it from an essential aspect of human behaviour; to remarry law and emotion returns law to where it belongs, back to its humanity.

Bibliography

Cases

ANZ Banking Group Ltd v Alirezai BC200400178

Attorney-General for the Commonwealth v Kevin and Others (2003) 30 Fam LR 1

Balfour v Balfour [1919] 2 KB 571

Barclays Bank Plc v O'Brien [1994] 1 AC 180

Bartlett v Bartlett (1933) 50 CLR 3

Bellinger v Bellinger [2001] EWCA Civ 1140

Berry (1988) 10 Cr App R (S) 15

Birch v Taubmans Ltd [1956] 57 SR (NSW) 93

Birmingham Southern Railway Co v Lintner (1904) 141 ALA 420

Brown v Commissioner for Superannuation (1995) 21 AAR 378

Burns v Radio 2UE Sydney Pty Ltd & Ors [2004] NSW ADT 267 (22 Nov 2004)

C v C (A Minor) (Custody Appeal) [1991] (3) Fam LR 174

Campbell v Campbell (1974) 9 SARS 25

Commonwealth Bank of Australia v Allregal Enterprises Pty ltd [1999] WASC 186

Corbett v Corbett (Otherwise Ashley) [1970] 2 All ER 33

Crabtree v Crabtree (No 2) [1964] ALR 820

Dubois v Chee-Teong Ong BC 200403050

Dunn v Dunn [1948] 2 All ER 822

European Asian of Australia Limited v Kurland (1985) 8 NSWLR 192

Fielding v Fielding (1921) NZLR 1069

Fisher v Fisher (1986) 161 CLR 438

Fisher v Smithson (1977) 17 SASR 223

Forster v Forster (1790) 161 ER 504

Gallie v Lee [1971] AC 1004

Garcia v National Australia Bank Ltd [1998] CLR 395

Garcia v National Australia Bank Ltd BC 9301944 Supreme Court of NSW Equity Division 1993

Garcia v National Australia Bank Limited S132/1996 (13 February 1997)

Gregory Brown and Commissioner of Superannuation [1995] AATA 130; (1995) 21 AAR 378 (15 May 1995)

Hasaganic v Minister for Education [1973] 5 SARS 554

H v J and Anor (2006) 36 Fam LR 316

Hein v Hein (1976) 1 Fam LR 11,128

Hyde v Hyde and Woodmansee [1861–1873] All ER Rep 175

In the Marriage of A and J (1995) 19 Fam LR 260

In the Marriage of BA and RW Spry (1997) 3 Fam LR 11,330

In the Marriage of Brook GE and Brook HL (1977) FLC 90–325

In the Marriage of C and D (falsely called D) (1979) 5 Fam LR 636

In the Marriage of C and JA Doyle (1992) 15 Fam LR 274

In the Marriage of N and H (1982) 8 Fam LR 577

In The Marriage of L (1984) 178 FLR 460

In The Marriage of L and L (1984) 9 Fam LR 1033

In the Marriage of O'Reilly NP and O'Reilly ECB (1977) FLC 90–300

In the Marriage of Pavey (1976) 1 Fam LR 11,358

In the Marriage of PC and PR (1975) 5 Fam LR 352

In the Marriage of Schmidt (1979) 5 Fam LR 421

In the Marriage of Shepherd RW and Shepherd SA (1979) FLC 90–729

In the Marriage of Spry [1977] 3 Fam LR 11,334

In the Marriage of Todd (No 2) (1976) 1 Fam LR 11,186

Jarman v Lloyd (1982) 8 Fam LR 878

Kealley v Jones [1979] 1 NSWLR 723

Liu v Adamson [2003] 12 BPR 22,205

Louth v Diprose (1992) 175 CLR 621

Meadows and Meadows v Maloney [1973] 4 SASR 567

Munro v Munro [1950] 1 All ER 832

National Australia Bank v Garcia [1996] NSWSC 253 http://www.austlii.edu.
au/au/cases/nsw/NSWSC/1996/253.html date accessed 1/09/2008

N v N and W (1976) 2 Fam L R 11,493

NSW v Layoun [2001] NSWSC 113

Orme v Orme (1824) 2 Add 382

Papadimitropoulos v R [1957] 98 CLR 249

PGA v The Queen (2012) 245 CLR 355

R v Clarence (1888) QB 23

R v Clarke [1949] 2 All ER 448

R v George Allan Pryor BC200105198 Supreme Court of Queensland Court of
Appeal unreported Aug 2001

R v Jackson [1822] 8 Car & P 266

R v L (1991) 174 CLR 379

R v Lister (1721) 1 Str 477

R v McMinn [1982] VR 53

R v Miller [1954] 2 QB 282

R v O'Brien [1974] 2 All ER 663

R v R [1991] 2 WLR 1065

R v Rammage Vic Court of Criminal Appeal no 146 unreported 1993

R v Saunders [1838] 8 Car & P 266

R v Spencer Queensland Court of Criminal Appeal CA no 80 unreported 1991

Re Cochrane (1840) 8 Dowl 630

Re K (1994) 17 Fam LR 357

Re J and M: Residence Application (2004) 32 Fam LR 668

Re Kevin (Validity of Marriage of Transsexual) (2001) 28 Fam LR 158

Re Mark (An application relating to parental responsibilities) (2004) 31 Fam LR 162

Re Patrick: An Application Concerning Contact (2002) FLC 93–096

Re Wakin; exparte McNally (1999) 198 CLR 511

Secretary, Department of Social Security v "SRA" [1993] FCA 573; (1993) 118 ALR 467 (1993) 43 FCR 299 (1993) 18 Aar, (1993) 31 ALD 1 (1 December 1993)

Synge v Synge [1900–03] All ER Rep 452

Taylor v Johnson (1983) 151 CLR 422

Tew v Tew (1921) NZLR 1071

Warburton v Whitely (1989) 5 BPR 97388

Watt v State Bank of New South Wales [2003] ACTCA 7

Wily v Wily (1918) P1

Yerkey v Jones [1939] 63 CLR 649

Statutes

Civil Partnership Act ACT (2009)

Civil Union Act ACT (2006)

Family Law Act Cth (1975)

Infant Custody Act (1839)

Marriage Act Cth (1956)

Married Women's Property Act UK (1870)

Married Women's Property Act UK (1882)

Married Women's Property Act UK (1893)

Matrimonial Causes Act UK (1857)

Matrimonial Causes Act UK (1973)

Matrimonial Causes Act Cth (1959)

Treaty Establishing the European Community (1957) http://eur-lex.europa.eu/
en/treaties/index.htm#founding accessed 06/01/2011

Media Reports

AAP, 'ACT Introduces Gay Marriage Legislation' 28/03/2006 *The Age* http://
www.theage.com.au/news/national/act-introduces-gay-marriage-
legislation/2006/ accessed 2/05/2008

AAP, 'Gay Marriage Comments Appalling' 23/2/2006 *Sydney Morning Herald*
http://www.smh.com.au/news/National/Gay-marriage-comments-
appalling/2006/02/23 accessed 2/05/2008

AAP, 'PM Opposes ACT Gay Laws' 30/03/2006 http://www.theage.com.
au/news/national/Govt-to-legislate-against-gay-unions/2006/ accessed
19/04/2006

AAP, 'PM Targets Gays in Marriage Law' 27/05/2004 *Sydney Morning Herald*
http://www.smh.com.au/articles/2004/05/27/1085461876842.html accessed
24/09/2007

AAP, 'Same-Sex Law Changes "Overdue"' 30/04/2008 *Sydney Morning Herald* http://
www.smh.com.au/news/national/samesex-law-changes-overdue/2008/04/30/120
accessed 2/05/2008

ABC, 'ACT Set To Legalise Civil Union Ceremonies' *ABCNews* 11/11/2009
http://www.abc/net.au/news/stories/2009/11/11/2739165.htm accessed
20/11/2009

ABC, 'Assembly Passes Civil Unions Law' 9/05/2008 *ABC News* http://www.
abc.net.au/news/stories/2008/05/09/2239625.htm accessed 15/05/2008

ABC, 'Christian Lobby Welcomes Same-Sex Backdown' *ABC News* 5/05/2008
http://www.abc.net.au/news/stories/2008/05/05/2235174.htm accessed
5/05/2008

ABC, 'Gay Marriage' *First Hour* 4/05/2008 http://www.abc.net.au/cgi-bin/
common/printfriendly.pl?http://www.abc.net.au/sundayn. accessed
5/05/2008

ABC, 'Gay Marriage Debate –Tony Jones Talks to Jim Wallace and Bob Brown' *Lateline* 20/02/2008 http://www.abc.net.au/lateline/content/2007/s2168241. htm accessed 2/05/08

ABC, 'Gay Marriage Bill Passes Britain's House of Commons' *ABC News* 22/02/2013 http://www.abc.net.au/news/2013-05-22/britains-gay-marriage-bill-passes-major-hurdle/4704878 accessed 14/06/2013ABC, 'G-G to Disallow Civil Union Laws' *ABC News* 13/06/2006 http://www.abc.net.au/ cgibin/common/printfriendly.pl?http://www.abc.net.au/news/n accessed 26/06/2008

ABC, 'Greens win Gay Marriage Motion' 11/18/2010 *ABCNews* http://www. abc.net.au/news/stories/2010/11/183069810.htm accessed 18/11/2010

ABC, 'Labour vs Labour Over Same Sex Marriage' *AM* 1/05/2008 http://www. abc.net.au/cgi-bin/common/printfriendly.pl?http://www.abc.net.au/am/ cont accessed 2/05/2008

ABC, 'Legal Ceremonies for Same-Sex Couples' *News* 11/11/2009 http://www. abc.net/news/stories/2009/11/11/2739661.htm accessed 20/11/2009

ABC, 'New Zealand Court Hears Man Murdered Wife Because She Didn't Give Him a Son'[02/06/09] *PM* http://www.abc.net.au/pm/content/2008/ s2587484.htm accessed 3/06/2009

ABC, 'NSW MPs Pass Gay Adoption Bill' 02/09/2010 *ABC News* http://www. abc.net.au/news/stories/2010/09/02/3000652.htm accessed 02/09/2010

ABC, 'Obama's Evolution On Gay Marriage' *ABC News* http://abcnews.go.com/ Politics/obamas-evolution-gay-marriage/story?id=19150614 accessed 14/06/2013

ABC, 'Power of Love Driving Gay Marriage Debate' 15/11/2010 *ABCNews* http://www.abc.net.au/news/stories/2010/11/15//3067122.htm accessed 18/11/2010

ABC, 'The Pitch: Republic of Everyone' *Gruen Nation* episode 3 10/07/2010 http://www.youtube.com/watch?v=O4jI1atQwp4 accessed 23/08/2010

ABC, 'Wilkie Calls for Gay marriage Conscience Vote' 22/10/2010 *ABC News* http://www.abc.net/au/news/stories/2010/10/22/3045375.htm accessed 10/22/2010

ABC Radio National, 'ACT, Commonwealth Battle Over Same-Sex Marriage Laws' 30/03/2006 *The World Today* http://www.abc.net.au/cgibin/common/ printfriendly.pl?http://www.abc.net.au/worldto accessed 2/05/2008

ABC Radio National, 'The Emotional Brain: Part I, Sexual Desire' *All in the Mind* 26/11/2005 http://www.abc.net.au/rn/sceince/mind/styories/s1514225.htm accessed 5/12/2005

ABC Radio National, 'Finding Fault' *Hindsight* 15/08/10 http://www.abc.net.au/rn/hindsight/stories/2010/2977277.htm accessed 02/09/2010

ABC Radio National, *The Law Report* 3/11/2009 http://www.abc.net.au/rn/lawreport/stories/2010/2858962.htm accessed 17/07/10

ABC Radio National, 'Love Trap' *Catalyst* 30/09/2004 http://www.abc.net.au/cgibin/common/printfriendly.pl?/catalyst/stories/s1210487.htm accessed 30/05/2007

ABC Radio National, 'Why We Fall In Love' *Breakfast* 24/02/2004 http://search.abc.net.au/search/cache.cgi?collection=abconline&doc=http/www.abc.net accessed 30/05/2007About.com.marriage, 'What Do Others Have to Say About Marital Rape' http://marriage.about.com/cs/maritalrape/f/maritalrape.htm accessed 8/04/2010

Alexander C, 'Corbell to Revive Gay Union Act' 30/11/2007 *TheCanberra Times* http://canberra.yourguide.com.au/news/local/news/general/corbell-to-revive-gay-union accessed 13/05/2008

Alexander C, 'Stanhope Digs in on Gay Unions' 5/12/2007 *The Canberra Times* http://canberra.yourguide.com.au/news/local/news/general/stanhope-digs-in-on-gay-u accessed 13/05/2008

Arndt B, 'Women Need to Say Yes to Sex' *Canberra Times* 2/03/09 http://www.canberratimes.com.au/news/opinion/editorial/general/women-need-to-say-yes-to-sex/1447294.aspx# accessed 29/06/10

The Australian, 'Fresh Bid on Gay Marriage Laws' 14/06/2006 http://www.theaustralian.news.com.au/stroy/o,20867,19467767-29277,00.html accessed 2/05/2008Australian Christian Lobby, 'ACL Calls for Marriage and Family Safeguards in Same-Sex Law Changes' Media Release 30/04/2008 http://www.acl.org.au/act/media.stw accessed 16/12/2008

Australian Christian Lobby, 'ACL Welcomes Federal Intervention to Fulfil Election Promise to Protect Marriage' Media Release 4/05/2008 http://www.acl.org.au/act/media.stw accessed 16/12/2008

Australian Christian Lobby, 'Guy Barnett Has it Right on Gay Discrimination' Media Release 24/10/2006 http://www.acl.org.au/act/media.stw accessed 16/12/2008

Australian Christian Lobby, 'Rudd's Change on Marriage Sets Up a New Stolen Generation' Media Release 21/05/2013 http://www.acl.org.au/2013/05/mr-ridd%e2%80%99s-change-on-marriage-sets-up-a-n.... Accessed 1/06/2013

BBC, 'Australia- Muslim Cleric Asked By Prime Minister to Apologise For Statements on Marital Rape and Abuse' 22/01/2009 http://news.bbc.co.uk/2/hi/asia-pacific/7843909.htm accessed 12/04/2010

Breen G, 'Call to Rewards Couples with Cash' *ABC News* 13/07/2010 http://www.abc.net.au/news/stories/2010/08/13/2982063.htm accessed 15/08/2010

Burke J, 'Rape Within Marriage No Less a Crime' *Sydney Morning Herald* 10/09/2007 http://www.smh.com.au/news/opinion/rape-within-marriage-no-less-a-crime/2007/09/ accessed 12/04/2010

Burke K, 'To Love and Submit: A Marriage Made in 2012' 25/08/2012 Sydney Morning Herald http://www.smh.com.au/nsw/to-love-and-to-submit-a-marriage-made-in-2012-20120824-24ru7.html accessed 1/06/2013

Carey B, 'Crazy For You – Here's the Scan to Prove it' 1/6/05 *Sydney Morning Herald* 1, 14

Carthew A, interview with Prince Charles and Lady Diana ITN 24/02/1981 http://news.bbc.co.uk/onthisday/hi/dates/stories/february/24/newsid_2516000/2516759.stm accessed 1/12/2010

Cath News, 'No Church Wedding for Impotent Man' 12/06/2008 http://www.cathnews.com/article.aspx?aeid+7581 accessed 13/07/2009

CNN.com, 'Researchers: Marriage Doesn't Make you Happy' http://cnn.health.pritnthis.clickability.com/pt/cpt?action+cpt&title+CNN.com+-+rese accessed 23/07/2010

Cooper G, 'History of Flesh and Fantasy' 8-9/03/2008 *Sydney Morning Herald* 35

Creative Spirits, 'Circle Sentencing' http://www.creativespirits.info/aboriginalculture/law/circle-sentencing.html accessed 17/07/10

Curry D, 'Canberra's First Same-Sex Civil Union' *Canberra Times* 3/06/2008 http://www.canberratimes.com.au/news/local/news/general/first-samesex-civil-union/7 accessed 3/07/2008

Dunn M, 'Cleric: Rape, Beating Ok for Wives' *The Daily Telegraph* 22/01/2009 http://www.dailytelegraph.com.au/news/cleric-rape-beating-ok-for-wives/story-e6freu accessed 12/04/2010

Farouque F, 'Why or Why Can't I Have a Civil Union' *The Age* 10/06/2006 http://wwwtheage.com.au/news/in-depht/why-oh-why-cant-I-have-a-civil-union/2006 accessed 22/05/2008

Foschia L, 'Ruddock Moves to Block ACT Gay Marriage Proposal' *ABC AM* 30/03/2006 http://www.abc.net.au/cgi-bin/common/printfriendly.pl?http://www.abc.au/am/con accessed 19/04/2006

Fraser A, 'Corbell Hopeful of Brokering Gay Union Compromise' *The Canberra Times* 2/05/2008 http://www.canberra.yourguide.com.au/printerfriendlypage.asp?story_id=1235863 accessed 2/05/2008

Glennie C, 'Family First Candidate Sparks Outrage Over Gay Marriage' *ABC PM* 09/07/2010 http://www.abc.net.au/pm/content/2010/s2977960.htm accessed 10/08/2010

Goward P, 'Gay Marriage: it's a Conservative Thing' 07/10/2010 *The Drum Unleashed* ABC http://www.abc.net.au.unleashed/39744.html accessed 07/10/2010

Green J, 'Australian Territory Legalises Gay and Civil Partnership Ceremonies' *PinkNews* 11/11/2009 http://www.pinknews.co.uk/2009/11/11/australian-territory-leglaises-gay-civil-partner accessed 13/11/2009

Gregory P, 'All we Need is Love, Concludes Retiring Judge' *The Age* 17/12/2008 http://www.theage.com.au/national/all-we-need-is-love-concludes-rtiring-judge-2008 accessed 12/05/2010

Hand J, 'Lovers Demand Equal Right to Wed' 2/8/10 *Sunday Canberra Times* 4

Heard J, 'Leave Wedded Bliss to Those Who Can Make Babies' 28/7/2009 *The Australian* http://www.tehaustralian.news.com.au/story/0,20867,21403376-7583,00.html accessed 5/08/2009

Horen A, 'Love Among Photocopiers' 8/9/05 *Sydney Morning Herald* 1, 6

Hughes R, 'First ACT Ceremony Takes Place' *ActGay* 25/11/2009 http://actgay.e-p.net/news/280-first-ceremony-takes-place-in-canberra accessed 2/12/2009

Jensen P, Anglican Archbishop of Sydney 'Unique Union' *The Australian* 8/05/2008 http://www.theaustralian.com.au/news/unique-union/story-e6frg73o-1111116275570 accessed 25/07/10

Lynch A, 'How Can Same-Sex Unions Possibly be a Threat to Marriage? *The Age* 7/6/2006 http://www.theage.com.au/news/opinion/how-can-samesex-unions-possibly-be-a-thre accessed 24/09/2007

Macey J, 'Same-Sex Adoption bill in NSW Parliament' *ABC PM* 31/08/2010 http://www.abc.net.au/pm/content/2010/s2998784.htm accessed 1/09/2010

McCabe K, 'Same Hurdles to Gay Marriage' *The Daily Telegraph* 01/05/2008 htpp://www.news.com.au/dailytelegraph/story /o,22049,23623686-5001030,00.html accessed 2/05/2008

Miller B, 'Joy, Anger as France Legalises Same-Sex Marriage' http://www.abc. net.au/news/2013-04-24/joy-anger-as-france-legalises-same-sex-marriage Accessed 24/04/2013

Miller N, 'Gay Unions Have Many Critics with Little Logic' *The West Australian* 31/12/2005 http://www.galewa.asn.au/index2.php?option+com_ content&task+view&id+542&Ite accessed 19/04/2006

Neustatter A, 'Falling in Love Again? Don't!' *Guardian.co.uk* 27/6/1999 http://www.guardian.co.uk/world/1999/jun/07/gender.uk/print accessed 28/10/2009News.com.au, 'Vote on Same-Sex Marriage Unlikely To Go Ahead' http://www.news.com.au/national-news/vote-on-same-sex-marriage-unlikely-to-go-ahead/story-fncynjr2-1226652218249 accessed 14/06/2013

O'Brien K, 'McClelland Strikes Out Against Discrimination Against Same sex Couples' *ABC The 7.30 Report* http://www.abc.net.au/7.30/content/2007/ s2232028.htm accessed 2/05/2008

Out Now Global, 'Young, Gay and Married (And Divorced)' http://www. theage.com.au/news/national/govt-to-legislate-against-gay-unions/2006/ accessed 19/04/2006

Peake R, 'Angry Corbell Adandons Gay Plan' 5/5/2008 *Canberra Times* http://www.canberra.yourguide.com.au/printerfriendlypage.asp?story_ id+1237202 accessed 5/05/2008

Pink News, 'Australian Territory Legalises Gay Civil Partnership Ceremonies' http://www.pinknews.co.uk/2009/11/11/australian-territory-legalises-gay-civil-partnership-ceremonies/ accessed 13/11/2009

Reuters, *Just Woman@asiaOne* 21/12/2007 http://www.asiaone.com/ Just%2BWoman/News/Women%2BIn%2BThe%2BNews/Story/ A1Story20071221-42037.html accessed 19/05/10

Ruddock P, 'ACT Civil Partnerships Bill Does Not Remove Concerns' (Press Release, 6/02/2007)

Rudra N, 'Same-Sex Legal Union Push' 3/07/2008 *Canberra Times* http://www.canberratimes.com.su/news/local/news/general/samesex-legal-union-push/ accessed 4/07/2008

Stanhope J, Chief Minister ACT, 'ACT to Legislate for Civil Unions' Media Release 2/12/2005 http://www.chiefmininster.act.giov.au/media.asp?media=927&id=927 accessed 2/05/2008

Wolf N, 'The Porn Myth' *New York News and Features* http://nymag.com/nymetro/news/trends/n_9437/ accessed 29/06/10

Parliamentary Debates

Australian Capital Territory, Parliamentary Debates Legislative Assembly March 28 2006, 655-659 http://www.hansard.act.gov.au/start.htm accessed 12/05/2008

Australian Capital Territory, Parliamentary Debates Legislative Assembly May 3 2006, 1077-1519 http://www.hansard.act.gov.au/start.htm accessed 12/05/2008

Australian Capital Territory, Parliamentary Debates Legislative Assembly May 11 2006, 1596-1651 http://www.hansard.act.gov.au/start.htm accessed 12/05/2008

Australian Capital Territory, Parliamentary Debates Legislative Assembly June 7 2006, 1842-1843 http://www.hansard.act.gov.au/start.htm accessed 12/05/2008

Australian Capital Territory, Parliamentary Debates Legislative Assembly June 8 2006, 2033-1914 http://www.hansard.act.gov.au/start.htm accessed 12/05/2008

Australian Capital Territory, Parliamentary Debates Legislative Assembly Dec 12 2006, 3953-3956 http://www.hansard.act.gov.au/start.htm accessed 12/05/2008

Australian Capital Territory, Parliamentary Debates Legislative Assembly Dec 4 2007, 3910-3911 http://www.hansard.act.gov.au/start.htm accessed 12/05/2008

Australian Capital Territory, Parliamentary Debates Legislative Assembly April 2 2008, 850 http://www.hansard.act.gov.au/start.htm accessed 12/05/2008

Australian Capital Territory, Parliamentary Debates Legislative Assembly May 8 2008, 1749-1773 http://www.hansard.act.gov.au/start.htm accessed 12/05/2008

Australian Capital Territory, Parliamentary Debates Legislative Assembly November 11 2009, 4781-4909 http://www.hansard.act.gov.au/start.htm accessed 12/05/2008

Commonwealth, Parliamentary Debates House of Representatives May 27 2004 (Phillip Ruddock) http://parlinfoweb.aph.gov.au/piweb/view_document. aspx?ID=2259205 accessed 14/04/2008

Commonwealth, Parliamentary Debates House of Representatives June 16 2004 (Anthony Albanese) htpp://parlinfoweb.aph.gov.au/piweb/view_document. aspx?ID+2263289 accessed 13/05/2008

Commonwealth, Parliamentary Debates House of Representatives June 16 2004 (Arch Bevis) http://parlinfoweb.aph.gov.au/piweb/view_document. aspx?ID=2262773 accessed 13/05/2008

Commonwealth, Parliamentary Debates House of Representatives June 16 2004 (Scott Bruce) http://parlinfoweb.aph.gov.au/piweb/view_document. aspx?ID=2262777 accessed 13/05/2008

Commonwealth, Parliamentary Debates House of Representatives June 16 2004 (Alan Cadman) http://parlinfoweb.aph.gov.au/piweb/view_document. aspx?ID=2262785 accessed 13/05/2008

Commonwealth, Parliamentary Debates House of Representatives June 16 2004 (Michael Danby) http://parlinfoweb.aph.gov.au/piweb/view_document. aspx?ID=2262781 accessed 13/05/2008

Commonwealth, Parliamentary Debates House of Representatives June 16 2004 (Peter Dutton) http://parlinfoweb.aph.gov.au/piweb/view_document. aspx?ID=2262761 accessed 13/05/2008

Commonwealth, Parliamentary Debates House of Representatives June 16 2004 (Patrick Farmer) http://parlinfoweb.aph.gov.au/piweb/view_document. aspx?ID=2263233 accessed 13/05/2008

Commonwealth, Parliamentary Debates House of Representatives June 16 2004 (Martin Ferguson) http://parlinfoweb.aph.gov.au/piweb/view_document. aspx?ID=2262789 accessed 13/05/2008

Commonwealth, Parliamentary Debates House of Representatives June 16 2004 (David Hawker) http://parlinfoweb.aph.gov.au/piweb/view_document. aspx?ID=2262793 accessed 13/05/2008

Commonwealth, Parliamentary Debates House of Representatives June 16 2004 (Brendan O'Connor) http://parlinfoweb.aph.gov.au/piweb/view_document. aspx?ID=2262797 accessed 13/05/2008

Commonwealth, Parliamentary Debates House of Representatives June 16 2004 (Christopher Pearce) http://parlinfoweb.aph.gov.au/piweb/view_document. aspx?ID=2262593 accessed 13/05/2008

Commonwealth, Parliamentary Debates House of Representatives June 16 2004 (Nicola Roxon) http://parlinfoweb.aph.gov.au/piweb/view_document.aspx?ID=2262589 accessed 13/05/2008

Commonwealth, Parliamentary Debates House of Representatives June 16 2004 (Stephen Smith) http://parlinfoweb.aph.gov.au/piweb/view_document.aspx?ID=2262765 accessed 13/05/2008

Commonwealth, Parliamentary Debates House of Representatives June 16 2004 (Barry Wakelin) http://parlinfoweb.aph.gov.au/piweb/view_document.aspx?ID=2262769 accessed 13/05/2008

Commonwealth, Parliamentary Debates House of Representatives June 17 2004 (Anthony Albanese) http://parlinfoweb.aph.gov.au/piweb/view_document.aspx?ID=2263289 accessed 13/05/2008

Commonwealth, Parliamentary Debates House of Representatives June 17 2004 (Peter Andren) http://parlinfoweb.aph.gov.au/piweb/view_document.aspx?ID=2263245 accessed 13/05/2008

Commonwealth, Parliamentary Debates House of Representatives June 17 2004 (Robert Baldwin) http://parlinfoweb.aph.gov.au/piweb/view_document.aspx?ID=2263225 accessed 13/05/2008

Commonwealth, Parliamentary Debates House of Representatives June 17 2004 (Michael Danby) http://parlinfoweb.aph.gov.au/piweb/view_document.aspx?ID=2263293 accessed 13/05/2008

Commonwealth, Parliamentary Debates House of Representatives June 17 2004 (Peter King) http://parlinfoweb.aph.gov.au/piweb/view_document.aspx?ID=2263241 accessed 13/05/2008

Commonwealth, Parliamentary Debates House of Representatives June 17 2004 (Carmen Lawrence) http://parlinfoweb.aph.gov.au/piweb/view_document.aspx?ID=2263229 accessed 13/05/2008

Commonwealth, Parliamentary Debates House of Representatives June 17 2004 (Roger Price) http://parlinfoweb.aph.gov.au/piweb/view_document.aspx?ID=2263237 accessed 13/05/2008

Commonwealth, Parliamentary Debates House of Representatives June 17 2004 (Paul Neville) http://parlinfoweb.aph.gov.au/piweb/view_document.aspx?ID=2263249 accessed 13/05/2008

Commonwealth, Parliamentary Debates House of Representatives June 17 2004 (Michael Organ) http://parlinfoweb.aph.gov.au/piweb/view_document.aspx?ID=2263261 accessed 13/05/2008

Commonwealth, Parliamentary Debates House of Representatives June 17 2004 (Tanya Plibersek) http://parlinfoweb.aph.gov.au/piweb/view_document. aspx?ID=2263253 accessed 13/05/2008

Commonwealth, Parliamentary Debates House of Representatives June 17 2004 (Tanya Plibersek) http://parlinfoweb.aph.gov.au/piweb/view_document. aspx?ID=2263305 accessed 13/05/2008

Commonwealth, Parliamentary Debates House of Representatives June 17 2004 (Phillip Ruddock) http://parlinfoweb.aph.gov.au/piweb/view_document. aspx?ID=2263269 accessed 13/05/2008

Commonwealth, Parliamentary Debates House of Representatives June 17 2004 (Phillip Ruddock) http://parlinfoweb.aph.gov.au/piweb/view_document. aspx?ID=2263281 accessed 13/05/2008

Commonwealth, Parliamentary Debates House of Representatives June 17 2004 (Phillip Ruddock) http://parlinfoweb.aph.gov.au/piweb/view_document. aspx?ID=2263297 accessed 13/05/2008

Commonwealth, Parliamentary Debates House of Representatives June 17 2004 (Phillip Ruddock) http://parlinfoweb.aph.gov.au/piweb/view_document. aspx?ID=2267273 accessed 13/05/2008

Commonwealth, Parliamentary Debates House of Representatives June 17 2004 (Phillip Ruddock) http://parlinfoweb.aph.gov.au/piweb/view_document. aspx?ID=2263309 accessed 13/05/2008

Commonwealth, Parliamentary Debates House of Representatives June 17 2004 (Alby Shultz) http://parlinfoweb.aph.gov.au/piweb/view_document. aspx?ID=2263265 accessed 13/05/2008

Commonwealth, Parliamentary Debates House of Representatives June 17 2004 (Anthony Smith) http://parlinfoweb.aph.gov.au/piweb/view_document. aspx?ID=2263257 accessed 13/05/2008

Commonwealth, Parliamentary Debates House of Representatives June 17 2004 (Warren Snowden) http://parlinfoweb.aph.gov.au/piweb/view_document. aspx?ID=2263317 accessed 13/05/2008

Commonwealth, Parliamentary Debates House of Representatives June 24 2004 (Kerry Bartlett) http://parlinfoweb.aph.gov.au/piweb/view_document. aspx?ID=2268309 accessed 13/05/2008

Commonwealth, Parliamentary Debates House of Representatives June 24 2004 (Michael Organ) http://parlinfoweb.aph.gov.au/piweb/view_document. aspx?ID=2267281 accessed 13/05/2008

Commonwealth, Parliamentary Debates House of Representatives June 24 2004 (Michael Organ) http://parlinfoweb.aph.gov.au/piweb/view_document. aspx?ID=2267293 accessed 13/05/2008

Commonwealth, Parliamentary Debates House of Representatives June 24 2004 (Michael Organ) http://parlinfoweb.aph.gov.au/piweb/view_document. aspx?ID=2267297 accessed 13/05/2008

Commonwealth, Parliamentary Debates House of Representatives June 24 2004 (Nicola Roxon) http://parlinfoweb.aph.gov.au/piweb/view_document. aspx?ID=2267277 accessed 13/05/2008

Commonwealth, Parliamentary Debates House of Representatives June 24 2004 (Phillip Ruddock) http://parlinfoweb.aph.gov.au/piweb/view_document. aspx?ID=2267285 accessed 13/05/2008

Commonwealth, Parliamentary Debates House of Representatives August 12 2004 (Lindsay Tanner) http://parlinfoweb.aph.gov.au/piweb/view_document. aspx?ID=22673817 accessed 13/05/2008

Commonwealth, Parliamentary Debates Senate June 15 2006 (Lyn Allison) http://parlinfoweb.aph.gov.au/piweb/view_document.aspx?ID=23454465 accessed 13/05/2008

Commonwealth, Parliamentary Debates Senate June 17 2004 (Guy Barnett) http://parlinfoweb.aph.gov.au/piweb/view_document.aspx?ID=2014889 accessed 15/05/2008

Commonwealth, Parliamentary Debates Senate June 23 2004 (Guy Barnett) http://parlinfoweb.aph.gov.au/piweb/view_document.aspx?ID=2017929 accessed 13/05/2008

Commonwealth, Parliamentary Debates Senate June 15 2006 (Andrew Bartlett) http://parlinfoweb.aph.gov.au/piweb/view_document.aspx?ID=2345429 accessed 13/05/2008

Commonwealth, Parliamentary Debates Senate June 15 2006 (Ron Boswell) http://parlinfoweb.aph.gov.au/piweb/view_document.aspx?ID=23454453 accessed 13/05/2008

Commonwealth, Parliamentary Debates Senate June 15 2006 (Bob Brown) http:// parlinfoweb.aph.gov.au/piweb/view_document.aspx?ID=2345425 accessed 13/05/2008

Commonwealth, Parliamentary Debates Senate June 15 2006 (Kim Carr) http:// parlinfoweb.aph.gov.au/piweb/view_document.aspx?ID=2345433 accessed 13/05/2008

Commonwealth, Parliamentary Debates Senate June 15 2006 (Steve Fielding) http://parlinfoweb.aph.gov.au/piweb/view_document.aspx?ID=2345445 accessed 13/05/2008

Commonwealth, Parliamentary Debates Senate June 15 2006 (Gary Humphries) http://parlinfoweb.aph.gov.au/piweb/view_document.aspx?ID=2345437 accessed 13/05/2008

Commonwealth, Parliamentary Debates Senate June 15 2006 (Joe Ludwig) http://parlinfoweb.aph.gov.au/piweb/view_document.aspx?ID=2345421 accessed 13/05/2008

Commonwealth, Parliamentary Debates Senate June 15 2006 (Christine Milne) http://parlinfoweb.aph.gov.au/piweb/view_document.aspx?ID=2345449 accessed 13/05/2008

Commonwealth, Parliamentary Debates Senate June 15 2006 (Nick Minchin) http://parlinfoweb.aph.gov.au/piweb/view_document.aspx?ID=2345417 accessed 13/05/2008

Commonwealth, Parliamentary Debates Senate June 15 2006 (Kerry Nettle) http://parlinfoweb.aph.gov.au/piweb/view_document.aspx?ID=2345413 accessed 13/05/2008

Commonwealth, Parliamentary Debates Senate June 15 2006 (Rachel Siewart) http://parlinfoweb.aph.gov.au/piweb/view_document.aspx?ID=23454461 accessed 13/05/2008

Commonwealth, Parliamentary Debates Senate June 15 2006 (Ruth Webber) http://parlinfoweb.aph.gov.au/piweb/view_document.aspx?ID=23454457 accessed 13/05/2008

Commonwealth, Parliamentary Debates Senate June 15 2006 (Penny Wong) http://parlinfoweb.aph.gov.au/piweb/view_document.aspx?ID=23454451 accessed 13/05/2008

Books and Articles

Abrams K, (2009) 'Barriers and Boundaries: Exploring Emotion in the Law of the Family' *Virginia Journal of Social Policy and the Law* 16 301–321

Abrams K, 'Legal Feminism and the Emotions: Three Moments in an Evolving Relationship' (2005) 28 *Harvard Journal of Law and Gender* 327

Abrams K, '"Fighting Fire with Fire": Rethinking the Role of Disgust in Hate Crimes' (2002) 90 *California Law Review* 1423–1464

Abrams K, 'The Progress of Passion' (2002) 100 *Michigan Law Review* 1602–1620

Abrams K, 'Sex Wars Redux: Agency and Coercion in Feminist Legal Theory' (1995) 95 *Columbia Law Review* 304–376

Abrams K, 'Songs of Innocence and Experience: Dominance Feminism in the University' (1993–94) 103 *Yale Law Journal* 1533–1560

Abrams K, 'Unity, Narrative and Law' (1993) 13 *Studies in Law, Politics and Society* 3–35

Abrams K, 'Hearing the Call of Stories' (1991) 79 *California Law Review* 871–1052

Abrams K & H Keren, 'Who's Afraid of Law and the Emotions?' (2010) 94 *Minnesota Law Review* 1997–2074

Abrams K & H Keren, 'Law in the Cultivation of Hope' (2007) 95 *California Law Review* 319–382

Ackelsberg M, 'Whatever Happened to Feminist Critiques of Marriage?' (2010) 6 *Politics and Gender* 119–120

Acorn A, *Compulsory Compassion: A Critique of Restorative Justice* (University of British Columbia Press, Vancouver 2004)

Acorn A, 'Besieged by Beneficence: Love, Justice and the Autonomous Self' (2000) 63 *Saskatchewan Law Review* 69–86

Adamo S A, 'The Injustice of the Marital Rape Exemption: A Survey of Common Law Countries' (1989) 4 *American University Journal of International Law & Policy* 555–590

Amato P R, 'Institutional, Companionate, and Individualistic Marriages: Change Over Time and Implications for Marital Quality' in Garrison & Scott (eds), *Marriage at the Crossroads* 107–125

Anderson M J, 'Lawful Wife, Unlawful Sex: Examining the Effect of the Criminalization of Marital Rape in England and The Republic of Ireland' (1998) 27 *Georgia Journal of International & Comparative Law* 139–166

Anderson T, *The Movement and the Sixties* (Oxford University Press, New York 1995)

Aristotle, *Nicomachean Ethics* trans H Rackman Loeb Classical Library (Harvard University Press, Cambridge 1982)

Aristotle, *The Art of Rhetoric* trans J H Freese Loeb Classical Library (Harvard University Press, Cambridge 1975)

Atria F & N MacCormick (eds), *Law and Legal Interpretation* (Ashagate, Dartmouth 2003)

Auchmuty R, 'The Fiction of Equity' in Susan Scott-Hunt and Hilary Lim (eds), *Feminist Perspectives on Equity and Trusts* (Cavendish, London 2001)

Austin G W, 'Queering Family Law' (1999) 8 *Australasian Gay & Lesbian Law Journal* 39–56

Austin J, J Brown (ed), *The Austinian Theory of Law: Being an Edition of Lectures I, V and VI of Austin's 'Jurisprudence' and of Austin's 'Essay on the Uses of the Study of Jurisprudence'* (John Murray, London 1906)

Australian Bureau of Statistics, *Special Article: Marriage and Divorce in Australia* http://www.abs.gov.au/ausstats/abs@.nsf/0/AE4E953ED4BAA64DCA256C3 800817456?OpenDocument accessed 9/11/2010

Australian Journal of Family Law Developments and Events, 'Abolition of the Marital Rape Exemption at Common Law' (1992) 6 *Australian Journal of Family Law* 1–3

Averill J R, 'The Social Construction of Emotion' in K J Gergen & K E Davis (eds), *The Social Construction of the Person* (Springer, New York 1985) 89–109

Averill J R & P Boothroyd, 'On Falling in Love in Conformance with the Romantic Ideal' (1977) 1 *Motivation and Emotion* 235–247

Baird R & S E Rosenbaum (eds), *Same-Sex Marriage: the Moral and Legal Debate* (Prometheus Books, New York 1997)

Baker K K, 'Gender and Emotion in Criminal Law' (2005) 28 *Harvard Journal of Law & Gender* 447–466

Baker R, K J Wininger & F Elliston (eds), *Philosophy and Sex* (Prometheus Books, New York 1975)

Balkin J M, 'Understanding Legal Understanding: The Legal Subject and the Problem of Legal Coherence' (1993) 103 *Yale Law Journal* 105–176

Balos B & M L Fellows, 'Guilty of the Crime of Trust: Nonstranger Rape' (1991) 75 *Minnesota Law Review* 599–618

Banaker R & M Travers, (eds) *An Introduction to Law and Social Theory* (Hart, Oxford 2002)

Bandes S, (ed) *The Passions of Law* (New York University Press, New York 1999)

Bandes S, 'Empathy, Narrative and Victim Impact Statements' (1996) 63 *University of Chicago Law Review* 361–412

Bandes S, 'Fear Factor: The Role of Media in Covering and Shaping the Death Penalty' (2003–04) 1 *Ohio State Journal of Criminal Law* 585–598

Bandes S, 'Patterns of Injustice: Police Brutality in the Courts' (1999) 47 *Buffalo Law Review* 1275–1342

Bandes S, 'Repression and Denial in Criminal Lawyering' (2006) 9 *Buffalo Criminal Law Review* 339–390

Bandes S, 'What's Love Got To Do With it?' (2001) 8 *William & Mary Journal of Women & Law* 97–106

Bandes S, 'When Victims Seek Closure: Forgiveness, Vengeance, and the Role of Government' (2000) 27 *Fordham Urban Law Journal* 1599–1606

Barbalet J M, *Emotion, Social Theory, and Social Structure: A Macrosociological Approach* (Cambridge University Press, UK 1998)

Bartlett K, 'MacKinnon's Feminism: Power on Whose Terms?' (1987) 75 *California Law Review* 1559–1570

Barton C & K Painter, 'Rights and Wrongs of Marital Sex' (1991) 141 *New Law Journal* 394

Barton J L, 'The Story of Marital Rape' (1992) 108 *Law Quarterly Review* 260–271

Barwin-Legros B, 'Intimacy and the New Sentimental Order' (2004) 52 *Current Sociology* 241–250

Bateman M, 'Lesbians, Gays and Child Custody an Australian Legal History' (1992) 1 *Australasian Gay & Lesbian Law Journal* 47–72

Bauman Z, 'On Post Modern Uses of Sex' (1995) 15 *Theory Culture and Society* 19–34

Bayer B, 'Not Interaction But Melding — The Russian Dressing Theory of Emotions: An Explanation of the Phenomelogy of Emotions and Rationality with Suggested Related Maxims for Judges and Other Legal Decision Makers' *Mercer Law Review* (2000–01) 52 1033–1086

Beck U & E Beck-Gernsheim, *The Normal Chaos of Love* trans M Ritter and J Wiebel (Polity Press, Cambridge 1995)

Becker M, 'The Passions of Battered Women: Cognitive Links Between Passion Empathy and Power (2001–02) 8 *William & Mary Journal of Women & Law* 1–72

Bell D and J Binnie, *The Sexual Citizen: Queer Politics and Beyond* (Polity Press, Cambridge 2000) 128.

Benjamin D N, *The Home: Words, Interpretations, Meanings and Environments* (Avery, Aldershot 1995)

Bentham J, *An Introduction to the Principals of Morals and Legislation* J H Bruns & H L A Hart (eds) (Methuen, London 1982)

Bentham J, *A Comment on the Commentaries: A Criticism of the William Blackstone's Commentaries on the Laws of England* (Clarendon Press, Oxford 1978)

Bentham J, H L A Hart (ed), *An Introduction to the Principles of Morals and Legislation* (Methuen, London 1970)

Bentham J, H L A Hart (ed), *Of Laws in General* (Athalone Press, London 1970)

Berlant L (ed), *Intimacy* (University of Chicago Press, Chicago 2000)

Berlant L, 'Love: A Queer Feeling' in T Dean & C Lane (eds), *Psychoanalysis and Homosexuality* (Chicago University Press, Chicago 2000) 432–451

Berlant L, *The Queen of America Goes to Washington City: Essays on Sex and Citizenship* (Duke University Press, Durham 1997)

Berlant L & M Warner, 'Sex in Public' (1998) 24 *Critical Inquiry* 547–566

Berns S, 'Regulation of the Family: Whose Interests Does it Serve?' (1992) 1 *Griffith Law Review* 152–209

Bernstein A (ed), *Marriage Proposals: Questioning a Legal Status* (New York University Press, New York 2006)

Bersani L & A Phillips, *Intimacies* (University of Chicago Press, Chicago 2008)

Bix B, *A Dictionary of Legal Theory* (Oxford University Press, Oxford 2004)

Bix B, 'Bargaining in the Shadow of Love: The Enforcement of Premarital Agreements and How We Think About Marriage' (1998–1999) 40 *William & Mary Law Review* 145–208

Bix B (ed), *Analysing Law: New Essays in Legal Theory* (Clarendon Press, Oxford 1998)

Blackstone Sir William, *Commentaries on the Laws of England in Four Volumes*, vol 1 (Garland Publishing Inc, New York 1978)

Blackstone Sir William, *Commentaries on the Laws of England*, vol 1 fifteenth edition (T Cadell and W Davies, London 1809)

Blake S H, *Law of Marriage* (Barry Rose Publishers Ltd, Chichester 1982)

Bloxham C & M Picken, *Love and Marriage* (Webb & Bower, Exeter 1990)

Boden S & S J Williams, 'Consumption and Emotion: The Romantic Ethic Revisited' (2002) 36 *Sociology* 493–512

Borneman J, 'Caring and Being Cared For: Displacing Marriage, Kinship, Gender, and Sexuality' in J D Faubon (ed), *The Ethics of Kinship Ethnographic Inquiries* (Rowan & Little Field Publishers, Boston 2001) 29–46

Bottomley A, (ed) *Feminist Perspectives on the Foundational Subjects of Law* (Cavendish Publishing, London 1996)

Bottomley A & S Wong, (eds) *Changing Contours of Domestic Life, Family and Law: Caring and Sharing* (Hart Publishing, Oxford 2009)

Bottomly S & S Parker, *Law In Context* (Federation Press, Sydney 1997)

Bowen C, *The Lion and the Throne: The Life and Times of Sir Edward Coke* (1552–1634) (Little Brown, Boston 1980)

Boyd B (ed), *Challenging the Public/Private Divide: Feminism, Law and Public Policy* (University of Toronto Press, Toronto 1997)

Bradley G V, 'Law and the Culture of Marriage' (2004) 18 *Notre Dame Journal of Law Ethics & Public Policy* 189–217

Bradley G V, 'Same-Sex Marriage: Our Final Answer' (2000) 14 *Notre Dame Journal of Law Ethics & Public Policy* 729–752

Braithwaite J, 'Narrative and "Compulsory Compassion"'(2006) 31(2) *Law and Social Inquiry* 425–446

Brenna W J jnr, 'Reason, Passion and the "The Progress of Law"' (1988) 10 *Cardozo Law Review* 3–24

Brennan T & C Pateman, '"Mere Auxiliaries to the Commonwealth": Women and the Origins of Liberalism' (1979) 27 *Political Studies* 183–200

Brett P & L Waller, *Criminal Law: Text and Cases*, fourth edition (Butterworths, Sydney 1977)

Brett P, L Waller & C R Williams, *Criminal Law Texts and Cases*, sixth edition (Butterworths, Sydney 1989)

Bright S & J Dewar (eds), *Land Law Themes and Perspectives* (Oxford University Press, Oxford 1998)

Brown R, *Analyzing Love* (Cambridge University Press, New York 1987)

Bruckener P, *The Paradox of Love* trans S Randall (Princeton University Press, Princeton 2012)

Burnett G, 'The Life and Death of Sir Mathew Hale (South Hacehnsach, New Jersey 1972)

Busch R & N Robinson, '"What's Love Got to do With it?" An Analysis of an Intervention Approach to Domestic Violence' (1993) 1 *Waikato Law Review* 109–140

Butler J, 'Is Kinship Always Already Heterosexual?' (2002) 13 *Differences* 21–44

Butler J, 'Gendering the Body: Beauvoir's Philosophical Contributions' in Garry A & Pearsall M (eds), *Women Knowing and Reality: Explorations in Feminist Philosophy* (Unwin Hyman, Boston 1989) 253–62

Calhoun C, *Feminism, the Family, and the Politics of the Closet: Lesbian and Gay Displacement,* (Oxford University Press, New York 2000)

Calhoun C, 'Making Up Emotional People: The Case of Romantic Love' in Bandes (ed), *The Passions of Law* (New York University Press, New York 1999) 217–240

Calhoun C, 'Family's Outlaws: Rethinking the Connections Between Feminism, Lesbianism and the Family' in H Nelson (ed), *Feminism and Families* (Routledge, New York 1997) 131–150

Calhoun C, 'Sexuality Injustice' (1995) 9 *Notre Dame Journal of Law Ethics & Public Policy* 241–274

Calhoun C, 'Denaturalising and Desexualising Lesbian and Gay Identity' (1993) 79 *Virginia Law Review* 1859–1875

Calhoun C & R Solomon, *What is an Emotion?: Classical Readings in Philosophical Psychology* (Oxford University Press, New York 1984)

Campbell T, 'Grounding Theories of Legal Interpretation' in J Goldsworthy & T Campbell (eds), *Legal Interpretation and Democratic States* (Ashgate, Dartmouth 2002)

Capellanus A, *The Art of Courtly Love* trans J J Parry (Frederick Ungar Publishing, New York 1941)

Cartledge S & J Ryan, (eds) *Sex and Love: New Thoughts on Old Contradictions* (The Women's Press, London 1985)

Carver T, 'Through the Looking Glass: Wrongful Death, Remarriage and Australian Law Reform' (2005) 5 *QUT Law & Justice Journal* 1–27

Case M A, 'Couples and Coupling in the Public Sphere: A Comment on the Legal History of Litigating for Lesbian and Gay Rights' (1993) 79 *Virginia Law Review* 1643–1694

Chalmers A, *What Is This Thing Called Science?*, second edition (University of Queensland Press, St Lucia 1982)

Chambers D L & N D Polikoff, 'Family Law and Gay and Lesbian Family Issues in the Twentieth Century' (1999–2000) 33 *Family Law Quarterly* 523–544

Christian L K, *Becoming a Woman Through Romance* (Routledge, New York 1990)

Cobbe F 'Wife Torture in England' in *The Contemporary Review* April 1878 http://www.keele.ac.uk/history/currentundergraduates/tltp/WOMEN/ HANNAM/TEXT/HAN19IIA.HTM accessed 17/01/2013

Code L, (ed) *Encyclopedia of Feminist Theories* (Routledge, London 2000)

Coleman J & B Leiter, 'Determinacy, Objectivity and Authority' (1993)142 *University of Pennsylvania Law Review* 549–637

Coleman J L, 'Truth and Objectivity in Law' (1995) 1 *Legal Theory* 33–68

Collier B, 'The Rule in Yerkey v Jones: Fundamental Principles and Fundamental Problems' (1996) 4 *Australian Property Law Journal* 181–222

Collins M, *Modern Love: An Intimate History of Men and Women in Twentieth-Century Britain* (Atlantic Books, London 2003)

Collins R & S Coltrane, *Sociology of Marriage and the Family: Gender Love and Property* fourth edition (Nelson Hall Publishers, Chicago 1995)

Conway M, 'Equity's Darling?' in S Scott-Hunt & H Lim (eds), *Feminist Perspectives on Equity and Trusts* 43

Cook A E, 'The Death of God in American Pragmatism and Realism: Resurrecting the Value of Love in Contemporary Jurisprudence' (1993–94) 82 *Georgetown Law Journal* 1431–1518

Cook A E, 'Reflections on Post-Modernism' (1991–92) 26 *New England University Law Review* 751–782

Coontz S, *Marriage: A History — How Love Conquered Marriage* (Penguin Books, New York 2005)

Cooper D, 'For Richer or For Poorer, in Sickness and in Health: Should Australia Embrace Same-Sex Marriage?' [2005] 19 *Australian Journal of Family Law* http://www.lexisnexis.com/au/legal/search/homesubmitForm.do accessed 10/08/2010

Cotterrell R, *Politics of Jurisprudence: A Critical Introduction to Legal Philosophy*, second edition (Lexis Nexis, UK 2003)

Cotterrell R, *The Sociology of Law: An Introduction*, second edition (Butterworths, London 1992)

Craft-Ruben G & J G Heller, 'Restatement of Love' (1994) 104 *Yale Law Journal* 707–730

Crenshaw K (ed), *Critical Race Theory: The Key Writings that Formed the Movement* (The New Press, New York 1995)

D'Arcy M C, *The Mind and Heart of Love: Lion and Unicorn a Study in Eros and Agape* (Collins The Fontana Library, London 1962)

Daicoff S, *Law as Healing Profession: The 'Comprehensive Law Movement'* (New York Law School Clinical Research Institute Research paper series 05/06#12 http://cdn.law.ucla.edu/SiteCollectionDocuments/workshops%20and%20colloquia/clinical%20programs/susan%20daicoff.pdf accessed 17/07/10)

Dal Pont G, 'The Varying Shades of Unconscionable Conduct: Same Term Different Meaning' (1999) 19 *Australian Bar Review* 135–166

Darwin C, *The Expression of the Emotions in Man and Animals* (John Murray, London 1872: NY Philosophical Library 1955)

Davies M, *Asking the Law Question:The Dissolution of Legal Theory*, second edition (Lawbook Co, NSW 2002)

Davis G, B Sullivan & A Yeatman (eds), *The New Contractualism?* (Macmillan Education, Australia 1997)

Davis J M (ed), *A Handbook of the Troubadours* (University of California Press, Berkeley 1995)

De Lauretis T (ed), *Feminist Studies: Critical Studies* (Indiana University Press, Bloomington 1986)

De Rougemeont D, *Love in the Western World* trans M Belgion (Princeton University Press, Princeton [1983] c1956)

De Sousa R, 'The Rationality of Emotions' in Rorty A (ed), *Explaining Emotions* (University of California Press, Berkley 1980) 128–151

DeBeauvoir S, *The Second Sex* trans H M Parshley (Alfred A Knopf, New York 1953)

Deigh H, 'Nussbaum's Defence of the Stoic Theory of Emotions' (2000) 19 *Quarterly Law Review* 293–308

Delaney N, 'Love and Loving Commitment: Articulating a Modern Ideal' (1996) 33(4) *American Philosophical Quarterly* 339–356

Delgado R & J Stefancic, 'Critical Race Theory: An Annotated Bibliography' (1993) 79 *Virginia Law Review* 461–516

Delgado R, 'Storytelling for Oppositionists and Others' (1989) 87(8) *Michigan Law Review* 2411–41

Dickey A QC, 'Relief From the Performance of Marital Obligations' (1995) 69 *Australian Law Journal* 402–403

Diduck A & F Kaganas, *Family Law, Gender and the State: Text, Cases and Materials* (Hart, Oxford 2006)

Diski J, *The Sixties* (Profile, London 2009)

Dixon T, *From Passions to Emotions: The Creation of a Secular Psychological Category* (Cambridge University Press, Cambridge 2003)

Dobson J C, 'Marriage is the Foundation of the Family' (2004) 18 *Notre Dame Journal of Law Ethics & Public Policy* 1–6

Douglas C A, *Love and Politics: Radical Feminist and Lesbian Theories* (Ism Press, San Francisco 1990)

Douglas K S, D R Lyon & J R Ogloff, 'The Impact of Graphic Photographic Evidence on Mock Jurors' Decisions in a Murder Trial: Probative or Prejudicial?' (1997) 21 *Law and Human Behaviour* 489–509

Douzinas C, *Law and the Emotions: Prolegomena for a Psychoanalytic Approach to Legal Studies* (European University Institute, EUI Working Paper 1998/8)

Douzinas C & A Gearey, *Critical Jurisprudence the Political Philosophy of Justice* (Hart, Oxford 2005)

Douzinas C & R Warrington, *Justice Miscarried: Ethics and Aesthetics in Law* (Harvester Wheatsheaf, New York 1994)

Douzinas C, P Goodrich & Y Hachamovitch, *Politics, Postmodernity and Critical Legal Studies: The Legality of the Contingent* (Routledge, London 1994)

Douzinas C, R Warrington with S McVeigh, *Postmodern Jurisprudence: The Law of Text in the Texts of Law* (Routledge, London 1991)

Dovey K, 'Home: An Ordering Principle in Space' (1978) 22 *Landscape* 27–30

Dunn K, 'Yakking Giants': Equality Discourse in the High Court' (2000) 24 *Melbourne University Law Review* 427–461

Dunn K, 'Splitting the Difference: Superannuation, Equality and Family Law' (1998) 12 *Australian Journal of Family Law* 214–239

Dworkin R, 'Objectivity and Truth: You'd Better Believe it' (1996) 25 *Philosophy and Public Affairs* 87–139

Dworkin A, *Intercourse* (The Free Press, New York 1987)

Dworkin A, *Right Wing Women* (Wideview/Perigree Books, New York 1983)

Easteal P, 'Marital Rape: Conflicting Constructions of Reality' (1997) 3 *Women Against Violence: An Australian Feminist Journal* 23–30

Eichner M, 'Marriage and the Elephant: The Liberal Democratic State's Regulation of Intimate Relationships Between Adults' (2007) 30 *Harvard Journal of Law & Gender* 25–66

Eisenberg M A, 'The World of Contract and the World of Gift' (1997) 85 *California Law Review* 821– 866

Eskridge W N jnr, 'A History of Same-Sex Marriage' (1993) 79 *Virginia Law Review* 1419–1513

Estrich S, 'Rape' (1985–86) 95 *Yale Law Journal* 1087–1184

Evans D, *Emotions: The Science of Sentiment* (Oxford University Press, Oxford 2001)

Evans D & P Cruse, *Emotion, Evolution and Rationality* (Oxford University Press, Oxford 2004)

Evans M, 'A Critical Lens on Romantic Love: A Response to Bernadette Barwin Legros' (2004) 52 *Current Sociology* 259–264

Evans M, 'Book Review: Talk of Love How Culture Matters' (2005) 39 *Sociology* 172–173

Evans M, 'Falling in Love is Falling for Make Believe: Ideologies of Romance in Post-Enlightenment Culture' (1998) 15 *Theory Culture and Society* 265–276

Faubion J, (ed) *The Ethics of Kinship: Ethnographic Inquiries* (Rowland & Littlefield, Maryland 2001)

Featherstone M, 'Love and Eroticism: An Introduction', special edition (1998) 15 *Theory Culture and Society* 1–18

Fehlberg B, *Sexually Transmitted Debt: Surety Experience and English Law* (Clarendon Press, Oxford 1997)

Fehlberg B, 'Women in "Family" Companies: English and Australian Experiences' (1997) 15 *Company and Securities Law Journal* 348–365

Fehlberg B, 'The Husband, the Bank, the Wife and her Signature the Sequel' (1996) 59 *Modern Law Review* 675–694

Fehlberg B, 'The Husband, the Bank, the Wife and her Signature' (1994) 57 *Modern Law Review* 467–75

Fehlbergh B & J Behrens, *Australian Family Law: The Contemporary Context — Teaching Materials* (Oxford University Press, Victoria 2009)

Fehlbergh B & J Behrens with R Kaspiew, *Australian Family Law: The Contemporary Context* (Oxford University Press, Victoria 2008)

Feigenson N R, 'Sympathy and Legal Judgement: A Psychological Analysis' (1997) 65 *Tennessee Law Review* 1–78

Feldman H L, 'Law Psychology and Emotions' (2000) 74 *Chicago-Kent Law Review* 1423–1430

Feldman H L, 'Objectivity in Legal Judgement' (1994) 92 *Michigan Law Review* 1187–1255

Fierstein H, *Torch Song Trilogy* (Villard Books, New York 1983 c 1979)

Fineman M A, 'The Meaning of Marriage' in A Bernstein (ed), *Marriage Proposals: Questioning Legal Status* (New York University Press, New York 2006)

Fineman M A, *The Autonomy Myth: Theory of Dependency* (New York Press, New York 2004)

Fineman M A, 'Contract, Marriage and Background Rules' in B Bix (ed), *Analysing Law: New Essays in Legal Theory* (Clarendon Press, Oxford 1998)

Fineman M A, (ed) *Mothers in Law: Feminist Theory and the Legal Regulation of Motherhood* (Columbia University Press, New York 1995)

Fineman M A, *The Neutered Mother, The Sexual Family and Other Twentieth Century Tragedies* (Routledge, New York 1995)

Fineman M A, 'The Neutered Mother' (1991–1992) 46 *University of Miami Law Review* 653–669

Finlay H A, *To Have But Not to Hold: A History of Attitudes to Marriage and Divorce in Australia 1858–1975* (Federation Press, NSW 2005)

Finlay H A, 'Divorce and The Status of Women: Beginnings in Nineteenth Century Australia' 20 Sept 2001 Australian Institute of Family Studies seminar paper www.aifs.gov.au/institute/seminar/finlay.html accessed 21/03/2013

Finnis J, 'The Good of Marriage and the Morality of Sexual Relations: Some Philosophical and Historical Observations' (1997) 42 *American Journal of Jurisprudence* 97–134

Finnis J, 'Law, Morality and "Sexual Orientation"' (1995) 9 *Notre Dame Journal of Law Ethics and Public Policy* 11–39

Finnis J, *Natural Law and Natural Rights* (Clarendon Press, Oxford 1980)

Firestone S, *The Dialectic of Sex: The Case for Feminist Revolution* (Bantam Books, New York 1970)

Fisher H, *Why We Love the Nature and Chemistry of Romantic Love* (Henry Holt and Company, New York 2004)

Fiss O M, 'Reason In all Its Splendor' (1990) 56 *Brook Law Review* 789–804

Fitzpatrick P, *Mythology of Modern Law* (Routledge, London 1992)

Foorde K, 'Imagine There are no Lesbians: Psychoanalysis, Queer Theory and the Legal Recognition of Same-Sex Parenting' (2007) 27 *Australian Feminist Law Journal* 3–22

Foucault M, *The History of Sexuality* trans R Hurley (Pantheon Books, New York 1987)

Fox L, *Conceptualising Home* (Hart, Oxford 2007)

Franke K, 'The Curious Relationship of Marriage and Freedom' in Garrison & Scott (eds), *Marriage at the Crossroads* 87–106

Fraser D, 'What a Long, Strange Trip It's Been: Deconstructing Law From Legal Realism to Critical Legal Studies' (1988–89) *Australian Journal of Law & Society* 35–43

Fraser D, 'What's Love Got to do With it?: Critical Legal Studies, Feminist Discourse, and the Ethic of Solidarity' (1988) 11 *Harvard Women's Law Journal* 53–82

Freeman M, 'Contracting in the Haven: *Balfour v Balfour* Revisited' in Halson R (ed), *Exploring the Boundaries of Contract* (Dartmouth, Aldershot 1996)

Freeman M A, (ed) *Lloyd's Introduction to Jurisprudence*, seventh edition (Sweet and Maxwell, London 2001)

French P A & H K Wettstein, *The Philosophy of Emotion*, Midwest Studies in Philosophy XXII (University of Notre Dame, Indiana 1998)

Frew C, 'The Social Construction of Marriage in Australia' (2011) 28 *Law in Context* 81

Fridja N H & J M Robinson, 'Bob Solomon's Legacy' (2010) 2 *Emotion Review* 2–4

Friedell D, 'But Stoney Was Bold' 31(4) *London Review of Books* 17–18

Friedman M, *Autonomy, Gender, Politics* (Oxford University Press, New York 2003)

Friedman M, 'Romantic Love and Personal Autonomy' in French P A & H K Wettstein (eds), *Midwest Studies in Philosophy, XXII (1998): The Philosophy of Emotion* (University of Notre Dame Press, Indiana 1998) 162–181

Fudge J & R Owens (eds), *Precarious Work, Women, and the New Economy: The Challenge to Legal Norms* (Hart, Oxford 2006)

Fus T, 'Criminalizing Marital Rape: A Comparison of Judicial and Legislative Approaches' (2006) 39 *Vanderbilt Journal of Transnational Law* 481–517

Gajowski E, *The Art of Loving: Female Subjectivity and Male Discursive Traditions in Shakespeare's Tragedies* (University of Delaware Press, Delaware 1992)

Gallagher M, 'Rites, Rights and Social Institutions: Why and How Should the Law Support Marriage?' (2004) 18 *Notre Dame Journal of Law Ethics and Public Policy* 225–241

Gardner J, *The Logic of Excuses and the Rationality of Emotions* (University of Oxford Legal Research Papers 35/2008)

Gardner S, 'Rethinking Family Property' (1993) 109 *Law Quarterly Review* 263–300

Garrison M & E S Scott (eds), *Marriage at the Crossroads: Law, Policy and the Brave New World of Twentieth Century Families* (Cambridge University Press, Cambridge 2012)

Garton S, *Histories of Sexualities* (Equinox Publishing, London 2004)

George R P & G V Bradley, 'Marriage and the Liberal Imagination' (1995) 84 *Georgetown Law Journal* 301–320

Gerwitz P, 'On "I Know it When I See it"' (1996) 105 *Yale Law Journal* 1023–1047

Giddens A, *The Transformation of Intimacy: Sexuality Love and Eroticism in Modern Societies* (Polity Press, Cambridge 1992)

Gilligan G, *In a Different Voice: Psychological Theory and Women's Development* (Harvard University Press, Cambridge Massachusetts 1982)

Glasman C, 'Women Judge the Courts' (1991) 141 *New Law Journal* 395

Goldie P, 'Love for a Reason' (2010) 2 *Emotion Review* 61–67

Goldman E, 'Marriage and Love' in A K Sullivan (ed), *Red Emma Speaks: Selected Writings and Speeches* (Random House, New York 1972)

Goldsworthy J, 'Legislative Intentions, Legislative Supremacy, and Legal Positivism' in J Goldsworthy & T Campbell (eds), *Legal Interpretation and Democratic States* (Ashgate, Dartmouth 2002)

Goode W, 'The Theoretical Importance of Love' (1959) 24 *American Sociological Review* 38–47

Goodrich P, *The Laws of Love: A Brief Historical and Practical Manual* (Palgrave Macmillan, London, 2006)

Goodrich P, 'Erotic Melancholia: Law Literature, and Love' (2002) 14 *Law & Literature* 103– 129

Goodrich P, 'Amatory Jurisprudence and the Querelles des Lois' (2000) 76 *Chicago-Kent Law Review* 751–778

Goodrich P, 'Reviews Hanne Peterson (ed) Love and Law in Europe' (2000) 63 *Modern Law Review* 134–137

Goodrich P, 'The Laws of Love: Literature, History and the Governance of Kissing' (1998) 24 *New York University Review of Law & Social Change* 183–234

Goodrich P, 'Epistolary Justice: The Love Letter as Law' (1997) 9 *Yale Journal of Law & Humanities* 245–295

Goodrich P, 'Law in the Courts of Love: Andreas Capellanus and the Judgements of Love' (1996) 48 *Stanford Law Review* 633–675

Goodrich P, *Law in the Courts of Love: Literature and Other Minor Jurisprudences* (Routledge, London 1996)

Goodrich P, 'Gynaetopia: Feminine Genealogies of Common Law' (1993) 20 *Journal of Law & Society* 276–308

Goodrich P, 'Poor Illiterate Reason: History, Nationalism and Common Law' (1992) 1 *Social and Legal Studies* 7–28

Goodrich P, 'Law and Modernity' (1986) 49 *Modern Law Review* 545–559

Goodwin R, *Personal Relationships Across Cultures* (Routledge, USA 1999).

Graft Rubin G & J M Heller, 'Restatement of Love (tentative draft)' (1994–95) 104 *Yale Law Journal* 707–730

Graycar R, 'Love's Labour's Cost: the High Court Decision in Van *Gervan v Fenton*' (1993) 1 *Torts Law Journal* 122–136

Graycar R & J Millbank, 'From Functional Family to Spinster Sisters: Australia's Distinctive Path to Relationship Recognition' (2007) 24 *Journal of Law and Policy* 160–61

Graycar R & J Morgan, *The Hidden Gender of Law*, second edition (Federation Press, Sydney 2002)

Green K & H Lim, 'Weaving Along the Borders: Public and Private, Women and Banks' in S Scott-Hunt & H Lim (eds), *Feminist Perspectives on Equity and Trusts* (Cavendish, London 2001) 85–109

Green P, 'Homobesottedness' 8 May 2008 *London Review of Books* 21–23

Greenlee M B, 'Echoes of the Love Command in the Halls of Justice' (1995–96) 12 *Journal of Law and Religion* 255–270

Greer G, *The Female Eunuch* (Grafton Books, London 1971)

Grenfell L, 'Making Sex: Law's Narratives of Sex, Gender and Identity (2003) 23 *Legal Studies* 66–102

Griffin S M & R Moffat, *Radical Critiques of Law* (University Press of Kansas, Kansas 1997)

Grisez G, *The Way of the Lord Jesus,* vol 2: Living a Christian Life (Franciscan Press, Quincy University 1993)

Guggisberg M, 'Intimate Partner Violence: A Significant Risk Factor for Female Suicide' (2008) 20 *Women Against Violence: An Australian Feminist Journal* 9–17

Haigh R & S Hepburn, 'Bank Manager Always Rings Twice: Stereotyping in Equity After Garcia' (2000) 26 *Monash University Law Review* 275–311

Hale Sir Matthew, *History of the Pleas of the Crown 1736* vols 1–2 P R Glazebrook (ed) (Professional Books LTD, London 1971)

Hale Sir Matthew, *The History of the Common Law of England* CM Gray (ed) (University of Chicago Press, Chicago 1971)

Halley J, 'Behind the Law of Marriage (I): From Status/Contract to the Marriage System' (2010) 6 *Unbound* 1–58

Harris A, 'Race and Essentialism in Feminist Legal Theory' (1990) 42 *Stanford Law Review* 581–616

Harris A P & M M Shultz, 'A(nother) Critique of Pure Reason: Toward Civic Virtue in Legal Education' (1993) 45 *Stanford Law Review* 1773–1805

Harris J W, 'Unger's Critique of Formalism in Legal Reasoning: Hero, Hercules and Humdrum' (1989) *52 Modern Law Review* 42–63

Harrison M, 'Australia's Family Law Act: The First Twenty-Five Years' (2002) 16 *International Journal of Law Policy and the Family* 1–21

Harrison M, 'The Legal System and De Facto Relationships' (1991) 30 *Family Matters* 30–33

Hartog H, 'What Gay Marriage Teaches About the History of Marriage' http://historynewsnetwork.com/articles/4400.html accessed 26/06/2006

Hasday J E, 'Intimacy and Economic Exchange' (2005) 119 *Harvard Law Review* 491–530

Hazo R G, *The Idea of Love* (Frederick A Prager Publishers, New York 1967)

Hedley S, 'Keeping Contract in its Place: Balfour v Balfour and the Enforceability of Informal Agreements' (1985) 5 *Oxford Journal of Law and Society* 391–415

Helm B W, *Emotional Reason: Deliberation, Motivation, and the Nature of Value* (Cambridge University Press, Cambridge 2001)

Henderson L, 'The Dialogue of the Heart and Head' (1988–89) 10 *Cardozo Law Review* 123–148

Henderson L, 'Legality and Empathy' (1986–87) 85 *Michigan Law Review* 1574–1654

Hendrick S & C Hendrick, *Romantic Love* (Sage Publications, Newbury Park 1992)

Hewitt B and J Baxter, 'Who Gets Married in Australia?: The Characteristics Associated with a Transition Into First Marriage 2001–6' (2012) 48 *Journal of Sociology* 43–61

Hill Collins P, *Black Feminist Thought: Knowledge, Consciousness and the Politics of Empowerment* (Unwin Hyman, Boston 1991)

Hirshman L R & J E Larson, *Hard Bargains: The Politics of Sex* (Oxford University Press, New York 1999)

Hoeflich M H, 'Law and Geometry: Legal Science from Leibniz to Langdell' (1986) 30 *American Journal of Legal History* 95–121

Hoffman Baruch E, *Women Love and Power Literary and Psychoanalytic Perspectives* (New York University Press, New York 1991)

Holbrook E, 'The Changing Meaning of Consortium' (1923) 22 *Michigan Law Review* 1–9

Holcombe L, *Wives and Property: Reform of the Married Women's Property Law in Nineteenth Century England* (Martin Robertson, Oxford 1983)

Hollibaugh A, 'Desire for the Future: Radical Hope' in Vance (ed), *Pleasure and Danger* 403–04

Holmes A S, 'The Double Standard in the English Divorce Laws, 1857–1923' (1995) 20(2) *Law and Social Inquiry* 601–620

Honore T, *Sex and Law* (Duckworth, London 1978)

Horder J, 'Cognition, Emotion, and Criminal Culpability' (1990) 106 *Law Quarterly Review* 469–486

Huang P H, 'Reasons With Passions: Emotions and Intentions in Property Rights Bargaining Critical Approaches to Property Institutions' (2000) 79 *Oregon Law Review* 435–478

Hudson A, *New Perspectives in Property Law, Human Rights and the Home* (Cavendish Publishing, London 2004)

Hunt A, *Explorations in Law and Society: Towards a Constitutive Theory of Law* (Routledge, New York 1993)

Hunt A, 'The Theory of Critical Legal Studies' (1986) 6 *Oxford Journal of Law and Society* 1–45

Hunter R, 'Decades of Panic' (2005–06) 10 *Griffith Review* 55–63

Hunter R, R Ingleby & R Johnstone, *Thinking About Law: Perspectives on the History, Philosophy and Sociology of Law* (Allen & Unwin, NSW 1995)

Huntington C, 'Repairing Family Law' (2008) 57 *Duke Law Journal* 1244–1319

Hutchinson A, *Dwelling on the Threshold* (Carswell Company, Toronto 1988)

Illouz E, *Why Love Hurts: A Sociological Explanation* (Polity, Cambridge 2012)

Illouz E, 'The Lost Innocence of Love: Romance as a Postmodern Condition' (1998) 15 *Theory Culture and Society* 161–186

Illouz E, *Consuming the Romantic Utopia: Love and the Cultural Contradictions of Capitalism* (University of California Press, Berkeley 1997)

Ingraham C, 'Book Review: Revolutions of the Heart — Gender, Power and Delusions of Love' (2001) 1 *Feminist Theory* 131–132

Jackson S, 'Even Sociologists Fall in Love: An Exploration in the Sociology of Emotions' (1993) 27 *Sociology* 201–220

Jackson S, 'Love and Romance as Objects of Feminist Knowledge' in M Kennedy, C Lubelska & V Walsh (eds), *Making Connections: Women's Studies, Women's Movements, Women's Lives* (Taylor & Francis, London 1993)

Jackson S, *Heterosexuality in Question* (Sage Publications, London 1999)

Jacose A, *Queer Theory* (Melbourne University Press, Victoria 1996)

Jagger A M, 'Love and Knowledge: Emotion in Feminist Epistemology' in G Lloyd (ed), *The Man of Reason: Male and Female in Western Philosophy*, second edition (Routledge, London 1993) 129–155

Jaggar A M, 'Love and Knowledge: Emotion in Feminist Epistemology' in A Garry and M Pearsall (eds), *Women Knowledge and Reality: Explorations in Feminist Philosophy* (Unwin Hyman, Boston 1989)

Jagger A M & I M Young (eds), *A Companion to Feminist Philosophy* (Blackwell, Massachusetts 1998)

James W, *Principles of Psychology* (Dover Publications, New York 2001)

Jamieson L, 'Intimacy Transformed? A Critical Look at the Pure Relationship' (1993) 33 *Sociology* 477–494

Jeffrey S, *Anticlimax: A Feminist Perspective on the Sexual Revolution* (New York University Press, New York 1990)

Johnson P, *Love, Heterosexuality and Society* (Routledge, London 2005)

Johnson P & S Lawler, 'Coming Home to Love and Class' *Sociological Research Online* (2005) 10(3) www.socresonline.org.uk/10/3/johnson.html accessed 16/10/2009

Jonasdottir A, 'What Kind of Power is Love Power?' in A Jonasdottir *et al* (eds), *Sexuality, Gender and Power* (Routledge, London 2011)

Jonasdottir A & A Ferguson, (eds) *Love a Question for Feminism in the Twentieth Century* (Routledge, Oxon 2014)

Jones C, *Expert Witnesses: Science, Medicine and the Practice of Law* (Clarendon Press, Oxford 1994)

Jones O D, 'Law, Emotions and Behavioural Biology' (1999) 39 *Jurimetrics* 283–290

Josephson J, 'Romantic Weddings, Diverse Families' (2010) 6(1) *Politics and Gender* 128–133

Joske P E, *Joske's Marriage and Divorce,* vol 2: Matrimonial Causes, fourth edition (Butterworths, Sydney 1961)

Kahan D M, (1999) 'The Progressive Appropriation of Disgust' in S Bandes (ed), *The Passions of Law* (New York University Press, New York 1999)

Kahn-Freund O, 'Inconsistencies and Injustices in the Law of Husbands and Wife' (1952) 15 *Modern Law Review* 133–154

Kaspiew R, 'Rape Lore: Legal Narrative and Sexual Violence' (1995–96) 20 *Melbourne University Law Review* 350–382

Kaye M, 'Equity's Treatment of Sexually Transmitted Debt' [1997] 5(1) *Feminist Legal Studies* 35–55

Keller S, 'Viewing and Doing: Complicating Pornography's Meaning' (1993) 81 *Georgia Law Journal* 2195–2242

Kemp S & J Squires (eds), *Feminisms* (Oxford University Press, Oxford 1997)

Keren H, 'Considering Affective Consideration'(2009–10) 40 *Golden Gate University Law Review* 165–234

Keyes M & K Burns, 'Contract and the Family: Wither Intention?' (2002) 26 *Melbourne University Law Review* 577–595

Kindregan C P jnr, 'Same-Sex Marriage: The Cultural Wars and the Lessons of Legal History' (2004–05) 38 *Family Law Quarterly* 427–448

Kirby M, Hon Justice, 'But the Greatest of These is Love' address Griffith University 16/12/2008 http://www.nbpatterson.com/Influences/Justice_Michael_Kirby/justice_michael_kirby accessed 12/05/2010

Kittay E F, *Love's Labour: Essays of Women, Equality and Dependency* (Routledge, New York 1999)

Koedt A & E Levine & A Rapone (eds), *Radical Feminism* (Quadrangle Books, New York 1973)

Koff G, *Love and the Law* (Simon Schuster, New York 1988)

Koppleman A, 'Is Marriage Inherently Heterosexual?' (1997) 42 *American Journal of Jurisprudence* 51–95

Kravaritou Y, *Love and Law in Europe: Complex Interrelations* (European Institute, EUI Working Paper 2000/02)

Krusman R L, 'Judicial Personality: Rhetoric and Emotion in Supreme Court Opinions (2002) 59 *Washington & Lee Law Review* 193–236

Kutz C L, 'Just Disagreement: Indeterminacy and Rationality in the Rule of Law' (1994) 103 *Yale Law Journal* 997–1030

Labbe J, *The Romantic Paradox: Love, Violence and the Uses of Romance* (St Martins' Press, New York 2000)

Laird J, 'Lesbian and Gay Families' in F Walsh (ed), *Normal Family Processes*, second edition (Guilford Press, New York 1993)

Langhamer C, 'Love and Courtship in Mid-Twentieth-Century England' (2007) 50 *The Historical Journal* 173–196

Langford W, 'Gender, Power and Self-Esteem: Women's Poverty in the Economy of Love' (1994) 3 *Feminist Theology* 94–115

Langford W, *Revolutions of the Heart: Gender, Power and the Delusions of Love* (Routledge, London 1999)

Laquer T W, *Making Sex: Body and Gender From the Greeks to Freud* (Harvard University Press, Cambridge 1990)

Larcombe W, *Compelling Engagements: Feminism, Rape Law and Romance Fiction* (Federation Press, Sydney 2005)

Larcombe W & M Heath, 'Case Note Developing the Common Law and Rewriting the History of Rape in Marriage in Australia: *PGA v The Queen*' (2012) 34 *Sydney Law Review* 785–807

Laster K & P O'Malley, 'Sensitive New Age Laws: the Reassertion of Emotionality in Law' (1996) 24 *International Journal of the Sociology of Law* 21–40

Lauw I, 'Recognition of Same-Sex Marriage: Time for Change?'(1993) 3 *Murdoch University Electronic Journal of Law* http://www.austlii.edu.au/au/journals/MurUEJL/1994/13.html accessed 29/06/10

Lee K, *The Positivist Science of Law* (Avebury, Aldershot 1989)

Lee P & R P George, 'What Sex Can Be: Self Alienation, Illusion or One-Flesh Union' (1997) 42 *American Journal of Jurisprudence* 135–157

Leiter B (ed), *Objectivity in Law and Morals* (Cambridge University Press, Cambridge 2001)

Leiter B, 'Book Review: Objectivity and the Problem of Jurisprudence' (1993) 72 *Texas Law Review* 187–209

Leites E, 'The Duty to Desire: Love, Friendship, and Sexuality in Some Puritan Theories of Marriage' (1982) 15 *Journal of Social History* 383–408

Leonard J & M Ashe (eds), *Legal Studies as Cultural Studies: A Reader in (Post) Modern Critical Theory* (State University of New York Press, Albany 1995)

Levy T M, 'At the Intersection of Intimacy and Care: Redefining Family Through the Lens of a Public Ethic of Care' (2005) 1(1) *Politics and Gender* 65–95

Lim H, 'Messages From a Rarely Visited Island: Duress and Lack of Consent in Marriage' (1996) 4(2) *Feminist Legal Studies* 196–220

Lindenmayer T E, hon justice, 'When Bankruptcy and Family Law Collide' (1994) 8 *Australian Journal of Family Law* 111–140

Lindon Shanley M, *Feminism, Marriage and the Law in England, 1850–1895* (Princeton University Press, Princeton New Jersey 1989)

Little L E, 'Adjudication and Emotion' (2002) 3 *Florida Coastal Law Journal* 205–218

Little L E, 'Negotiating the Tangle of Love and Law' (2001) 86 *Cornell Law Review* 974–1001

Little M R, 'Consortium: A Survey of the Present Law' (1980–81) 19 *Journal of Family Law* 707–727

Lloyd G, *The Man of Reason: Male and Female in Western Philosophy*, second edition (Routledge, London 1993)

Lloyd G, 'The Man of Reason' in A Garry & M Pearsall (eds), *Women Knowledge and Reality: Explorations in Feminist Philosophy* (Boston Unwin Hyman, London 1989) 111–128

Luban D, 'Reason and Passion in Legal Ethics' (1999) 51 *Stanford Law Review* 873–901

Luhman N, *A Sociological Theory of Law,* trans E King & M Albrow (Routledge & Kegan Paul, London 1985)

Luhman N, *Love as Passion: The Codification of Intimacy*, trans J Gaines & D L Jones (Polity Press, Cambridge 1986)

Lyndon-Shanley M, *Just Marriage* J Cohen & D Chasman (eds) (Oxford University Press, New York 2004)

Lystra K, *Searching the Heart: Women, Men, and Romantic Love in Nineteenth-Century America* (Oxford University Press, New York 1989)

Macedo S, 'Homosexuality and the Conservative Mind' (1995–96) 84 *Georgetown Law Journal* 261–300

MacKinnon C, 'Feminism, Marxism, Method and the State: An Agenda for Theory' (1982) 7 *Signs* 515–544

MacKinnon C A, *Towards a Feminist Theory of the State* (Harvard University Press, Cambridge Massachusetts 1989)

MacKinnon K, *Feminism Unmodified: Discourses on Life and Law* (Harvard University Press, Cambridge 1987)

Mahoney J, 'Objectivity, Interpretation, and Rights: A Critique of Dworkin' (2004) 23 *Legal Philosophy* 187–222

Majumbar R, *Marriage and Modernity: Family Values in Colonial Bengal* (Duke University Press, Durham London 2009)

Manalansaniv F, 'Queer Love in the Time of War and Shopping' in G E Haggerty & M McGarry (eds), *A Companion to Lesbian, Gay, Bisexual, Transgender, and Queer Studies* (Blackwell Publishing, MA 2007) 77–86

Marazziti D, H S Kiskal, A Rossi & G B Cassano, 'Alternation of the Platelet Serotonin Transporter in Romantic Love' (1999) 29 *Psychological Medicine* 741–745

Marcus S, 'Fighting Bodies, Fighting Words: A Theory and Politics of Rape Prevention' in J W Scott and J Butler (eds), *Feminists Theorise the Political* (Routledge, New York 1992)

Marmor A, 'An Essay on The Objectivity of Law' in *Analyzing Law: New Essays in Legal Theory* B Bix (ed) (Clarendon Press, Oxford 1998)

Marmor A (ed), *Law and Interpretation: Essays in Legal Philosophy* (Clarendon Press, Oxford 1995)

Marmor A (ed), *Positive Law and Interpretation Essays in Legal Philosophy* (Clarendon Press, Oxford 1995)

Marmor A, *Positive Law and Objective Values* (Clarendon Press, Oxford 2001)

Maroney T, 'The Persistent Cultural Script of Judicial Dispassion' (2011) *California Law Review* 629–294

Maroney T, 'Law and Human Emotion: A Proposed Taxonomy of an Emerging Field'(2006) 30 *Law and Human Behaviour*, special issue on Emotion in Legal Judgement 119–142

Marriage Movement, 'The Marriage Movement's Statement of Principles' http://www.americanvalues.org/pdfs/marriagemovement.pdf accessed 23/08/2010

Marso L J, 'Marriage and Bourgeois Respectability' (2010) 6(1) *Politics and Gender* 145–154

Mason Sir Anthony, 'Future Directions in Australian Law' (1987) 13 *Monash University Law Review* 149–163

Massaro T M, 'Shame Culture and American Criminal Law' (1991) 89 *Michigan Law Review* 1880–1944

Massaro T M, 'Empathy, Legal Storytelling, and the Rule of Law: New Words, Old Wounds' (1988–89) 87 *Michigan Law Review* 2099–2127

May S, *Love: A History* (Yale University Press, New Haven 2011)

McClain L C, 'What Place for Marriage (E)quality in Marriage Promotion?' in Bernstein (ed), *Marriage Proposals* 106–144.

Mc Convill J & E Mills, '*Re Kevin*: Gender Dysphoria and the Right to Marry' *University of Western Sydney Law Review* (2002) 6 http://www.austlii.edu.au/cgibin/sinodisp/au/jounrals/UWSLRev/2002/10.html?quer accessed 27/02/2008

McCoin S, 'Law and Sex Status: Implementing the Concept of Sexual Property' (1997–98) 19 *Women's Rights Law Reporter* 237–245

Mellen S L W, *The Evolution of Love* (W H Freeman and Co, Oxford 1907)

Mendus S, *Feminism and Emotion: Readings in Moral and Political Philosophy* (MacMillan Press Ltd, GB 2000)

Mertus J, 'Human Rights of Women in Central and Eastern Europe' (1998) 6 *American University Journal of Gender & Law* 369–484

Metz T, 'Demands of Care and Dilemmas of Freedom: What We Really Ought to be Worried About' (2010) 6(1) *Politics and Gender* 121–22

Meyers D T, *Feminist Social Thought: A Reader* (Routledge, New York 1997)

Milulinger M & G S Goodman (eds), *Dynamics of Romantic Love: Attachment, Caregiving,* and Sex (Guildford Press, New York 2006)

Mill J S, *The Subjection of Women* S M Okin (ed)(Hackett Publishing Co, Indianapolis 1988)

Millbank J, 'Recognition of Lesbian and Gay Families in Australian Law: Part One — Couples' (2006) vol 34(1) *Federal Law Review* 2–44

Millbank J, 'Recognition of Lesbian and Gay Families in Australian Law: Part Two — Children' (2006) vol 34(1) *Federal Law Review* 205–259

Millbank J, 'If Australia Opened Its Eyes to Lesbian and Gay Families, What Would It See?' (1998) 12 *Australian Journal of Family Law* 99–139

Millbank J, '"Which, then would be the 'husband' and which the 'wife' ?": Some Introductory Thoughts on Contesting "The Family" in Court' (1996) 3(3) *Murdoch University Electronic Journal of Law* http://www.murdoch.edu.au/elaw/issues/v3n3/millbank.html accessed 5/11/10

Millbank J, 'Lesbian Mothers, Gay Fathers: Sameness and Difference' (1992) 2 *Australasian Gay & Lesbian Law Journal* 21–40

Milson S F C, *The Nature of Blackstone's Achievement* (Seldon Society, London 1981)

Moore W, *Wedlock* (Weidenfeld, London 2009)

Moran R F, 'Law and Emotion, Love and Hate' (2000–2001) 11 *Journal Contemporary Legal Issues* 747–784

Morgan S, 'Legal Recognition of Gay and Lesbian Relationships' (1993) 3 *Australasian Gay & Lesbian Law Journal* 57–66

Morgan W, 'Queer Law: Identity, Culture, Diversity, Law' (1995) 5 *Australasian Gay & Lesbian Law Journal* 1–44

Morris J H C, 'The Australian Matrimonial Causes Act, 1959' (1962) 11 *International and Comparative Law Quarterly* 641–650

Mount F, *The Subversive Family: An Alternative History of Love and Marriage* (Jonathon Cape, London 1982)

Mulcahy L & S Wheeler (eds), *Feminist Perspectives on Contract Law* (Glasshouse Press, London 2005)

Murphy J G & Hampton J, *Forgiveness and Mercy* (Cambridge University Press, Cambridge 1998)

Murphy W T & H Clark, *The Family Home* (Sweet Maxwell, London 1983)

Myers B, S Jay Lynn & J Arbuthnot, 'Victim Impact Testimony and Juror Judgements: The Effects of Harm Information and Witness Demeanour' (2002) 32 *Journal of Applied Social Psychology* 2393–2412

Naffine N, *Feminism and Criminology* (Polity Press, Cambridge 1997)

Naffine N, 'Possession: Erotic Love in the Law of Rape' (1994) 57 *Modern Law Review* 10–37

Naffine N, 'Windows on the Legal Mind: Evocation of Rape in Legal Writings' (1991–1992) *Melbourne University Law Review* 744–751

Naffine N, *Law and the Sexes: Explorations in Feminist Jurisprudence* (Allen and Unwin, Sydney 1990)

Naffine N & R Owens (eds), *Sexing the Subject of Law* (Law Book Co, NSW 1997)

Nelson H (ed), *Feminism and Families* (Routledge, New York 1997)

Neville A, *Classification, Denial and the Racial State: Cubillo v Commonwealth* (unpublished PhD thesis School of Law LaTrobe University Dec 2005)

Neville R, *Hippie Hippie Shake: The Trials, The Love-Ins, The Screw Ups: The Sixties* (William Heinemann, Melbourne 1995)

Nicholson A, The Hon, 'The Legal Recognition of Marriage' [2005] 29 *Melbourne University Law Review* 556–572

Nicholson A, The Hon, 'The Changing Concept of Family: The Significance of Recognition and Protection' (1997) 11 *Australian Journal of Family Law* 13–22

Nicholson L, 'The Myth of The Traditional Family' In H Nelson (ed), *Feminism and Families* (Routledge, New York 1997) 27–42

Noddings N, 'Thinking, Feeling, and Moral Imagination' in French P A & H K Wettstein (eds), *Midwest Studies in Philosophy, XXII (1998): The Philosophy of Emotion* (University of Notre Dame Press, Indiana 1998) 135–145

Noddings N, *The Challenge to Care in Schools: an Alternative Approach to Education* (New York Teachers College Press, New York 1992)

Noddings N, *Caring: A Feminine Approach to Ethics and Moral Education* (University of California Press, Berkeley 1984)

Norzik R, *Examined Life: Philosophical Meditations* (Simon and Shuster, New York 1989)

Nussbaum M C, *Upheavals of Thought: The Intelligence of Emotions* (University of Chicago Press, Cambridge 2001)

Nussbaum M C, '"Secret Sewers of Vice": Disgust, Bodies and the Law' in S Bandes (ed), *The Passions of Law* (New York University Press, New York 1999).

Nussbaum M C, *Sex and Social Justice* (Oxford University Press, New York 1999)

Nussbaum M C, 'Emotion in the Language of Judging' (1996) 70 *St John's Law Review* 23–30

Nussbaum M C, 'Skepticism About Practical Reason in Literature and the Law' [1994] 107 *Harvard Law Review* 714–744

Nussbaum M C, 'Equity and Mercy' (1993) 22 *Philosophy and Public Affairs* 83–125

Nussbaum M C & D Kahan, 'Two Conceptions of Emotion in Criminal Law' (1996) 96 *Columbia Law Review* 269–374

Nussbaum M C & J Sihvola, *The Sleep of Reason: Erotic Experience and Sexual Ethics in Ancient Greece* (University of Chicago Press, Chicago 2002)

Nygren A, *Agape and Eros: A Study of the Christian Idea of Love* trans A G Hebert (SPCK, London 1932–1939)

Oatley K, *Best Laid Schemes: The Psychology of Emotions* (Cambridge University Press, Cambridge 1992)

Oatley K & J M Jenkins, *Understanding Emotions* (Blackwell Publishers, Oxford 1996)

Okin-Moller S, *Women in Western Political Thought* (Virago, London 1979)

Olsen F, 'The Myth of State Intervention in the Family' (1985) 18 *University of Michigan Journal of Law Reform* 835–864

Olsen F, 'The Family and the Market a Study of Ideology and Legal Reform' (1983) 96 *Harvard Law Review* 107–138

Ortiz D R, 'Creating Controversy: Essentialism and Constructivism and the Politics of Gay Identity' (1993) 79 *Virginia Law Review* 1833–1857

Otlowski M, 'Doyle and Doyle; Family Court Awards Custody to Homosexual Father' (1992) 11 *University of Tasmania Law Review* 261–268

Otto D, 'A Barren Future? Equity's Conscience and Women's Inequality (1992) 18 *Melbourne University Law Review* 808– 827

Paglia C, *Sex, Art, American Culture* (Vintage Books, New York 1992)

Parkinson P, *Tradition and Change in Australian Law*, third edition (Lawbook Co, NSW 2005)

Parkinson P, *Australian Family Law in Context: Commentary and Materials*, fourth edition (Lawbook Co, Sydney 2009)

Parkinson P, 'Quantifying the Homemaker Contribution in Family Property Law' (2003) 31 *Federal Law Review* 1–56

Parkinson P, 'Property Rights and Third Party Creditors: The Scope and Limitations of Equitable Doctrines' (1997) 11 *Australian Journal of Family Law* 100–140

Pascoe J, 'Women Who Guarantee Company Debts: Wife or Director?' (2003) 8 *Deakin Law Review* 13–48

Pateman C, 'Feminist Critiques of the Public/Private Dichotomy' in A Phillips (ed), Feminism and Equality (Basil Blackwell, Oxford 1987) 103–126

Pateman C, *The Sexual Contract* (Polity Press, Cambridge 1985)

Pearce L & J Stacey (eds), *Romance Revisited* (Lawrence & Wishart, London 1995)

Pearson G & S Fisher, *Commercial Law: Commentary and Materials* (Law Book Company, NSW 2009)

Peterson H (ed), *Love and Law in Europe* (Ashgate, Dartmouth 1998)

Peterson H, 'Informal Law and/of Love in the European Community' in Peterson (ed), *Home Knitted Law Norms and Values in Gendered Rule Making* (Ashgate, Dartmouth 1996) 114–155

Peterson S, 'Poetic Justices and the Legalities of Love' (2000) 31 *Victoria University of Wellington Law Review* 103–116

Pettman D, 'Love in the Time of Tamagotchi' (2009) 26 *Theory Culture Society* 189–208

Pettman D, *Love and Other Technologies: Retrofitting Eros for the Information Age* (Fordham University Press, New York 2006)

Pillsbury S H, 'Emotional Justice: Moralizing the Passions of Criminal Punishment' (1989) 74 *Cornell Law Review* 655–710

Plato, *Phaedrus* trans Jowett B The Internet Classic Archive http://clasics.mit.edu/Plato/phaedrus.1b.txt accessed 21/07/2010

Plato, *The Republic I & II* trans P Shorey Loeb Classical Library (Harvard University Press, Cambridge 1975, 1980)

Plato, *Symposium* trans W R M Lamb Loeb Classical Library (Harvard University Press, Cambridge 1975)

Pohjonen S, 'Partnership in Love and Business' (2000) 8 *Feminist Legal Studies* 47–63

Polikoff N D, 'Why Lesbians and Gay Men Should Read Martha Fineman' (2000) 8 *American University Journal of Gender Social Policy & Law* 167–176

Polikoff N D, 'We Will Get What We Ask For: Why Legalising Gay and Lesbian Marriage Will Not "Dismantle the Legal Structure of Gender in Every Marriage"' (1993) 79 *Virginia Law Review* 1535–1875

Polletta F, 'The Laws of Passion' (2001) 35 *Law & Society Review* 467–494

Posner E, 'Law and the Emotions' (2001) 89 *Georgia Law Journal* 1977–2012

Post D, 'Why Marriage Should be Abolished' (1996–97) 18 *Women's Rights Law Reporter* 283–313

Postema G, 'Objectivity Fit for Law' in B Leiter (ed), *Objectivity in Law and Morals* (Cambridge University Press, Cambridge 2001) 99–143

Postema G, *Bentham and the Common Law Tradition* (Clarendon Press, Oxford 1986)

Poster M, *Critical Theory of the Family* (Seabury, New York 1980)

Poulter S, 'The Definition of Marriage in English Law' (1979) 42(4) *The Modern Law Review* 409–429

Presser S B, 'Marriage and the Law: Time for a Divorce?' in J A Nichols (ed), *Marriage and Divorce in a Multicultural Context: Multi-Tiered Marriage and the Boundaries of Civil Law and Religion* (Cambridge University Press, Cambridge 2012)

Price A W, *Love and Friendship in Plato and Aristotle* (Clarendon Press, Oxford 1989)

Probert R, *The Changing Legal Regulation of Cohabitation: From Fornicators to Family 1600–2010* (Cambridge University Press, Cambridge 2012)

Probert R, *Examining Law Through the Lens of Literature: The Formation of Marriage in the Eighteenth-Century England* (Hart, Oxford 2008)

Probert R (ed), *Family Life and the Law: Under One Roof* (Ashgate, London 2007)

Proctor R N, *Value Free Science?: Purity and Power in Modern Knowledge* (Harvard University Press, Cambridge 1991)

Pulcini E, 'Modernity, Love and Hidden Inequality' trans L Fraser *Love and Law in Europe: Complex Interrelations* (European University Institute, EUI Working Paper 2000/2)

Power C *et al*, 'Lovestruck: Women, Romantic Love and Intimate Partner Violence' (2006) 21 *Contemporary Nurse* 174–185

Radway J A, *Reading the Romance: Women, Patriarchy and Popular Literature* (University of North Carolina Press, Chapel Hill 1991)

Rakoff R M, 'Ideology in Everyday Life: The Meaning of House' (1977) 7 *Politics and Society* 85–104

Redman J & A Redman, 'What Has Love Got To With It?: When Personal Contracts are Built on Commercial Contracts' (1994) 16 *Law Society of South Australia* 31–33

Reilly A, 'The Heart of the Matter: Emotion in Criminal Defences' (1997–98) 29 *Ottawa Law Review* 117–154

Richman K, 'Lovers Legal Strangers, and Parents: Negotiating Parental and Sexual Identity in Family Law' (2002) 36(2) *Law & Society Review* 285–324

Risely A C, 'Sex, Housework and the Law' (1980–81) 7 *Adelaide Law Review* 421–456

Rorty A, *Explaining Emotions* (University of California, Press Berkeley 1980)

Rosati C S, 'Some Puzzles About the Objectivity of Law' (2004) 23 *Law and Philosophy* 273–323

Rothman R, *Hands and Hearts: A History of Courtship in America* (Harvard University Press, Cambridge 1987)

Rubin M, '"Butcher, Baker, Wafer-Maker" — Book Review of *The Good Wife's Guide: A Medieval Household*' 32(7) *London Review of Books* 27–28

Ryan E, 'The Discourse Beneath: Emotional Epistemology in Legal Deliberation and Negotiation' (2005) 10 *Harvard Negotiation Law Review* 231–286

Rybczynski W, *Home: A Short History of an Idea* (Penguin Books, New York 1986)

Rykwert J, 'House and Home' (1991) 58 *Social Research* 51–64

Salzman T A & M G Lawler, 'New Natural Law Theory and Foundational Sexual Ethical Principles: A Critique and a Proposal' (2006) 47 *The Heythrop Journal* 182–205

Samuels G, 'Transsexualism' (1983) 16 *Australian Journal of Forensic Sciences* 57–64

Sanger C, 'Legislating with Affect: Emotion and Legislative Law Making' in J M Fleming (ed), *Passions and Emotions* (New York University Press, New York 2013)

Sanger C, 'The Role and Reality of Emotions in Law' (2001–2002) 8 *William & Mary Journal of Women & Law* 107–113

Sarmas L, 'Storytelling and the Law: A Case Study of Louth v Diprose (1994) 19 *Melbourne University Law Review* 701–728

Schalg P, 'Law and Phrenology' (1997) 110 *Harvard Law Review* 877–921

Schauer F, 'Formalism' (1988) 97(4) *The Yale Law Journal* 509–548

Schwarzer A, *After the Second Sex: Conversations with Simone De Beauvoir* (Pathenon Books, New York 1984)

Scott E S & R E Scott, 'Marriage as Relational Contract' (1998) 84 *Virginia Law Review* 1225–1334

Scott-Hunt S & H Lim, *Feminist Perspectives on Equity and Trusts* (Cavendish, London 2001)

Secomb L, *Philosophy and Love: From Plato to Popular Culture* (Indiana University Press, Indiana 2007)

Seidman S, *Embattled Eros: Sexual Politics and Ethics in Contemporary America* (Routledge, New York 1992)

Seidman S, *Romantic Longings: Love in America, 1830–1980* (Routledge New York 1991)

Seuffert N, 'Domestic Violence, Discourses of Romantic Love, and Complex Personhood in the Law' (1999) 23 *Melbourne University Law Review* 211–240

Sharpe A N, 'From Functionality to Aesthetics: The Architecture of Transgender Jurisprudence' (2001) 8 *Murdoch University Electronic Journal of Law* http://www.murdoch.edu.au/elaw/issues/v8n1/sharpe81.html accessed 4/08/10

Sharpe A N, 'The Transsexual Marriage: Law's Contradictory Desires' (1997) 7 *Australasian Gay & Lesbian Law Journal* 1–14

Shaw-Spaht K, 'A Proposal: Legal Re-regulation of the Content of Marriage' (2004) 18 *Notre Dame Journal of Law Ethics & Public Policy* 243–262

Shum C, 'Protection of Married Women as Guarantors' (1996) 14 *Australian Bar Review* 229–251 http://www.lexisnexis.com/au/legal/search/homesubmitform.do accessed 7/12/2000

Siegel R B, '"The Rule of Love": Wife Beating as Prerogative and Privacy' (1996) 105 *Yale Law Journal* 2117–2207

Simmonds A, '"Promises and pie-crusts were made to be broke": Breach of Promise of Marriage and Regulation of Courtship in Early Colonial Australia' (2005) 23 *Feminist Law Journal* 99–120

Singer I, *Philosophy of Love: A Partial Summing Up* (The MIT Press, Cambridge Massachusetts 2009)

Singer I, *The Nature of Love,* vol 3: The Modern World (Chicago University Press, Chicago 1987)

Singer I, *The Nature of Love,* vol 2: Courtly and Romantic (Chicago University Press, Chicago 1984)

Singer I, *The Nature of Love,* vol 1: Plato to Luther (Chicago University Press, Chicago 1966)

Singer J W, 'The Player and the Cards: Nihilism and Legal Theory' (1984) 94 *The Yale Law Journal* 1–70

Slavin S, 'Instinctively, I'm Not Just a Sexual Beast: The Complexity of Intimacy Among Australian Gay Men' (2009) 12 *Sexualities* 79–96

Smart C, 'Can I Be Bridesmaid? Combining the Personal and Political in Same-Sex Weddings' (2008) 11(6) *Sexualities* 763–778

Smart C, *Personal Life* (Polity Press, Cambridge 2007)

Smart C, 'Same Sex Couples and Marriage: Negotiating Relational Landscapes with Families and Friends' (2007) 55 *The Sociological Review* 671–686

Smart C, 'Book Review: Love Heterosexuality and Society' (2006) 40 *Sociology* 973–974

Smart C, *Feminism and the Power of Law* (Routledge, London 1989)

Smart C, *The Ties That Bind: Law, Marriage and the Reproduction of Patriarchal Relations* (Routledge & Kegan Paul, London 1984)

Smith R, 'Keep Friendship Unregulated' (2004) 18 *Notre Dame Journal of Law, Ethics and Public Policy* 225–241

Soble A (ed), *The Philosophy of Sex: Contemporary Readings* (LittleField, New Jersey 1980)

Solomon R C (ed), *Thinking About Emotions: Contemporary Philosophers on Emotions* (Oxford University Press, Oxford 2004)

Solomon R C, *Thinking About Feeling: Contemporary Philosophers on Emotions* (Oxford University Press, New York 2004)

Solomon R C, *Emotions: An Essay in Aid of Moral Psychology* (Cambridge University Press, Cambridge 2003)

Solomon R C, *Not Passion's Slave: Emotions and Choice* (Oxford University Press, New York 2003)

Solomon R C, 'Love and Feminism' in R B Baker K J Wininger & F A Elliston (eds), *Philosophy and Sex*, third edition (Prometheus Books, New York 1998)

Solomon R C, 'The Politics of Emotion' in French P A & H K Wettstein (eds), *Midwest Studies in Philosophy, XXII (1998): The Philosophy of Emotion* (University of Notre Dame Press, Indiana 1998) 1–20

Solomon R C, *About Love: Reinventing Romance for Our Times* (Little Field Quality Paperbacks, Lanham MD 1994)

Solomon R C, 'Sympathy and Vengeance: The Role of Emotions in Justice' in Van Goozen S, van de Poll N & J Sergent (eds), *Emotions: Essays on Emotion Theory* (Hillsdale, New Jersey 1994)

Solomon R C, 'Emotions and Choice' in A Rorty (ed), *Explaining Emotions* (University of California Press, Berkeley 1980) 251–281

Solomon R C, *The Passions* (Anchor Books, New York 1977)

Solomon R C & K M Higgins (eds), *The Philosophy of (Erotic) Love* (University Press of Kansas, Kansas 1991)

Spender P, 'Resurrecting Mrs Salmond' (1999) 27 *Federal Law Review* 217–241

Spender P, 'Family Companies and Women's Proprietary Entitlements' (1997) 11 *Australian Journal of Family Law* 196–247

Spender P, 'Women and the Epistemology of Corporations Law' (1995) 6 *Legal Education Review* 195–206

Stearns C Z & Stearns P N (eds), *Emotion and Social Change: Toward a New Psycho-History* (Holmes and Meir, New York 1988)

Sterns P N, 'History of Love' (1982) 15, special issue *Journal of Social History*

Starr L, *Counsel of Perfection: The Family Court of Australia* (Oxford University Press, Melbourne 1996)

Stecker R, *Interpretation and Construction: Art, Speech, and the Law* (Blackwell Publishing, Massachusetts 2003)

Steiner L R, *Romantic Marriage: The Twentieth Century Illusion* (Chilton Books, Philadelphia 1963)

Sternberg R J, *Cupid's Arrow: The Course of Love Through Time* (Cambridge University Press, Cambridge 1998)

Sternberg R J & M L Barnes (eds), *The Psychology of Love* (Yale University Press, New Haven 1988)

Sternberg R J & K Weis (eds), *The New Psychology of Love* (Yale University Press, New Haven 2006)

Stewart R M (ed), *Philosophical Perspectives on Sex and Love* (Oxford University Press, New York 1995)

Stocker M & E Hegeman, *Valuing Emotions* (Cambridge University Press, New York 1996)

Stone E, 'The Distinctiveness of Garcia' (2006) 22 *Journal of Contract Law* 170–193

Stone E, 'Infants, Lunatics and Married Women: Equitable Protection in Garcia v National Australia Bank' (1999) 62 *Modern Law Review* 604–613

Stone L, *Broken Lives* (Oxford University Press, Oxford 1993)

Stone L, *Uncertain Unions: Marriage in England, 1660–1753* (Oxford University Press, Oxford 1992)

Stone L, *Road to Divorce: England 1530–1987* (Oxford University Press, Oxford 1990)

Stone L, *The Family, Sex and Marriage in England: 1500–1800* (Weidenfeld & Nicolson, London 1977)

Strang H & J Braithwaite (eds), *Restorative Justice and Civil Society* (Cambridge University Press, New York 2001)

Sugarman D, 'Legal Theory, The Common Law Mind and the Making of the Textbook Tradition' in W Twining (ed), *Legal Theory and Common Law* (Basil Blackwell, Oxford 1986) 26–61

Su-King Hii, 'From Yerkey to Garcia: 60 years on and Still as Confused as Ever!' (1997) 7 *Australian Property Law Journal* 47–75

Sullivan A (ed), *Same-Sex Marriage, Pro and Con: A Reader* (Vintage Books, New York 1997)

Sung-Mook Hing & C Bartley, 'Attitudes Towards Romantic Love: an Australian Perspective' (1986) 7 *Australian Journal of Sex, Marriage & Family* 166–170

Tebbit M, *Philosophy of Law*, second edition (Routledge, London 2005)

Teo Hsu-Ming, 'Love Writes: Gender and Romantic Love in Australian Love Letters' *Australian Feminist Studies* (2005) 343–529

Teo Hsu-Ming, 'The Americanisation of Romantic Love in Australia' in A Curthoys and M Lake (eds), *Connected Worlds: History in Transnational Perspective* (ANU E Press, Canberra 2005)

Thompson S, 'Speak Now or Forever Hold Your Peace? Why We Need a Queer Critique of Gay Marriage http://www.lespanthreresroses.org/yextes/critiqueofgaymarriage.htm accessed 26/06/2006

Thornton M, 'Rapunzel and the Lure of Equal Citizenship' (2004) 8 *Law Text Culture* 231–262

Thornton M, 'Intention to Contract Public Act or Private Sentiment' in N Naffine R Owens J Williams (eds), *Intention in Law and Philosophy* (Ashgate, Aldershot 2001) 217–237

Thornton M, 'The Judicial Rendering of Citizenship: A Look at Property Interests During Marriage' (1997) 24 *Journal of Law & Society* 486–503

Thornton M, 'Historicising Citizenship: Remembering Broken Promises' (1995–1996) 20 *Melbourne University Law Review* 1072–1086

Thornton M (ed), *Public and Private: Feminist Legal Debates* (Oxford University Press, Melbourne 1995)

Thornton M, 'Loss of Consortium: Inequality Before the Law' (1984) 10 *The Sydney Law Review* 259–276

Tipton E, 'Sex in the City: Chastity vs Free Love in Interwar Japan' (2005) issue 11 *Intersections: Gender and Sexuality in Asia and the Pacific* intersections.anu.edu.au/issue11_contents.html accessed 11/05/2010

Tobin J, 'Recognising Same-Sex Parents Bringing Legitimacy to Law' (2008) 33 *Alternative Law Journal* 36–40

Toose P, R Watson & D Benjafoeld, *Australian Divorce Law and Practice* (Law Book Company, Sydney 1968)

Trebilcock M J & S Elliott, 'The Scope and Limits of Legal Paternalism, Altruism and Coercion in Family Financial Arrangements' in P Benson (ed), *The Theory of Contract Law New Essays* (Cambridge University Press, New York 2001) 45–85

Trollope A, *He Knew He Was Right* (Penguin Classics, Great Britain 1869)

Turski W G, *Towards a Rationality of Emotions: An Essay in the Philosophy of Mind* (Ohio University Press, Athens 1994)

Tushnet M, 'An Essay on Rights' (1984) 62 *Texas Law Review* 1363–1403

Unger R M, *The Critical Legal Studies Movement* (Harvard University Press, Cambridge 1986)

Updike J, *Gertrude and Claudius* (Hamish Hamilton, London 2000)

Vance C (ed), *Pleasure and Danger: Exploring Female Sexuality* (Routledge Kegan Paul, Boston 1984)

Verene D P (ed), *Sexual Love and Western Morality: A Philosophical Anthology* (Jones & Bartlett, Boston c1995)

Vinaver E, *Lancelot and Guinevere: New Edition of the Romance of Lancelot and Guinevere* (The Folio Society, London 1953)

Wallbank R, '*Re Kevin* in Perspective' in special issue 'Transsexualism: The New International Jurisprudence' (2004) 9 *Deakin Law Review* 461–502

Walthoe J, *Baron and Feme or, the Law of Husbands and Wives* reprint of the 1700 edition (Garland Publishing Inc, New York 1978)

Ward I, *Introduction to Critical Legal Theory* (Cavendish, London 2004)

Waring R, *Counting for Nothing: What Men Value and What Women are Worth* (Allen & Unwin, New Zealand 1988)

Warner K, 'Sentencing in Cases of Marital Rape: Towards Changing the Male Imagination' (2000) 20(4) *Legal Studies* 593–94

Warner M (ed), *Fear of a Queer Planet: Queer Politics and Social Theory* (University of Minnesota Press, Minneapolis 1993)

Warner M, *The Trouble with Normal: Sex, Politics, and the Ethics of Queer Life* (Free Press, New York 1999)

Waye V, 'Rape and the Unconscionable Bargain' (1992) 16 *Criminal Law Journal* 94–105

Weeks J, 'The Sexual Citizen' (1998) 15 *Theory Culture and Society* 35–52

Weeks J, *Invented Moralities: Sexual Values in an Age of Uncertainty* (Polity Press, Cambridge 1995)

Weeks J, *Sexuality* (Ellis Horwood, Chichester 1986)

Weinrib E, 'Legal Formalism: On the Immanent Rationality of Law' (1998) 97 *Yale Law Journal* 949–1016

Weisbrod C, 'The Way We Live Now: A Discussion of Contracts and Domestic Arrangements' (1994) 2 *Utah Law Review* 777–815

Welch D, 'Ruling With the Heart Emotion Based Policy, (1997–98) 6 *Southern California Interdisciplinary Law Journal* 55–88

West D, *Reason and Sexuality in Western Thought* (Polity Press, Cambridge 2005)

Wexler D & M McMahon (eds), special issue 'Therapeutic Jurisprudence' (2002) 20(2) *Law in Context*

Wightman J, 'Intimate Relationships, Relational Contract Theory, and the Reach of Contract' (2000) 8 *Feminist Legal Studies* 93–131

Wilkinson S & C Kitzinger (eds), *Heterosexuality: A Feminism and Psychology Reader* (Sage, London 1993)

Williams G, 'Equitable Principles for the Protection of Vulnerable Guarantors: Is the Principle in Yerkey v Jones Still Needed?' (1994) 8 *Journal of Contract Law* 67–83

Williams G, *Textbook of Criminal Law* second edition (Stevens and Sons, London 1983)

Williams G, 'The Problem of Domestic Rape: Part I' (1991) 141 *New Law Journal* 205–06

Williams G, 'The Problem of Domestic Rape: Part II' (1991) 141 *New Law Journal* 246–247

Williams P, 'The Obliging Shell: An Informal Essay on Formal Equal Opportunity' (1989) 87 *Michigan Law Review* 2128– 2151

Williams S G, 'Indeterminacy and the Rule of Law' (2004) 24(3) *Oxford Journal of Law Society* 539–562

Wilson A, 'Feminism and Same-Sex Marriage: Who Cares?' (2010) 6(1) *Politics and Gender* 134–143

Wilson J, *Love Between Equals: A Philosophical Study of Love and Sexual Relationships* (St Martin's Press, New York 1995)

Wilcox W B & J Dew, 'Is Love a Flimsy Foundation?: Soulmate Versus Institutional Models of Marriage' (2010) 39 *Social Science Research* 687–699

Witte J jnr, *From Sacrament to Contract Marriage Religion and Law in the Western Tradition* (Louisville, Kentucky 1997)

Wittig M, *The Straight Mind* (Harvester Wheatsheaf, New York 1992)

Wolf N, *Fire with Fire: The New Female Power and How it Will Change the 21st Century* (Random House, New York 1993)

Wollheim R, *On the Emotions* (Yale University Press, New Haven 1999)

Wouters C, 'Balancing Sex and Love Since the 1960s Sexual Revolution' (1998) 15 *Theory Culture and Society* 187–214

Wright T, 'The Special Wives' Equity and the Struggle for Women's Equality' (2006) 31(2) *Alternative Law Journal* 66–69, 87

Yaloum M, *A History of the Wife* (Perennial, New York 2001)

Young I, *Inclusion and Democracy* (Oxford University Press, Oxford 1990)

Young L & G Monahan, *Family Law in Australia*, seventh edition (Lexis Nexis Butterworths, Australia 2009)

Zanghellini A, 'Marriage and Civil Union: Legal and Moral Questions'(2007) 35(2) *Federal Law Review* 264–297

Zelder M, 'Sex and Reason' book reviews (1993) 91 *Michigan Law Review* 1584–1608

Zelizer V, 'The Purchase of Intimacy' (2000) 25 *Law and Social Inquiry* 817–848

Zelizer V, 'Payments and Social Ties' (1996) 11 *Sociological Forum* 481–495

Index